ATLANTIC
CROSSINGS

ATLANTIC
CROSSINGS

*A Sailor's Guide to Europe
and Beyond*

LES WEATHERITT

Sheridan House

First published 2006 by
Sheridan House Inc.
145 Palisade Street
Dobbs Ferry, NY 10522
www.sheridanhouse.com

Library of Congress Cataloging-in-Publication Data
Weatheritt, Les.
    Atlantic crossings : a sailor's guide to Europe and beyond / Les
  Weatheritt.
       p. cm.
  Includes index.
  ISBN-13: 978-1-57409-231-8 (alk. paper)
  1. Sailing—North Atlantic Ocean. 2. North Atlantic Ocean—Description
and travel. I. Title.

  GV817.N73W43 2006
  797.12409163'1—dc22   2006019321

ISBN 1-57409-231-6
ISBN 978-157409-231-8

Printed in the United States of America

Contents

SECTION TWO
LIFE ON THE OTHER SIDE

SECTION THREE
ARE YOU READY: BOAT AND CREW

SECTION FOUR
TRIALS BY WEATHER

SECTION FIVE
A TASTE OF OCEAN PLEASURES

Foreword

The desire to sail across the Atlantic Ocean lurks somewhere in the heart of nearly every sailor. A few have lofty ideas of circumnavigating the globe but that is a complicated, time-consuming, life-altering commitment. Most dreams of sailing around the world remain just that, dreams. A passage across the Atlantic on the other hand is within reach of most sailors. If you can just find a month of uncluttered time you can sail from North America to the Mediterranean. If you can arrange a year away from the humdrum, you can complete a full circle of the Atlantic. You don't need to be a master mariner to make a crossing. You do need to be well prepared, have a seaworthy boat, a sense of perspective and a copy of Les Weatheritt's *Atlantic Crossings*.

Make no mistake about it; crossing the Atlantic in a sailboat is not a casual undertaking. It is challenging and potentially dangerous. It is also extremely rewarding. I have completed 15 Atlantic crossings. The thrill of seeing Cape St. Vincent, the dramatic headland that marks the western edge of Europe, loom out of the haze never wanes. The pure joy of spying the verdant hills of Antigua after a rollicking tradewind crossing from the Canary Islands is unsurpassed. Sailing across the Atlantic, whether you're the captain or crew, is a personal accomplishment that defies easy measurement. I call it the Columbus Syndrome. You will feel like the Admiral of the Ocean Sea himself when you complete an Atlantic crossing. And you'll whoop and yell and shout silly things like, Land Ho!

The passion to cross the Atlantic is one thing; understanding the mechanics of when and how to organize and execute a safe and successful passage is something else. *Atlantic Crossings* provides a sea bag full of practical information. Weatheritt covers all the essentials, from route planning, to understanding the weather patterns of the Atlantic, to up-to-date harbor guides, to preparing your boat specifically for the crossing. He also provides inspiration through many amusing anecdotes that just may be the best part of the book.

Les Weatheritt is an accomplished but refreshingly humble sailor. He's also a terrific writer. His book is wonderfully free of macho advice. He has hardwon opinions but he shares them gently. I like that he is also not afraid to offer suggestions that stray from conventional wisdom. He coins the phrase, the Mid-Atlantic Turnpike, the proven route that follows the prevailing westerly winds to Europe and he describes this route in detail. However, he also candidly discusses the advantages of making your crossing further south, in the Horse Latitudes. Although the winds may not always be favorable in these latitudes, they are often lighter and in some cases better suited for a small sailboat. Weatheritt provides solid information on every route across the Atlantic, not just the ones he has sailed. And he recognizes that not every sailor wants to see if he can survive a storm at sea.

Atlantic Crossings also offers worthwhile insights on living aboard, particularly on what he calls, "the other side." He has a soft spot for the Azores, the lonely Atlantic archipelago that stands as welcome waypoints for small boat sailors. I know of what he speaks. Horta, on the Azorean island of Faial just may be my favorite harbor. Café Sport, just up the hill from the marina is definitely my favorite watering hole. *Atlantic Crossings* offers the most complete description of the Azores that I have read.

Hurry up and read this book. Devour it. Don't waste any more time. Plan your own crossing. Before you know it, Faial will decorate the horizon. As soon as you clear customs and tie up in the new marina in Horta, make your way up to Café Sport. With a bit of luck you'll find Les Weatheritt at the bar. Buy him a drink.

John Kretschmer
May 2006

ATLANTIC
CROSSINGS

Introduction

Getting off first base

An ocean crossing is a life-enhancing adventure. If you have an itch to sail one, it is never too soon to set out. Life won't be easy. There will be ridicule and complaints from family and friends, storms and frustrating calms at sea, but at the end you will have a sense of achievement that is yours alone and will last forever.

Chance and uncertainty

This book is to help you plan a whole journey, from there and back again. Some of your plan will be fairly concrete. Some will be hopelessly vague. Don't confuse the two. The concrete bits are right at the beginning, when you are fairly sure of the when and where of your departure. After that, nothing is fixed, however much you might think it is or want it to be. Learn to live with the uncertainty in everything that is to come.

Part of this uncertainty comes from when you, as an ocean voyager, join the *camaraderie* of the sea. Other long distance sailors will change your ideas. They are sources of vital information and help to one another. You will discover that you don't have to be at home to fix your boat. In whichever port you happen to be, some other sailor will have solved your exact problem. When you change your passage plan in some sailing crossroads you will find someone to lend or sell or swap the charts and pilot books you need. Start to think like an ocean sailor now, before you become one.

On an ocean voyage you will spend longer on and dig deeper into the boat you are sailing, the crew you are with and the weather systems that surround you. This book aims to give you a thorough grounding in all of this.

Key points:

- Details make you safer and increase your confidence.

- This Atlantic crossing can be done on relatively benign routes but will still be different from what you may have done before.

- There is a lot of technical advice and personal stories available but nothing which "holds your hand" on a first crossing. This book addresses your emotional and personal needs as well as the technical.

- People who have done it learn a lot and they will tell you when you meet them. By then it will be too late. Read this book first.

- This book is for ordinary people rather than wacky heroes.

You don't have to be crazy to sail a small yacht across a huge ocean, but most of your friends and family will think you are. Cultivate the rare ones who think your plan is the height of sanity. But beware: they could be crazier than you. To avoid losing all credibility with the land-locked people who populate your onshore life you need to demonstrate the cautious good sense of your planned transatlantic dream. You need a whole load of facts about weather, routes, successful voyages, crew management and the beautiful places you will visit on the other side. Think of this book as the nautical almanac to give you an appearance of sanity. Master the facts. Quote them where and whenever best helps you. That is a good enough reason to have this book on your bedside table but the better reason is that the facts really will help you on your great adventure and help you enjoy it all the more.

This isn't a book of facts, though. It is a book of dreams disguised as facts. The important thing right now is to nurture your dream to the point of making it happen. That's why this book covers the full story of an Atlantic crossing. You will need other books focused on single topics, packed full of dense technicalities about diesel engines, 12-volt electrics, heavy weather sailing and delicate personal surgery. Use these books to fill out your knowledge. Read them when you need them. Make a library from them. Don't let them wear you down. They are essential, but don't expect to read them for pleasure.

For those who feel their next sailing challenge is to cross an ocean, the Atlantic is the best one to pick. Compared to the Pacific it is a compact, narrow stretch of water, only 5,900 miles at its widest although increasing by about one inch each year thanks to movement along the Mid-Atlantic Ridge, the great underwater mountain ridge running the length of the ocean.

Another reason to favor the Atlantic is that you don't have to go all the way round the world to get home. It can be done as a circuit in a single year if you are really in a hurry, or in two years if you are in slightly less of a hurry. Those who need to keep in touch with life back home, and may need to go back at short notice for business or family reasons, can break the journey into manageable sections. The Atlantic circuit has many places where you can safely tie up the boat and conveniently take a flight home. You don't have to decide on the more challenging routes to Europe until you have most of the crossing under your belt and if you don't feel like sailing north to Britain and Northern Europe you don't have to.

As a novice Atlantic crosser with only two crossings under my belt I make no excuses for preferring the easy route to the hard route. An ocean is a big enough challenge without looking for ice, gales, fog and head winds. On most days of the week I'd swap that lot for clear blue skies, gentle breezes and the occasional calm. This inevitably means that my preferred routes are as far south as I can sail in comfort. I'm not alone in this. When asked about their experience of really bad weather most long-distance live-aboards say they are rarely out in anything above a Force 7 and if they were they wouldn't be foolish enough to try sailing through it when the alternative is to heave-to and read a good book. How do they manage this? By working with the seasons and carefully choosing their routes.

The east-to-west and west-to-east crossings of the Atlantic differ considerably in the character of sailing on these softest, most southern routes. It isn't so much the weather that you'll meet here but the climatic boundaries you will be crossing. Given your initial choice of route your strategy will be to work your way most directly to the wind belt that offers the strongest, safest winds.

On the east-to-west crossing from Europe to America the choices are so clear that no navigator is likely to suffer a headache working them out. When I made that journey I naturally took the Trade Wind route on what Europeans call the Milk Run and made my landfall in the Caribbean. On the west-to-east crossing there is no Trade Wind route of blue skies, steady breezes and following seas. Even so, some routes come closer than others to being a Milk Run and this is what a sailor of my natural caution naturally prefers.

I make no bones about it. I am no stranger to anxiety when the nearest dry land is at least one thousand miles away and my boat is a lot smaller than the last wave that just went passed. I like to know before I go that I have minimized the dangers. I like to think that everyone else who sails oceans feels the same way. Give us reassurance, and give it to us now.

PETRONELLA log, somewhere in the Horse Latitudes
I never imagined that an ocean could be so calm. Day after day I look for signs of threatening weather but no threatening weather comes. I have read about the great area of calms along this route, of course, but what I absorbed from my reading were the complaints sailors made as they tipped their investment in equine stock overboard or the Spanish Galleon Mobile Lending Library ran out of improving books for old salts. Here I am in the Horse Latitudes and the wide

> Sargasso Sea finding that the endless visibility, cloudless blue skies, ankle-high waves and gentle swell is. . . . Just Wonderful! And what is most wonderful is that it seems as though it will go on forever without a gale, a downpour or even a little squall. I used to say that Nature had designed the Trade Wind Milk Run for ocean novices, but that was before I discovered the Horse Latitudes.

Reassurance is a hard thing to measure. Sailors making their first ocean crossing need a dump truck of reassurance before they can get down to the committed planning of the trip. But only when you lose yourself in the details and the practicalities do you begin to feel that you can manage this wonderful adventure. First, you feel less of a fool telling other people about your intentions if you have a clear idea of what routes you can choose, how wide the ocean is and how long it will take to get to the other side. Second, recite recipes about how to bake bread and quote statistics on how many showers will be allowed from a finite amount of water carried in at least two tanks. Then you will bore your friends to sleep before they injure your ego with tricky questions about the trip.

On the shoulders of giants

You will need to read many books before setting out on your Atlantic crossing. You may read them for fun, long before the seed germinates or the plans get firmer. You may already be well into the authors I love. The Hiscocks and the Smeetons, the Pardeys and Cornells, Webb Chiles and Hal Roth, Bernard Moitessier and of course Joshua Slocum, the great Nova Scotian who led the way. My little book cannot compete with these giants of bluewater sailing. But then, I'm not one of those giants and my book isn't being written for people like them. It's being written for you.

> On my first ocean crossing about 90 per cent of my worries came from the Sailing Heroes. You know who I mean. Fearless sailors inclined to mishap. They write all the books I most enjoy reading. Ripping yarns but frightening when you come to cast off from the pontoon. Where was the book by a sailing rabbit, the skipper who didn't spit in the eye of the storm, laugh scornfully at the iron-bound lee shore or whiplash the inadequates who dared call themselves crew? I never found it.

I love to read sailing books but in terms of preparing me for an ocean crossing something was missing from my shelf. None of those books quite tell the journey as it panned out. Take the physical conditions such as the weather. It was there on the page but somehow the weather we had was never quite as I had expected. There are good reasons for that and I can work them out now that I have been out there, but that didn't help me then to put orders of magnitude on what fears were justified and what were not. Second, take the social conditions of the trip. The issues of selecting and living with crew were barely covered in these books, or at least not in any way that lived up to the reality as we experienced it. Yet this is pivotal to the sailing adventure. Get it right and you can have the perfect crossing, regardless of much else. Get it wrong, and life afloat will be hell.

What was really missing from my library was the story of an ordinary Joe doing what I was planning to do. The nearest I got was probably reading "First Crossing," the account of their 1979 journey from New York to the Mediterranean by Malcolm and Carol McConnell. Here, in raw detail, was the account of two novices on a small boat who met storms that went on longer than they wanted, blind ships that passed too close, and a floating steel construction that nearly holed them in mid ocean. Here was a skipper driven to the verge of murderous violence by exhaustion and fear. I could empathize with this. Just about everything that could happen on the ocean happened to them. I didn't want to go to the brink with them, but I was pleased to know that a couple of ordinary Joes could go there and still come back. I was pleased that they, like me, could suffer frights and discomforts that landlubbers would regard as intolerable and yet still know that there is nowhere else they would rather be and nothing else they would rather be doing, and that landlubbers are wrong, wrong, wrong.

I know now, of course, that the best way to hear the stories of ordinary Joes is to meet them in the harbors of places like Trinidad or Antigua, Martinique or the Virgins, in Bermuda or the Azores. It is easy to meet these long distance cruising people when you are on a long distance cruising yacht of your own. It is easier still to bump into these people the further into your journey you go. When you throw your line ashore in Horta, Faial or Bayona, North West Spain, after weeks at sea you will be accepted into a new family of people who know what you have done without ever needing to ask why, who respect what you have done without passing judgment on your sanity, who regard crossing oceans in small boats as both a commonplace and a privileged way of life, but by then you are on your way, past the point where you still need the gentle push that this book will give you.

Life on Earth

> **Key points**
>
> - Get this in perspective. You don't have to become a sea-gypsy. For most people it's just like an extended cruise. Life back home must be maintained.
>
> - Detailed planning is essential and helps you arrive at the emotional commitment to go. But you must make that commitment at some stage.

Not all of us are wandering souls. Most of us like a bit of adventure and then to come back home for a hot shower and a TV dinner. If you are ready to cast off and not come home for the next decade, well and good, but I reckon it's usually best to give it a try for a month or year first. So it is worth doing a little bit of planning to make sure there is something to come back to.

There are three essential thought processes to go through before you arrive at the practical stage of dealing with your need to retain a grip on life back home. The first is so long and pointless that it should be dropped in the garbage can as soon as possible. You don't need to lose as much sleep contemplating the cruising life or an ocean crossing as I did.

This first stage is when you create a balance sheet of financial and social income and expenditures to show what will be irretrievably lost or damaged by your irresponsible wish to interrupt the comfortable life you have spent so long building just so that you can indulge this anti-social fantasy to sail across an ocean. The best hours spent on this complicated and insoluble calculus come as you cruise the highways at the wheel of your car, stare idly at your reflection in a window, or contemplate eternity as you sit in front of a TV soap opera. The worst hours are when your mind won't slow down to let you fall asleep or you wake in the middle of the night with the hot flush of a new fear of failure.

A balance sheet is not helpful in any real way, even if you learned to do them on a Harvard MBA. The fears that occupy you can't be added up. Filling in columns and rows on graph paper is displacement activity while you delay getting to the vital but brutal second stage.

This second stage is that brief moment of total irrationality when you finally say, "That's it. I'm going." There is no justification for your decision. No calculus to show its impact on your future. If you are lucky, this moment comes in a sudden blinding flash of inspiration, no more subject to analysis or reconsideration than any other half-cocked conversion. If you are unlucky, it comes in a long grinding period of vacillation until you can no longer bear the thought that you are more mouse than man, and you just jump.

The third stage is in form very like the first stage, in that it involves the detailed construction of an MBA-type social and financial balance sheet and many sleepless nights, but this stage is marked with purpose and deadlines. You are on your way now. It isn't just a matter of time. It's a matter of timing.

This adventure is not about burning all your bridges. Some of the most interesting questions faced by someone sailing a boat across an ocean are about the life they are leaving and how they will pick it up again. I mean, life at home may be getting you down just now but it will have a new and rosy glow after six months or more on a small ocean-going boat.

For many sailors an Atlantic crossing is just taking you further away from home than usual. You may have already left North America and spent a year or more cruising the Bahamas or the Caribbean, feeling that you are no more than just a quick jump from home. Perhaps the coasts of Europe and Africa and the Mediterranean Sea seem further from home, more foreign, less part of your own backyard. That doesn't mean that you can never return from them once you get there. Or that you won't meet people just like you over there.

An Atlantic circuit can, in theory, be done in a year if you are so inclined. This is more or less what I had in mind on my first crossing. I was not running away to sea for ever. I just wanted to see if I could sail the ocean and after that I wanted to return to real life ashore. I was happy to let the weather determine my timetable for a round trip. I wasn't going to rent out my home. I wasn't going to give up work. I wasn't going to put family and friends on hold. Lots of other people I met were treating their Atlantic crossing as a similar extended cruise. All of us, then, had to work out the most effective and least disruptive ways to leave our affairs ticking over for a longer period than usual. For me, if not for them, the extended period proved more extended than I could have imagined, but we'll come to that by and by.

The things I had to deal with are probably not very different from yours. I needed to maintain an apartment with a mortgage and various family and working relationships. I reckoned that a year playing at sailing was about all I could allow if I was to come back and revive the life I had left behind. Like many cruising sailors I have since met, the heart of my concern was financial. In those days I was a freelance research economist working on projects of two to six months. As such, I had in theory the flexibility to find time for long breaks within my pattern of work. In practice this never happens. Freelancing may be a quantum of personal freedom greater than conventional employment but for most of the time the effective freedom is to exploit yourself on behalf of clients who back-slappingly envy your autonomy while taking twice as much time on vacation as you dare.

Lady Luck sails with you

Fear of the unknown defines mankind. It certainly defines those who go to sea in small boats, if they have any sense or finer feelings. Fear of the unknown is perfectly reasonable but fear of the known is not to be despised either. Even those who have sailed a stretch of sea or ocean a hundred times can hardly claim to know it in any way which removes fear. The bigger the bit of water, the less you can know or predict what will happen while you are sailing on it. So accept that being afraid of undertaking this adventure is normal and don't let fear stop you from doing this or any of the other worthwhile things you have in mind.

What concerned me most before I set off, and ranks as a Class A Fear, was what conditions we would meet at sea and our probability of being overwhelmed by them. This is the mark of the practical sailor as well as the coward. Whichever I turn out to be, I was nail-bitingly aware as we cast off for my first crossing that we were going to be a long way offshore and well outside the range of the coast-guard service and that the ocean is as mean as the sea, but with a bigger and nastier attitude.

In my earlier sailing life there were many times when I came close to care-lessly being wrecked. I had already met storms that brought me near tears with frustration because the violent motion of the boat would not let me complete a simple task. If only the sea would be still for a minute I could use both hands to get the half-frayed end of that line through the block. If only the wind would stop screaming in my ears for thirty seconds I could think straight and work out how to get the bar-taut knotted sheets off the tangled jib. I had sailed in rock-strewn tidal channels in 300 feet visibility and suddenly found a line of white breaking water dead ahead. I have been on river bars at that heart-stopping moment when the depth meter shows zero and the following sea curls into a breaking crest and you are alone in a cruel place with nothing to expect but a jarring crash as ten tons of boat drops its narrow keel onto rock-hard sand rising through receding water. So I had no reason to fear these things as new experiences.

What was new and all too unknown for me was what might happen a thousand miles off land. Surely the storms were bigger, lasted longer, brewed monster waves and were relentlessly frequent. I know the Pilot Charts, showing in neat little diagrams all those weather observations that ships' captains have been wonderful enough to send in for the last few hundred years, do not lead to this conclusion for the routes I had in mind but I did worry that those trusty old ships' captains on their much larger vessels might not have noticed the gale force wind that only blows for an hour or two. But I would notice it. Those 20-foot waves are no problem to the ocean tanker, but they would be to me. Anyway, the past is not a certain guide to the future as any dinosaur would tell you. Look at the greater incidence of hurricanes in the last decade.

And I could have stayed awake all night in sweating fear of other things if I had put my mind to it. It isn't enough that these commercial captains might underestimate the tempests but what about the flotsam and jetsam they leave behind. All those 20-ton containers falling off their deck. A cargo container is a big and hard lump of steel for a sailing boat to hit at night and one full of ping-pong balls could be floating around the ocean for years knocking us sailors off like flies.

And it isn't just containers. One night, years ago, blown a hundred miles offshore by an unexpected gale, my skinny 24 footer and I sailed right up to a huge old concrete and steel thingy that was floating low in the water. I was lucky to see it as the last light of day drained from that ferocious sky. As I recall, the thing had incredible spikes sticking out that would have holed us as soon as say "Mayday, Mayday, Mayday." It floated away and I lost sight of it in the dark never to see it again. But it was there. I swear it.

And as for whales. This life force, so large and intelligent, just might want to take some revenge for your failure and mine to get the Russians and Japanese to join the international ban on commercial whaling. Such brainy beasts are hardly going to head-bang a 10,000 ton ship with sonar detectors and ready-primed explosive harpoons. Not likely. This marine Napoleon will find some little yacht carelessly bobbing up and down on the bright blue sea and give it such a slapping with its flukes *pour encourager les autres*.

If these external sources of disaster were not enough, what if a seacock jammed and water flooded in as we slept. Of course we would wake before this sank us but with gallons of briny in the bilges our boat would sit so low in the water that some rogue wave would poop us and disable us so that the next monster would swamp us completely. And we would go down because the bilge strainer was blocked by some trashy novel my crew dropped as they fell asleep all unawares of the tragic events about to unfold. No wonder I have trouble sleeping at night.

Honestly, a lot can frighten a sailor. I wanted to be told that none of this was going to happen to me, any more than I would fall overboard one dark night and watch PETRONELLA sail on with my crew asleep or drunk and the self steering soberly alert and steering us. All the world in its allotted place, apart from me.

The point is that I discovered no evidence that these fears should grow in proportion to distance offshore or depth of sea under the hull. We had stronger than expected winds as well as days of calm. We had brushes with ships that clearly weren't watching. We met a pod of killer whales that had reputedly attacked a French yacht. We didn't see pirates but we might have done. To be frank, I concluded after two crossings that good luck is more common than bad, else our species would not have survived.

It's never been easier

More and more cruising sailors are getting the confidence to venture farther offshore. Improved electronic navigation and reliable communications to other yachts as well as to shore give enormous comfort. Easier sail handling, self steering and powered equipment to handle ground tackle and dinghy hoisting enable smaller crews to handle bigger boats and get the greater stability, seaworthiness and creature comforts that really only come with size.

Generations of East Coast sailors have answered the question "Where next?" by the single word, "South." That one word is packed with magic. Palm trees, gentle surf on a golden beach, silky seas for swimming when the sun gets too hot, and always the exhilarating breeze of the Trade Winds to drive you to the next island in the chain. But more American sailors are turning to the wide ocean for their next passage, and a year or more exploring the many countries and cultures of Europe.

Europe is a good choice. It's a densely populated and highly developed union of countries with reliable mains electricity and excellent provision for sailing boats. You may not feel the need to gear up your ship as though you were off around the world to visit the extremes and least populated places. I agree. But even in Europe you can find extreme weather and remote anchorages. Prepare your boat for worse weather and more independence from the shore than you are used to. Also, you may, after a while, crave remoteness and distance from humanity. Why not, I do. So although you might get away with going light on some of my suggestions do it with careful thought. And remember, although this may start out as a one- or two-year circuit of the highly developed world of Europe you may end up north of Norway or coasting down Africa and Brazil and turning left or right for the truly remote parts of the world.

A crossing is a circuit

The Atlantic Ocean lends itself to a sailing circuit, thanks to the winds and currents and landfalls and the way that you can sail in summer breezes most of the way, keeping one step ahead of winter. You can, if you wish, leave home in May and cross via Bermuda and the Azores; visit the British Isles and other parts of northwest Europe between July and August and then head south to Spain and Portugal and the Atlantic islands between September and November; make your return crossing with the Trades in December or January; make landfall in Tobago or Trinidad to explore the Caribbean from south to north and be back in the office by May. Or if you think northern Europe is a long detour from the quick run from the Azores to Spain or Portugal you might spend more time on the Iberian coast, even visit the Mediterranean if the Levanter isn't blowing, or go further south and see West Africa and the Cape Verde islands before crossing to the Caribbean and heading home.

I planned a one-year circuit on my first Atlantic crossing until I realized that I wasn't an annual-circuit sort of sailor. I changed my plans after I arrived in the Caribbean from Africa. I thought I'd make my circuit last two or three years instead of one. I didn't mind having to tell friends back home that I had changed my mind. Changing your mind is a sign of mature judgment in the light of new experiences. And that's what you get when you go long distance cruising. Then I discovered that I was really more of a decade-circuit sailor. Ten years might just be time enough for this voyage. As it turned out I did finish a circuit in ten years but I might have misjudged myself. I didn't finish the circuit back in my home-port or anywhere near it. I made it back to the same continent, that's all, and then I started wondering where else I'd like to go out there on the deep Atlantic.

I made my first Atlantic crossing to see if I could. I wasn't interested in the places on the way. It wasn't as though I was going to discover a new continent or add to mankind's sum of knowledge. I was just indulging myself. I was finding out if I could manage such a big adventure, now that I had sailed my little boat everywhere else short of the ocean. This isn't a bad reason to get you started. The ocean is a good place to discover yourself.

I discovered that I really didn't want to do all that ocean sailing and NOT see the beautiful places on the way. Also, you meet lots of people who are on a slower track than you and you want to spend some time doing what they are enjoying. You meet people going on interesting side-trips who are willing to have you tag along. And, then, long distance cruising also involves a lot of down-time repairing and improving the boat. You soon realize that you don't need to rush home to wrenches and screwdrivers in the wet cold winter when you could park up in the tropics or some other warm dry place and explore a foreign land at the same time.

Welcome to Europe

Before you leave home you will need a document, such as your certificate of registration, to show you are a foreign registered vessel, a radio license, insurance papers, certificate of competence for the skipper and identity papers for each person on board. North Americans can offer a birth certificate as valid identification when re-entering their own country or coming into a British territory, but the one document that identifies you in all of the other countries you might visit on this adventure is your passport.

Apart from the papers mentioned above you may carry other documents relevant to your boats, from vaccination certificates to firearm certificate, but these are extras, special to your circumstances. Have them ready. Don't hide anything but equally don't show papers you innocently think might interest the official. Why raise a hostage to fortune?

> In France any vessel other than a beach craft (*engin de plage*) must be registered unless it is remarkably small and underpowered and never goes more than 300 meters from shore i.e. not an average yacht tender. It is very unlikely that any French official will demand to see the registration documents for your tender but it is not unheard of. In summer 2005 the Gendarmerie of Southern Brittany upset a number of visitors by demanding to see the registration documents for their tenders. So it may be prudent to put your tender on your registration document or get a new one for it before you leave home.

You will need to show the clearance papers from the last country you left. This is vital. Once in the European Union (EU) you will find that there are no border controls between the countries signed up to the Schengen Agreement 1995: Austria, Belgium, Denmark, France, Finland, Germany, Greece, Iceland, Italy, Luxembourg, the Netherlands, Norway, Portugal, Spain and Sweden. With non-signatories, such as the UK, there are still immigration controls as you arrive from another part of the Union.

The European Union allows non-EU flagged vessels a stay of 18 months and then they must clear out or pay value added tax (VAT) at the rate of that country on an agreed valuation of your boat. These foreign flagged vessels can always return again for another 18 months. Time spent away from the vessel, making land visits or returning home, doesn't count towards your 18-month allowance. Nor does time in a boat yard having essential repairs done. This is a European Union wide rule and the EU, as we all know, has a single, harmonized set of rules. But the EU is also a loose sort of conglomeration and its rules can be interpreted differently in different countries, depending on the discretion of the local officials. It is most unlikely that you, as a North American sailor, will be made to feel unwelcome. That isn't what the EU rules seek to do. But you may find that somewhere some official takes a hard line to your detriment and does this within the letter of the law.

Check any local anomalies first with other non-EU flagged sailors as you move through different member states, and then with the officials themselves. A good adage when dealing with all officials is "never ask a question when you don't already know the answer."

If you plan to stay more than a year or two in Europe here are a few tips. Try to figure out at the beginning of the sailing season where you will want to spend next winter, especially if you intend to leave the boat while you return home. Get full and up-to-date information on the local Customs and Immigration procedures, time limits and penalties. Remember, before you talk to the officials, talk to fellow cruisers.

One couple we met had sailed from Virginia to the Caribbean before crossing to the Mediterranean. After two years of full time cruising the wife returned to her teaching job and the couple switched to summer cruising around the Mediterranean. When she retired a few years later, they continued part time cruising but spending more time on the boat. They found the Mediterranean, like the Caribbean, ideally suited to part time cruising. Well-developed facilities for visiting yachts and easy access to flights home. As part time cruisers they wanted their time for sailing, not maintenance, and appreciated the reliable and experienced boat yards to keep the boat up to scratch.

IALA B to A

Europe and the Atlantic islands are in the IALA A region. North, Central and South America, as well as the Caribbean are in IALA B. Take care. It's a bit like finding they drive on the wrong side of the road when you arrive in Britain.

Until the mid 1970s the world had about 30 different buoyage systems, some of which were in the same region and conflicted with one another. The 1980 Tokyo Conference was convened by the International Association of Lighthouse Authorities (IALA) to harmonize this. As a result the world's oceans are now either IALA A or IALA B. The essential difference is how the port and starboard hand buoys are located when coming from seaward or from a direction specified on the chart.

In the North American IALA B region the red port hand buoys are to starboard as you approach the land from seaward—red right returning. In Europe and the Atlantic islands, such as the Azores, it is the other way round. Leave red to port as you approach from the sea.

In Britain's great academic institutions of Oxford and Cambridge, and at the highest tables of the land, when the meal is over the bottle of port is always passed around the dinner table clockwise or to your left. Port to port, the British say. No wonder they take to IALA A like ducks to water. So when the Master of Magdalen College, Oxford invites you to dine, don't forget which IALA region you are in. And by the way, at Oxford Magdalen is pronounced maudlin, which you have to hope isn't the quality of their dinners.

The lateral markers are the same in both IALA regions:

- port hand markers are can or spar shaped, any topmark will be a can and lights are red
- starboard hand markers are cone or spar shaped, any topmark will be a cone and lights are green.

Cardinal marks are the same too. They are named after the quadrant in which the danger lies. So pass a European north cardinal buoy to the north, and so on, just as you would back home.

A little courtesy

The yellow Q flag should be flown when you enter the 12-mile limit of a new country. Visiting foreign vessels fly the national flag of the country as an age-old courtesy to show they intend no threat. The flag is flown from the second most important signaling position on a vessel. On a sailing yacht this is the outer starboard crosstree. I don't know if technically it should be flown above or below your own national flag but I do know that following the local flag etiquette can be important in getting a welcome response from officials.

We had arrived in our third Portuguese harbor since Spain and the man who deliberately hadn't taken our lines even though we were struggling with the high dockside told us that we shouldn't be flying our national flag from the masthead if we could only raise the Portuguese flag to the spreaders. We weren't sure of his status in the office or if he was right. We had spent a year in the Portuguese Azores and no one had mentioned this, as G rather pleasantly but firmly pointed out to him. He became more charming as we joked about Azorean ways and let him tell us about his own time in the archipelago, but when we got back to the boat we lowered our big flag from the mizzen mast and ran a smaller one up the shroud to sit just beneath the Portuguese flag. Flags are a small thing to us. Staying on the right side of officials is a big thing.

Using this book

This book draws on my own knowledge of sailing in the Atlantic and Europe. It uses the experiences of many ocean sailors we have met on both sides of the Atlantic. It draws on a wide range of sources but in particular it takes a very practical look at the actual boats, crew sizes, passage times and routes of most Atlantic crossers in the four years 2001 through 2004 by analyzing data from harbor authorities in the Azores.

Section one is about the routes across the Atlantic and the way that the seasons, winds and currents lead you to decide the most appropriate route for you. Planning your route isn't exactly rocket science although there is plenty to confuse you if you are that way inclined. The point in Section one is to emphasize the simplicities.

Section one also tells you about your journey back, in case that is what you want to do.

Section two tells you what pleasures you will find in Europe and what sources of sailing information you should consult or carry with you. This section gives you a guide to Europe in a nutshell, so that you can plan an outline of your voyage to get the most life-enhancing sailing and cultural experiences.

Section three offers guidance on the two main practical concerns of choosing and preparing your boat and choosing and living with your crew. There is plenty of scope to get this right, just as there is plenty of scope to get it wrong.

Section three deals with the key practical issues you face as you step from being a coastal cruiser to being an ocean-crossing sailor. They all come from our experience and our reflections on things that have happened to us. You don't have to accept our views and conclusions. You do, though, have to address these issues for yourself. There are also many practical hints about boat handling and equipment that might otherwise take you a whole Atlantic circuit to realize.

Section four helps you prepare for heavy weather sailing, in case you get some, and light weather sailing, because you certainly will.

Section five tells you about two real-life mid-Atlantic experiences:

- the charm of the Horse Latitudes and why the place exists at all
- the charm of the Azores and why you might consider staying longer.

Appendices deal with more specific and technical aspects of bluewater sailing from grab bags to bin bags.

BON VOYAGE.

SECTION ONE

Route Planning

You could easily confuse yourself by looking at the whole length of the Atlantic seaboard of North America and then the equally long European seaboard and trying to work out the best place to begin and end an ocean crossing. This really isn't necessary.

The Atlantic crossing is a bit like driving on a turnpike. From many points of departure drivers funnel into a single stream, travel in convoy and then spread out at the end towards their separate destinations. So it is when crossing the Atlantic. From almost anywhere on the Eastern Seaboard the first step for most yachts is to head towards Bermuda. After that you join the pack running almost due east to the Azores. And after that you diverge onto one of a handful of well-traveled routes depending on where you want to go in Europe.

On your first crossing from the Eastern Seaboard, or if you want to make an ocean shakedown cruise, head towards Bermuda at 33°N by 65°W. From most of the Eastern Seaboard this will be a relatively short passage of 700 to 800 miles compared to the 3,000 or so miles of the full crossing.

> The harbor of Horta on the Azorean island of Faial is not huge. You could count the local and year-round visiting yachts on your fingers and toes, but during May and June it is packed with yachts crossing the Atlantic. Even early-season April has enough visiting yachts for the parties to begin and enough are still arriving in August to end the season in fine style. More than a quarter of these yachts stopped in Bermuda on their way over, shortening their major ocean-leg by a week or so.

Bermuda is a sailing crossroads, a jewel in the ocean, but it is the world's most northerly group of coral islands and the surrounding reefs are made more dangerous by the unpredictable speed and direction of the current over them. The only safe approach is from the south or southeast, where the coast is steep-to.

You don't have to stop there if you don't want to, but when you get to Bermuda you will have done one of the tough bits, the Gulf Stream crossing, and

Bermuda Island and Reefs

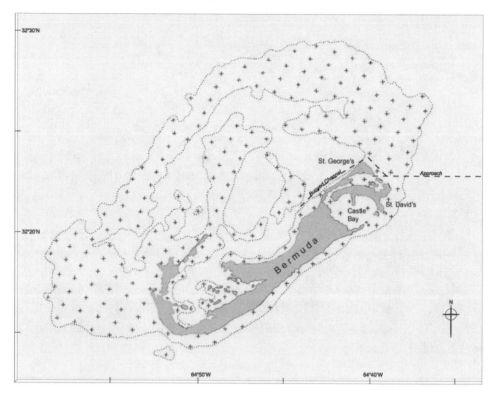

may want to check your gear thoroughly. Expect the place to be busy if you arrive during the Newport to Bermuda race in June.

> The locals say that Bermuda is a heavenly place to be but a hell of a place to get to. In the great days of sail hundreds of ships got lost in the strong winds and currents and poor visibility around the island and were wrecked on the reefs. Calms are common unless a depression tracks across from America. In May 2003 an American yacht heading for Norway via the Azores fought ten hours against a strong gale that came up just 20 miles from Bermuda. The skipper said they shipped more water than at any time since they had left but made it into St. George's Harbor in daylight. If they hadn't, they would have hung off for the night rather than try to enter that tricky place in the dark.

There are really only two alternatives to the mid-Atlantic turnpike. First, if you are already as far north, say, as Newport or Nova Scotia and aiming for Britain or Scandinavia, you might prefer the northern route. This reduces your distance from 2,500 or 3,000 miles to the enviably short 1,900 or so miles. But the northern route brings more chance of gales and you must take care to stay south of the ice line for that year. This book covers that route for those who really must sail amongst the bergs. But I would leave the northern route to the experienced, hard-bitten ocean type, not us sailing rabbits.

HB was no sailing expert. Perhaps he chose the northern route just to prove me wrong. There is always someone outside the envelope. He left New York in April for St John's, Newfoundland in a boat he had just bought, learning to sail as he went. When he left St John's in May the south coast of Greenland was still covered in ice. During the 23 days to reach Iceland he had one violent storm blowing 60 knots and five days of calm. He spent the winter in Iceland and sailed to Northern Norway via the Faeroes and Shetland. He coasted to Russia and then came back to spend another winter in Norway. It was a cold three years and he sailed without any particular plan, happy just to meet the people of the north and be seeing a part of the world that had always fascinated him. He must have had his compass adjusted in Trondheim fjord because after that he discovered south and sailed there, albeit slowly. Ten years after leaving the US he is exploring the Mediterranean with the new-found love of his life, has a beautiful cottage in an out-of-the-way place and is still sailing for half the year. Not bad for a guy who took the northern route.

The second reason not to head for Bermuda is if you are already in the Caribbean. From the northern Caribbean you can take the rhumb line route straight to the Azores on 38°N/39°N by 31°W/25°W, passing well to the southeast of Bermuda. This, like the northern route, saves a lot of miles. But it takes you through the often windless seas of the Horse Latitudes. This is the route for sailing rabbits who don't mind spending an extra week or two at sea and are brave enough to burn their entire diesel.

A rhumb line is not the same as a great circle.
A great circle is the shortest distance between two places on the surface of a globe. On our little yachts we sail on the three dimensional surface of a globe but we navigate with charts that are two dimensional, usually the Mercator projection named after the great 16th century Flemish cartographer himself. The straight line connecting

two places on a Mercator chart is a rhumb line, and that is what most of us use as our passage line. It is much easier to draw a straight line on a conventional chart and steer that course rather than invoke complicated spherical trigonometry or the use of gnomic charts. Fortunately, great circle sailing is not all that useful on an Atlantic cruise. It is more important to go with the right winds and currents.

Chaguaramas, Trinidad. You need to get very organized about jobs before crossing an ocean. Here, while re-rigging the boat, our little camp was just part of a wider community in Power Boats.

Speyside, Tobago. Looking out over the windward coast. Africa, the nearest land, is nearly 3,000 miles to the east.

The Turnpike and other routes

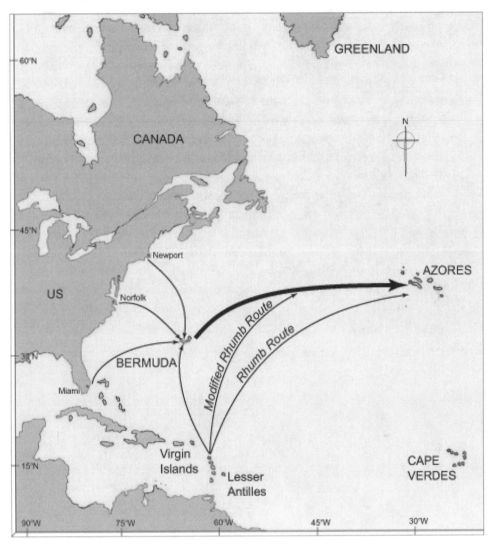

The Caribbean is the sailing backyard of North America and many of those who took their boats into the islands did so to try their hand at the sailing life. After a while even the worst hedonists among them will wonder about venturing further afield. In this they are typical of those who come off the mainland of North America, anywhere from Florida to Maine, to make their first Atlantic crossing.

The Caribbean is a fine sailing area in its own right. The conditions there can nurture the novice into a competent and confident sailor. It's also a place where North American sailors who might have day-hopped into the Caribbean can meet and learn from those who have already crossed an ocean.

I was in my favorite sailing bar at Chaguaramas, Trinidad. The Australian with a mass of frizzy hair was talking to the American with a long ponytail about Ponytail's plans to sail to Europe in the late spring. Frizzy lives on a lovely old 35 footer. He has sailed it from Australia and he's on his way back there. Mr Ponytail has a brute of a 40 footer which has been in bits for the last five years but is coming together now. I've never seen it in the water but I hear tell that its next trip will be the big one to Europe. Mr Ponytail is the strong silent type from somewhere in the Midwest, not given to long speeches and his sailing has not yet taken him a long way offshore, so for both those reasons he was mainly listening and sipping cold beer. So were many sailors at other tables, their minds only half with the company they were keeping. The rest of their mind was tuned to what Frizzy was telling Ponytail about crossing the Atlantic. The more I have come to meet American sailors in the southern end of the Caribbean sea the more I have sensed that for many of them a bigger agenda is developing, and that this means sailing out into the ocean.

1

That which prevails— weather, wind and current

Weather is about to become the most central part of your life.

> **Log of WINDSONG, 2003**
> The wind completely dominates life out here. I thought I would fill my log book with insights into the meaning of life and other fundamentals from my enforced life of contemplation but the only other topic that competes with the weather in my log book is how much sleep I am getting.

The weather may seem fickle and hard to forecast but we live in what is an essentially orderly natural world with clearly marked seasons, winds and currents. The great forces of Planet Earth create these and decide your route. When we go with them they make our sailing life easier. The winds and currents of the Atlantic are created first by the temperature differences between poles and tropics and second by the spinning of the planet. Our prime mid-ocean stopover, the peaks of underwater volcanoes at the Azores, comes courtesy of the powerful forces of tectonic plates and the release of volcanic pressures.

It never hurts to learn a little bit more about climate and weather. The prevailing winds and currents give us the big picture for sailing the Atlantic. The weather provides the final word. This crossing, like all great ocean journeys, has a distinct season. It is a journey to be made between the winter storms of the north and the summer hurricanes of the south. The information you need to make your plans comes at a number of levels:

- the very broadest level is the global picture of how winds and currents operate in the mid North Atlantic at different times of year

- next look at the Pilot Charts to see what weather has been experienced by ships over the last couple of centuries at the times of year you intend to make your crossing
- consider where you are likely to be when you set off and where you would like to be when you arrive. Your departure point may not have many degrees of freedom. If you have been in the Caribbean for the last five years, that is where you will be starting from. And if you have never yet left Chesapeake Bay, you will probably start from there. Your arrival in Europe is a very different matter. How much of Europe do you want to see and in what order? My experience is that sailing boats find it easier to travel from north to south down the Atlantic coast of Europe, and that is the way to be heading when winter chills the air
- decide how far you want to travel on your crossing. The northern route crosses the Atlantic at its narrowest, but at a cost of rougher weather. A great circle route can be much shorter than the rhumb line but a great circle is only worth sailing if it doesn't drive you away from favorable wind and current. On your west to east crossing you will come close enough to sailing a great circle route anyway
- do you want to sail non-stop or take a break or two? You don't have many choices but neither do you have to think too much about this. The northern route has a number of stepping stones. The southern route has Bermuda and the Azores. You can even decide whether or not to stop after you set off. You pass these places close enough whether you put in there or not.

All sailors travel within the same climatic and weather systems. Not all make the same choices.

Baz crossed the same year we did, but he left Trinidad much later. He left in May and by then was running late for his crossing. He was running even later after some weeks in Martinique making unexpected repairs. Baz was sailing on a tight schedule. Friends had arranged a big birthday party for him in England and he didn't want to miss it. He had no time for the windless Horse Latitudes. He sailed north towards Bermuda and turned right when he met the westerly winds. He never got close enough to stop at Bermuda. He made good time in his slippery S&S34 but ran into calms when north of the Azores. The forecast was for strong winds in a bad depression followed by nothing much. Baz could have put into the Azores but he needed the good sailing wind to make the party on time. He stayed at sea, rode the fronts, took a bit of a hammering off Ireland and put in at Bantry Bay for a rest. It was a quick crossing but hard and wet.

Not all of them have the same luck.

Hans Christian left Virginia in May 2001 and kept below 40°N because there was still a danger from ice up there. He missed Bermuda but stayed a few days in the Azores then on to the Scillies and Scandinavia. He had eight gales on his crossing in weather far worse than he had expected. It is a good looking plastic ketch with slender wooden masts and a broad stern but in need of maintenance and had bad deck leaks by the time he made Europe. To add to his discomfort Hans Christian had total electrical failure. One of his crew turned the master battery switch off and when the engine ran it burnt out the alternator circuits. The gauge was faulty so Hans Christian wasn't surprised to see no sign of charging. What alerted him was not being able to run any of his electronic gear, from navtex to nav lights, or get water to clean his teeth.

Blowing with the wind

The air of our atmosphere is driven first by the different rates of surface heating from the sun, and second by the rotation of the earth.

The earth receives and absorbs most radiation energy from the sun at the equator and least at the poles. This is not because the equator is any nearer to the sun. The different level of heating and energy absorption is because the sun's rays strike the earth more or less at a right angle at the equator and much less directly at the poles:

- at the equator the sun-heated air expands and rises. Lighter air means lower pressure at the earth's surface
- cold polar air is dense and therefore heavy. It sinks, bringing higher atmospheric pressure at the earth's surface.

Nature abhors disequilibrium. Air tries to balance out these pressure differences by moving from high pressure to low pressure in the same way that water will always try to flow from high to low. This isn't always easy. Warm and cold air in

Wind regions of the oceans

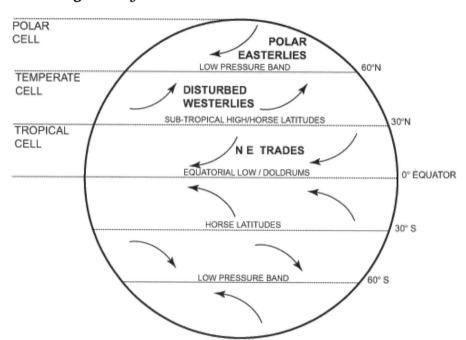

the atmosphere, like warm and cold water in the oceans, don't want to mix. The warm air at the equator rises until it reaches the tropopause, the name given to a natural barrier between this air and the upper atmosphere. Once at the tropopause this air is deflected towards the poles, moving north in the northern hemisphere and south in the southern hemisphere. As it begins to move it becomes subject to the Coriolis Force, the force exerted on all moving objects by the rotation of the earth and a vital factor in producing winds and ocean currents. In the northern hemisphere the Coriolis Force deflects moving air to the right, or clockwise, and to the left or counter-clockwise in the southern hemisphere.

Winds don't travel directly from the equator to the poles in a single loop but form three distinct smaller loops or "cells" either side of the equator: the tropical, temperate and polar cells.

The rising equatorial air, moving north towards the pole and deflected east by the Coriolis Force, cools as it moves. At the edge of the tropics, about 30°N, it begins to fall back towards the earth's surface so adding to the amount of air already at these latitudes. This results in a region of high atmospheric pressure, typified by light winds and little or no rain. This is the desert belt of the world. In the ocean it is called the Horse Latitudes.

On either side of this region of light winds are the main wind belts of the Atlantic. To the south, between around 10°N to 30°N, the North East Trade

Winds move air towards the equator to replace the rising air. To the north, around 30°N to 50°N, are the Disturbed or Prevailing Westerlies. Beyond the Prevailing Westerlies is a narrow belt of low pressure between 50°N and 60°N which separates the Westerlies from the high pressure region of the pole.

These wind belts do not remain in the same place throughout the year. They move with the seasons, as the sun moves north and south across the equator. The conditions in each belt and the curious ways they interact at their boundaries give us our expectations on wind and weather conditions, and our choices for an Atlantic crossing.

High and low pressure systems work in different ways with significantly different effects on the weather.

- high pressure systems, called cyclones, pull air down from the upper atmosphere. As the cold air falls it warms and is able to absorb moisture. The sky is characteristically clear and blue. Winds spin clockwise round the center of high pressure and outwards at about 15 degrees.
- low pressure systems, known as depressions or anticyclones, suck air upwards, pulling moisture from the sea. As the air rises it cools and forms clouds. Winds blow counter-clockwise around the center of the low and inwards at about 15 degrees.

The four regions of wind that most concern us on this Atlantic crossing blow between the equator and 50°N. They were given names by our sailing predecessors. These old names carry a weight of meaning.

The Doldrums

This low pressure area around the equator is known to meteorologists as the Intertropical Convergence Zone (the ITCZ) because it is the boundary area between the North East Trade Winds in the northern hemisphere and the South East Trade Winds in the southern hemisphere. I think the old name given to it by sailors carries more weight. Not for nothing has the word doldrums been taken to mean anything which prevents action and induces a listless, apathetic state of mind. In this narrow band of unstable weather the thunderstorms, intense rain, high humidity and light winds make sailing very difficult.

The Doldrums travel north and south across the equator in line with the seasonal movement of the sun but not at quite the same time or speed. It lags the sun by a couple of months. The sun is at its northern maximum in June but the convergence zone is not at its maximum until August to September.

The shifting location of the ITCZ has important influences on Caribbean weather and then on the Eastern Seaboard. The northward movement of the

Zone heralds the end of the main Caribbean sailing season and the beginning of the tropical hurricane season. In April or May, at about the time the ITCZ moves north, the first tropical wave will be reported coming off the coast of Africa. Later, in the main period of the hurricane season, tropical waves will be forming every few days. Some of these will develop into hurricanes. This northward movement of the ITCZ is one of the key factors in determining when to leave the Caribbean or the Eastern Seaboard and cross the Atlantic. You never want to be out in a hurricane.

The Trade Winds

The Trade Winds are the most persistent of all the great wind belts of the world. They got their name from their vital role in helping maritime commerce in the days of sail. Characterized by blue skies and the fleecy rainless clouds, these are the winds that sailors dream of. Trade Winds lie between 10°N and 30°N. They have blown European sailors to the Americas ever since Columbus and cover the Caribbean island chain the whole year round. They blow at ten to 25 knots, stronger in winter than summer and have occasional periods of calm or rushes of intense squalls.

For sailors in the Caribbean there are many local factors influencing the strength and direction of these persistent winds. Mastering these makes for much more comfortable passage-making as you head north to leave the Antilles and start your ocean voyage.

The Horse Latitudes

This region of sub-tropical high pressure north of the Trades around latitudes 25°N to 35°N got its name from the time when the great Spanish galleons were forced by slow progress in light airs to jettison their horses to save water. This is a region of sparklingly clear air and flat seas but not a lot of wind.

The Horse Latitudes are not the Doldrums.
A landlubber friend thought the Doldrums and the Horse Latitudes were the same region of the ocean. I can understand his confusion. The old ocean sailing ships didn't like either of them and the literature of the sea tends to lump the two together as regions which ships struggle to escape from, but they are different geographically and meteorologically.

The winds in the Doldrums and the Horse Latitudes vary in several fundamental ways. In the Doldrums the air moves vertically, with little of the horizontal movement loved by sailing ships. Hot rising air sucks moisture from the sea to create the cloudy, turbulent and often unpleasant weather characteristic of low atmospheric pressure.

In the persistent high pressure of the Horse Latitudes, where conditions are wonderfully clear and cloudless, the surface winds do blow but only lightly.

PETRONELLA **log, 2003**
The sea isn't as flat as a millpond but the waves are often no more than ripples. Visibility in the mornings is diamond sharp. In the afternoon thin clouds build and sit along the horizon. Some clouds form dark banks or cumulus towers and travel towards us, sometimes passing over us, but they are all pussy cats with no wind and only the lightest of rain. In the night the cloud is rarely enough to trouble the stars. The skies are magnificent. I lie awake looking for shooting stars.

The Disturbed Westerlies

North of the Horse Latitudes, from about 30°N to about 50°N, is a region of predominantly westerly winds. These Westerlies are not as steady as the Trade Winds. At their northern boundary they are disturbed by the great depressions that travel the Atlantic from west to east, and which do so much to encourage North European sailors to cross to the Caribbean.

Here, where the warm moist air of the tropics meets but may not want to mix with the cold dry air from the pole, a small disturbance along the polar front will create a vortex and the start of a depression. In the developing depression the warm and cold fronts mark the boundaries between airs of different temperature.

At some point on a crossing from west-to-east, most of us will sail in this region of westerly winds. How far we venture into it depends on our route. What weather we experience depends on conditions that year. But in this region frontal weather systems will be marching across the ocean with you.

From breeze to hurricane

Fronts and depressions can bring strong winds and a yacht crossing the Atlantic must be prepared for a gale on whatever route it takes. But you never want to be caught by a hurricane. Nothing can prepare a yacht for a hurricane. The centrifugal force inside these wild storms can generate 120mph winds, sometimes 200mph. They bring thunder, lightning, monstrous seas and torrential rain. You just don't want to be there.

The sea between the Eastern Seaboard and Bermuda is a pathway for hurricanes. In the past Bermuda has been hit by early rather than late season hurricanes but forecasters say that predicting events within the hurricane season is becoming harder. Hurricanes are becoming more frequent later in the season, even extending the season from the traditional November to December, and are more extreme. Hurricanes this far north, however, are reckoned to be more settled and predictable and have been longer in the sights of the forecasters. You might get information to help you take evasive action. My advice, though, is to cast off before the season gets underway, leave with a good forecast, and hope to be clear of Bermuda before a big beast arrives.

> The Pardeys were caught by the first hurricane of the season in their mid-1970s crossing from the Chesapeake to the Azores on SERAFFYN, their 24-foot cutter. They were sheltering from a near gale in the old Cape Charles ferry harbor when Hurricane Agnes rose again from being a tropical storm and reformed over the Virginia Capes and southern Chesapeake, right on their spot. Lin Pardey's description of their night of fear in "Cruising in SERAFFYN" is beautifully downbeat, given the danger they were in.

Hurricanes generally pass round the Sargasso Sea and the Horse Latitudes but can occasionally slip down from northeast of Bermuda and even track down as far as 30°N before curving up to head to the Azores. Occasionally hurricanes can stay in the eastern half of the Atlantic, usually heading almost due north until they run out of energy around 40°N. Very, very rarely they head to Spain or North Africa, as happened in the exceptional year 2005. The official hurricane season starts on June 1 and runs till November 30. Nature is already changing the small print on this.

Tropical hurricanes are not a pressure region like the Doldrums, the Trades and the Westerlies. They are interlopers, weather events created in the boundary between the Doldrums and Trade Winds. They are a phenomenon of the western Atlantic basin. Hurricanes go hunting in the islands of the Caribbean, the Gulf of Mexico and up the Eastern Seaboard. They are part of the equation for planning your sailing strategy.

Life cycle of the hurricane

Hurricanes are seeded on the central to western side of the Atlantic Ocean because the sea temperatures of the east are rarely enough to support these massive storms. The water on the east side of the ocean basin is cool, being brought down from the north. It picks up heat from the sun's radiation as it stays in the equa-

Tropical storm tracks 2005

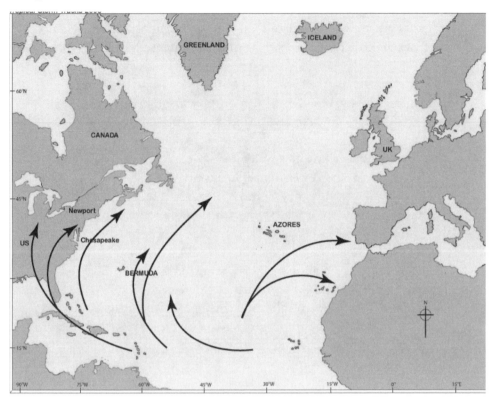

torial belt, traveling west. The temperature of the sea must rise to 80°F (27°C) in order to fuel a hurricane. They are a revolving storm and cannot start to revolve until more than five degrees off the equator, where the Coriolis Force is strong enough to divert winds from a straight path.

When hurricanes first form, as varying intensities of tropical storm, they blow west at the speed of the Trades, which is about 15 knots. The typical track of hurricanes is to bend to the right as they approach the western coast of the Atlantic and re-curve to such an extent that they go back out into the Atlantic in a northeasterly direction from about 40°N.

Because tropical hurricanes arise in a very specific way weather forecasters can recognize them early and monitor them as they mature. Hurricanes gain their energy from heat drawn from evaporating water as moist air rises in the cloud masses of tropical thunderstorm cells along the northern boundary of the Doldrums. As the air column becomes warmer and lighter, barometric pressure at the surface falls and more moist air is sucked into the thunderstorm system, positively fuelling itself. The tropical depression is classed as a tropical storm when winds reach Beaufort Force 8 to 11, from 35 knots upwards, and becomes a hurricane when they reach Force 12 with winds of 64 knots and over—"that which no canvas could withstand."[1]

Hurricanes are graded from 1 to 5 on the Saffir-Simpson Scale. Category 3 to 5 hurricanes are collectively known as major or intense hurricanes.[2]

As you listen to forecasts in the months running up to hurricane season it will help you to understand the terms forecasters use:

- tropical disturbance, tropical wave and upper level troughs will be mentioned frequently in broadcasts. They are nothing in themselves to worry about. They are just poorly organized weather systems interrupting the Trades with rain of varying intensity
- tropical depressions, the next rung up, bring rain and strong winds but are highly variable. The winds can be 35 knots or can be no more than the normal Trades
- tropical storm is trouble. This brings intense rain and winds up to gale force. Tropical storms are given names. If the storm worsens it will turn into a hurricane.

Most tropical storms won't develop into full hurricanes but they can still produce extensive damage ashore. For a small yacht facing a Force 11 storm the difference between tropical storm and hurricane may be academic. Most hurricanes do not blow harder than 90 knots, but even this is greater than a very bad Atlantic gale.

You need as much warning as possible to cope with a hurricane. At sea you must get out of the way of the eye, the center of the vortex. Forecasters now have sophisticated computer simulations to help you. When a tropical storm or hurricane is forecast a storm watch is included in the Marine Advisory issued every six hours from 0300 by the Tropical Prediction Center in Miami. The Advisory reckons to give 36-hour notice. When the storm watch is upgraded to a storm warning the Advisory gives 24-hour notice. You can get information from www.noaa.org.

It helps if you know the technical limitations of these predictions. Roughly speaking, the computer model predicts the position of the eye up to five days in advance and compares this with satellite images of the actual position. If the predicted and the actual positions are within about 40 nautical miles, the pre-

---

1. Admiral Beaufort, describing his highest category of wind strength
2. See Appendix 2

diction is reckoned to be good and more forecasts are attempted for one, two, three, four and five days in advance. The practical point for sailors is that this good prediction cannot forecast the center of a hurricane more than four to five days in advance, with an error limit of about 440 nautical miles. After the first 24-hour forecast the several tracks predicted at each time period begin to diverge increasingly widely.

You also get advance warning of a hurricane from natural signs. A deep fall in barometric pressure, especially if you are in the tropics where pressure is otherwise remarkably steady, is a good indication. A long, low swell will come in advance of the storm. Wind strength will increase markedly or switch direction, and the clouds will show the classic formation of an advancing depression. From an unusually clear sky come cirrus, altostratus and broken cumulus. When the dark line of cloud arrives, so does hurricane force wind.

To understand these changes carry a good barometer and one of those informative picture books on weather systems. But above all carry a good radio. *In extremis*, seek help from Buys Ballot.

Buys Ballot's Law

In the 19th century mariners used Buys Ballot's Law to help forecast the location of the storm. If you, in the northern hemisphere, stand facing the wind you will have the center of low pressure about 100 degrees to your right, which is just a little behind you. If the wind followed the isobars exactly the center would be precisely at right angles to you. But it doesn't. The wind in a low-pressure system blows slightly inward along the isobar. This is greatest in the leading edge where the forward movement of the depression adds to the pressure gradient. Point your left hand, palm down, into the wind and extend your thumb as far as you can. Your thumb will be pointing towards the center of the storm. Now you can predict the direction of the expected wind and your position relative to the worst parts of the storm.

Hurricanes, like other northern hemisphere depressions, spiral counter-clockwise, with winds drawn into the eye or vortex of the storm. They normally travel to the north or northwest. Because of this movement the dangerous half of the storm is its front side or northern semicircle and its most dangerous quadrant is the northwest. The southern semicircle is known as the navigable semicircle. Winds in the dangerous semicircle are up to 50% stronger than in the navigable semicircle.

The worst winds, cloud cover, rain and seas are around the eye. This can reach from ten to 100 miles in diameter. The eye itself is an area of thin cloud and light winds with monstrous chaotic seas sweeping in from all sides. Beyond the eye, the vicious winds of the feeder bands can reach out hundreds of miles.

The safest strategy with hurricanes is to avoid them. A yacht cannot outrun the storm. It must try to escape the center, hence your need to know the direction of track. Most hurricanes move to the northwest as they come into the region but progressively turn northwards and then northeast. Where the track is at its maximum curve is known as the point of recurvature. At any moment they can stall, curve the wrong way or loop their own loop. The problem is to know when they will change their track.

Hurricanes can travel faster than you can prepare for them at the last moment, and their final track is notoriously unpredictable. If the wind veers (that is, shifts clockwise or to the right) you are in the dangerous semicircle. If it backs (that is, shifts counter-clockwise), you are in the navigable circle. If the wind strengthens but its direction remains steady and the barometer falls, you are in the path of the eye. If the wind weakens but its direction remains steady and the barometer rises, the eye is moving away from you.

The storm is most extreme in the second stage of hurricane development, when it has turned from tropical depression and tropical storm to a mature hurricane. Here winds near the center can be ferocious. If sailing in rough seas in the dangerous semicircle go close hauled or heave-to with the wind on your starboard side. In the navigable semicircle run under jib or bare poles on a course at right angles to the assumed track of the storm. Your tactics will depend on how much sea room you have and the behavior of the boat when hove-to or running in big seas. Do what you can. Remember, there are no hard rules to ensure your survival.

In the third stage of its life the hurricane is decaying and maximum winds usually drop below a Force 12. Don't relax yet. The storm forces are still very dangerous for yachts. At this third stage the storm's energy is no longer contained in an intense but relatively small center. Now it blows strong to gale force winds over a much larger area.

The Eastern Seaboard is prone to hurricanes. Most land-falling hurricanes hit the Florida coast but hurricanes can strike almost anywhere. Cape Hatteras is particularly hard hit, perhaps because it protrudes out into the path of hurricanes paralleling the coast to its south.

The leading edge of weather

Tropical squalls

Boats coming up from Panama or starting from elsewhere in the Caribbean Sea will meet many interesting weather phenomena. Apart from the hurricane, the most interesting is the tropical squall. Bad squalls are more common in the tropics than in the temperate latitudes. With a few clues you can tell if a bad one is coming. You need to know when to hide and when to use the wind that comes with them.

The bigger the cloud mass, and the taller it is, the greater the chance of unwelcome strong winds. If you get wind before rain then the additional wind that comes with the squall will probably not be as great as when you get rain before wind. The barometer is no help in the tropics, so close to the equator. Watch for the clouds changing, the dark line approaching and a sudden drop in temperature. The greater the fall in temperature, the more wind you should expect. And of course, you will see the wind on the water before it hits your sails.

> I was looking out to sea at Hope Bay on the Atlantic side of Bequia, chatting idly to another sailor. "Do you see those islands?" I said. "What islands?" he replied. "The ones that have just disappeared," I said and we both started to run for shelter.

Caribbean squalls move east-to-west at the speed of the local Trade Winds, turned slightly to the right of the Trades by the Coriolis Force. This means that a black cloud down to the south of you may well be coming your way and if it does you will get a clockwise wind shift of 15 to 20 degrees and a possible increase of 20 to 30 knots. This usually lasts for less than half an hour, but it can be longer.

Sometimes you will be left in a flat calm for an hour or two after the squall and before the Trades find their way back. If you were running and saw a not-too-worrisome squall on its way you might chose to alter course to stay in front of it in the enhanced winds. If you were beating you might chose to go to windward to avoid the stronger winds.

Most squalls happen at night. At night the cloud tops can radiate heat back into the upper atmosphere and this enhances their ability to grow. In day time the cloud tops absorb energy from the sun and don't suck up as much warm moist air from sea level. In the deep dark of night you will not get much visible warning of an approaching squall. Night makes them all the more dangerous. Be cautious especially when sailing in the tropics and reduce sail at night.

> I was singlehanding from Dominica to St Vincent in the Caribbean and asleep in what had been a quiet night when the boat heeled the wrong way and rolled me to the floor. I came up on deck like a jack-in-the-box to see why. We had been sailing close-hauled to the south. Now we were reaching due north. The wind had gone from a light southeasterly to a very breezy northwesterly and despite the backed genoa the boat was driving hard towards the shore of

Dominica less than ten miles away. I was grateful for being tipped out of my berth. If the wind had been less breezy this dramatic change in wind direction would have left me sleeping soundly as we drove onto that rocky coast.

Fronts and depressions

Fronts are a feature of life in the middle and higher latitudes of the Atlantic, where the prevailing Westerlies blow.

A mid-latitude depression begins at the edge of two air flows, the tropical air moving east and the polar air moving west along the polar front. The key to their formation is the great temperature difference between the two air masses and their unwillingness to mix. Perhaps because of friction between the two air flows, a wave-type distortion appears on the polar front with a local fall of pressure at the tip of the wave. This can then turn into the vigorous depression common to sailors in northern Europe, when the warm and cold fronts march across the sea and across the weather forecasts.

Middle and higher latitude depressions move more slowly and are less intense in the summer but as they pass the wind and weather will change rapidly, not always as expected. The southeasterly winds will veer to southwest as the barometric pressure drops and the front approaches. The warm front brings heavy rain and southwesterly winds. As the cold front crosses the wind shifts sharply into the northwest and you get squalls and showers until the front is through, when the skies clear and visibility improves.

A front is named after whichever type of air is the advancing one. When warm air is over-running cold air, you will be facing a warm front. As the warm air rises up over the colder air, the moisture in it condenses out into cloud and rain. The cloud thickens and rises from cirrus, at the leading edge of the front, through cirrostratus to heavier altostratus. You may not see the nimbostratus until the rain eases.

Warm fronts typically bring milder weather than cold fronts but they move more slowly, sometimes at half the speed of a cold front, and will be overtaken, caught and merged by the cold front into an occluded front. An occluded front, if one arrives, brings less turbulent weather. Most of the energy of the depression will already have been lost.

Cold fronts are more active than warm fronts and potentially more of a problem. They bring towering cloud mass, more intense rain, greater falls in temperature, and a more extreme shift in the wind direction. They also bring stronger gusts than a warm front. The gust can increase wind speed by 30% to 70%. Since wind force increases by the square of wind speed, this is a huge increase in pressure on your sails.

Four stages of a depression

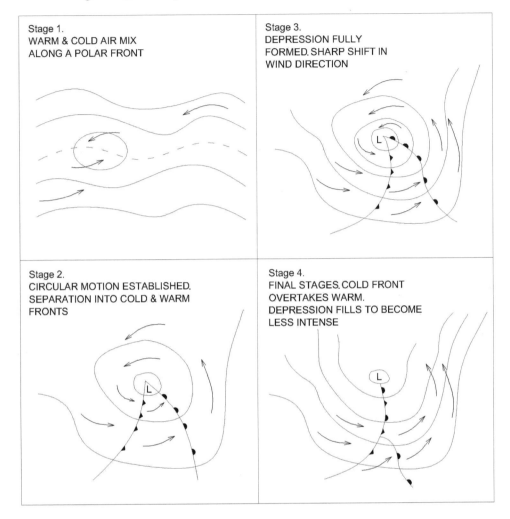

Stage 1.
WARM & COLD AIR MIX
ALONG A POLAR FRONT

Stage 3.
DEPRESSION FULLY
FORMED. SHARP SHIFT IN
WIND DIRECTION

Stage 2.
CIRCULAR MOTION ESTABLISHED.
SEPARATION INTO COLD & WARM
FRONTS

Stage 4.
FINAL STAGES. COLD FRONT
OVERTAKES WARM.
DEPRESSION FILLS TO BECOME
LESS INTENSE

Precisely what wind shifts you get depends where you are relative to the center of low pressure. Winds blow counter-clockwise around the center of the low and inwards at about 15 degrees. Because the depression moves east across the ocean, the movement of the system strengthens the wind in the southeast quadrant.

Take extra care when the fronts pass. Waves may become more of a hazard, changing direction or breaking suddenly and without warning. The new wind may be no more than a Force 6 but it may come with line squalls and severe gusts. Sudden gusts, strong and from new directions, are much harder to cope with than a steady gale. Records from one of the Fastnet races show the dramatic impact of a passing front. The average wind remained no more than a fresh to strong breeze, Force 5 to 6, but the gusts were storm Force 10. The sail you need

A depression passes

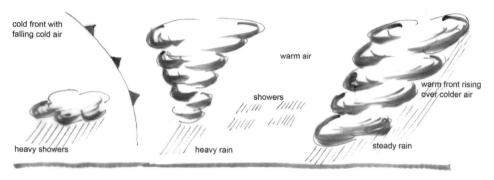

cold front with
falling cold air

warm air

showers

warm front rising
over colder air

heavy showers

heavy rain

steady rain

to make headway in rough water in a 25-knot breeze will broach you and knock you down in a 50-knot gust.

Depressions are always associated with falling barometric pressure and thickening cloud. In summer they often last four to five days. As they fill, pressure rises and they die. However, it is not uncommon for secondary centers of low pressure to form as this happens. These secondaries always form on the southern side of the main depression. They have shorter lives than the main depression but can be an intensifying weather system and more violent. Up to four secondaries might form before the main depression matures and dies and leaves the ocean to whatever new main depression is now forming.

Depressions bring gales and local conditions can make storms worse than the Pilot Charts suggest. In mid-July, on their "First Crossing," Carol and Malcolm McConnell were on the northern route from New York to the Azores, somewhere above 39°N, when they were hit by a storm that pounded them and made them fear they would be rolled. The unusually strong gale came out of an Arctic low drawn south by the jet stream from a tropical depression moving over the Ohio Valley from the Gulf of Mexico. The Arctic low produced a steep pressure gradient between its center and the Azores High. With a wind against the east going Gulf Stream current, and the Gulf Stream running faster due to the pressure of the Labrador Current to the north, the 50-knot winds and stronger gusts raised waves of more than 20 feet. With the barometer falling and the waves rising the McConnells feared they might be in the path of a hurricane. But no, just another nasty Gulf Stream storm.

Outside the envelope—global warming and you

Freaky weather may be becoming the norm. Scientists warn of the effects of global warming. Industrialists run counter claims. Politicians often sit on the fence. American scientists produce evidence of rising carbon dioxide in the atmosphere and the resultant greenhouse effects, but at the time of writing America hasn't joined Kyoto and at the G8 summit in 2005 political doubts were cast on scientific findings about global warming. America is a major contributor to global warming, generating 25% of the world's pollution. China is poised to become the biggest manufacturer in the global economy. India, the world's largest democracy, is coming up fast. Taken together, these countries have to bring tens of millions of people out of grinding poverty. How high can they place carbon emissions and sustainability against better living standards at any price? Neither China nor India have yet chosen to go clean or dirty. It looks like the world will get warmer.

It takes decades for the oceans to absorb heat and warm up, but they are noticeably warmer since my childhood. It is likely that they will take decades to shed their heat and cool again. Whatever the causes, a process is underway that may change the nature of the world for us and the next few generations. If the ice caps start melting it won't just be wet feet in London and New York as sea levels rise. All manner of freakishness may follow. The Gulf Stream may be reversed by the cold fresh water coming down from the north. Icebergs could block up Broadway. Make your Atlantic crossing now, while we still have the Gulf Stream and a familiar climate.

An amateur meteorologist in Fair Isle, Shetland, has been recording weather for the last 30 years. His data show 2005 to be the most chaotic year in his records. Sea temperatures not only differed from the long-term average but went up and down without reference to winter, spring, summer or fall. And the life that usually arrives at different times of the year, expecting temperatures that supports it, was just as confused as the meteorologist but suffered more. The nutrients that plankton expected and the plankton that the fish and sea mammals were expecting just never arrived.

Global warming produces freak effects because it interferes with the patterns of global heat exchange. Air and ocean currents need to travel faster to cope with the greater amount of heat. They need to push into new regions of the earth to find new heat sinks. The effects are more extreme than we have been used to. The growing desertification of the last half century becomes both a cause and effect of wider desertification as heavier winter rains fall further north. But these winter rains don't fall as welcome contributions to top up the aquifers emptied during the hotter northern summers. They come as torrential rain storms that scour soil from the land and turn flooded rivers into enemies.

Of course, extreme weather isn't new, not even since the last ice age ended some 10,000 years ago. Tennyson wrote a fine poem about a 16th century battle between the little British warship, THE REVENGE, and 53 Spanish ships of war one summer off the island of Flores in the Azores. THE REVENGE had 90 wounded crew ashore. By the time she had brought them back on board it was too late to run and she would not strike her colors so with 100 fit men on deck and 90 wounded below she fought. She sailed into the Spanish fleet until she fell into the wind shadow of a giant galleon, and there she stayed for a day and a night, engaged time after time by groups of galleons, and boarded but always repelling the boarders. At the end of the battle, when she had neither crew nor weapons with which to fight, but had sunk or smashed enough Spanish ships to dissuade the others, the wounded captain Sir Richard Grenville ordered THE REVENGE to be sunk. He died before his order was carried out, and his ship was taken by a prize crew. But as it and the Spanish fleet limped away from the battle field a huge storm and monstrous seas came through to sink THE REVENGE and many of the huge galleons. Who knows, perhaps it was part of a hurricane.

> When the weather is unseasonable elsewhere, there is a good chance it will be unseasonable on these ocean routes. Some friends were telling us about winter storms in the Azores when one of them happened to mention they had 45-knot winds right in the middle of Horta Harbor in April 2003. I wondered about this. "Ana?" I asked. The exceptionally early tropical revolving storm that had sat over Bermuda in Easter 2003 had lasted long enough to produce unseasonably strong gales in the Azores. And Ana wasn't even much of a tropical revolving storm.

I have learned from experience of many different places that the weather is never what it is supposed to be. Even so, I didn't let on to the world how shaken I was by tropical storm Ana in Easter 2003. Ana was profoundly worrying for two reasons:

- she came six weeks before the official start date of the hurricane season. She was a record breaker who also blew away the comforting thesis that storms were now only coming late in the season. Ana confirmed the growing unpredictability of the seasons.
- Ana had not been reported in weather forecasts until she arrived over Bermuda with storm force winds and torrential rains. Now the meteorologists kicked in, naming her and describing her feeder bands and the way she was sucking moisture from Colombia to Bermuda along a 300-mile-wide corridor which left the islands of the southern Caribbean with clear skies and brisk winds. They had plenty to say now, but none of it hid the

fact that they had not seen Ana coming. All that monitoring of thunder cells, jet streams, Sahel rain fall, sea temperatures and easterly waves, all of which supposedly gives a Caribbean sailor several days warning of a tropical storm, doesn't seem to get switched on until midnight May 31st.

Perhaps 2003 was just a taster. We personally know that 2004 was a dangerous year, because G's son in the Caymans lost his home and all his possessions when Hurricane Ivan struck, and the hurricane-proof several-storey office building he worked in was completely washed away. He was lucky to survive. But the hurricane season of 2005 is the one which will go down in the meteorological history books. It broke all records for number and intensity of storms. Katrina's devastation of Louisiana and Mississippi will be long remembered, but the evacuees were barely returning when Rita came in to hit Florida, the Texas/Louisiana border, and forced yet further massive evacuations along the Gulf Coast. Hurricane Wilma in October had the lowest central pressure of any Atlantic hurricane (882mb). Wilma dropped over 60 inches of rain on the Yucatan Peninsula before making landfall in Florida. Hurricane Vince became a hurricane in the eastern Atlantic and tracked northeast, missing Madeira but making landfall in Spain, the first time a tropical cyclone has been known to touch Spain.

Back in 1933 meteorologists agreed to assign 22 names a year to hurricanes. In 2005 they had run out of names by November and new tropical storms were called by Greek letters. Alpha, Beta, Gamma, Delta and Epsilon were named, well beyond the usual number, and they were themselves unusual. Delta formed in the central Atlantic in late November 2005 then swept 100-knot winds over the Canaries and Madeira before hitting Morocco. Tropical Storm Epsilon formed far east of Bermuda on November 29 and survived into December, one of the strongest and longest lasting December hurricanes on record. We couldn't believe it when Zeta formed in the Atlantic on December 30. This was so late that we wondered if it was the last tropical storm of 2005 or the first of the 2006 season. Only one other named storm has formed so late since records started in 1851.

> Scientists said that unless Delta proves to be an isolated incident caused by an unusual combination of weather in the North Atlantic, it points to serious climate change. Sailors on the Trade Wind route be warned.

The 2005 season had not gone as forecast and not all the storms conformed to computer model tracks.

So what of 2006? Word is that 2006 will be a La Niña year. La Niña conditions favor increased Atlantic hurricane activity.

The director of NOAA said "I would like to forecast a mild hurricane season for 2006 but I just can't do that . . . trends indicate that the atmospheric patterns, the temperature of the sea, lower wind shear and other factors probably will force another above normal storm season for 2006."

If you run into really bad and unseasonal weather on what should be a trip through permanent summer, be flexible enough to sit it out if you can. You're doing this for pleasure, remember.

Flowing with the current

The clockwise circulation of water in the Atlantic Ocean is like a conveyor belt that not only carries boats across but brings warm water from the tropics to keep northern Europe warm when the American side is icy wastes. Many of us find it surprising that equable London is further north than most of cold and stormy Newfoundland. Whichever direction you cross the Atlantic you are simply sailing in the same great circulation of air and water round the northern hemisphere, but the way they behave on the western side of the ocean compared to the eastern side is as different as the start and finish of a running race.

The great ocean currents behave in a similar way to the great ocean winds. They behave differently on the eastern side of the Atlantic basin compared to the west. Although in reality wind and current circulate endlessly it helps to visualize them as beginning on the eastern side of the ocean, because this is where they run slowest. The Trade Winds, for example, pick up speed as they cross from Africa to the Caribbean and then are bent round to the north and northeast by the land mass of the Americas and the earth's Coriolis Force. The North Equatorial Current similarly runs from Africa to the Caribbean and is a huge amount of water driven west by the Trade Winds. The bulk of this water pushes up into the Gulf of Mexico. A minor shoot branches off to the northwest and heads for Florida as the Antilles Current. This joins the great flow of water looping out of the Gulf of Mexico and together as the Gulf Stream carries warm water north to northeast along the American seaboard and into the North Atlantic where it becomes the North Atlantic Current.

Between about 50° to 64°N and 10° to 30°W, the North Atlantic Current becomes the slower-moving North Atlantic Drift Current. These two currents take Gulf Stream tropical waters towards the pole and into major sub-Arctic currents. The Drift Current takes warm waters to latitudes higher than in any other ocean. This is why Britain and western Scandinavia have moderate climates.

The waters of the Gulf Stream also turn east and south in mid-Atlantic towards the Iberian Peninsula. This branch runs down the coasts of Spain and Portugal as the Portuguese Current, and down the African coast as the Canaries Current, until it catches the tail of the North Equatorial Current and turns west for the Caribbean. And then the cycle begins all over again.

Only a small amount of Gulf Stream water barely crosses the Mid-Atlantic Ridge. Inside the major cross-ocean flow sits a smaller, weaker loop revolving clockwise in the region between Bermuda and the Azores. This weak flow is significant for those crossing the ocean through the Horse Latitudes. Data from drift buoys show that the weakening currents at the edge of the main stream loop and eddy about seamounts and other ocean-bed topography, as though the currents feel and respond to changes in the sea floor.

PETRONELLA log, Horse Latitudes
We have learned something about the area of variable currents shown on the Pilot Charts midway between the Caribbean and the Azores. When becalmed for a whole night we drifted a mile and a half northeast for part of the night and then to the southeast for the rest. Later, making five to six knots and with the bow wave to prove it the GPS has us making less than four knots over the ground. Adverse current, of course.

This sets the big picture for any Atlantic crossing. The aim must be to catch these currents and air flows. Where you catch them depends on the season of the year. The seasons are important for two reasons:

- to catch the good winds and currents
- to avoid the worst of bad weather.

Atlantic currents

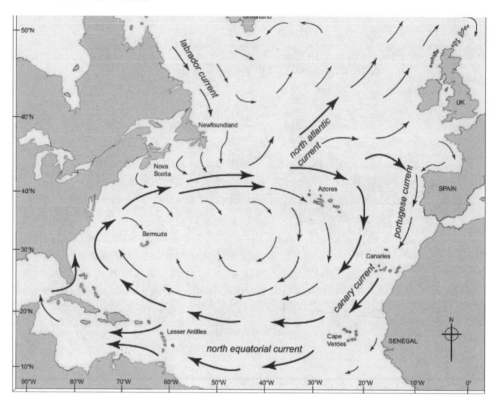

What's happening on the Eastern Seaboard

The North American Eastern Seaboard is dominated by two great currents: the Gulf Stream, bringing warm salty water north from the equator, and the Labrador Current, bringing cold, fresh water down from the ice fields of the Arctic. The Gulf Stream is the current which most directly affects most boats leaving the Eastern Seaboard although some of the features that bother us most are due to the reaction between the different types of water in the two currents.

Gulf Stream

The enduring obstacle when leaving the Eastern Seaboard is to cross the unstable weather of the Gulf Stream. As you leave the gentle breezes of the coast you may find the barometer will fall, the grey clouds build and the wind freshens to gale force and ugly seas kick at your hull. A day later the skies clear, the wind drops to a fine sailing breeze and the boat romps away. Even if you start out with a good forecast, be ready to reef or heave-to. This may be the place where you

Atlantic winds – May

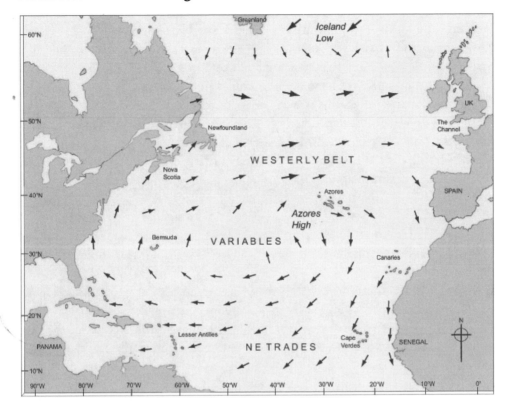

practice for real your heavy weather tactics, long before you reach the deep ocean. This is where all your sailing experience may get its hardest test.

M&J sailed through the Caribbean and the Bahamas north to Miami before starting out across the Atlantic. They had barely cleared the Florida coast when they hit a classic Gulf Stream storm. M was in the cockpit steering. J was down below reading the pilot book. M described the conditions and J told him what would happen next. The dark cloud mass. The torrential rain. Wind on the water. Wild lightning and roaring thunder. Lightning struck so close to the boat that M thought they must surely be hit. He was terrified. He had little faith in the heavy copper wire I had given him to tie to the rigging and hang overboard. When they cleared the Gulf Stream and the storm M couldn't believe how accurately the pilot book had predicted the changing events.

The Trade Wind-driven equatorial currents become known as the Gulf Stream in the channel between the Florida Keys and Cuba. In the Florida Strait the flow is called the Florida Current until it reaches Cape Hatteras. It can run as fast as 2.5 knots in the Strait. The axis of the Stream along the Eastern Seaboard is roughly a little way east of the continental shelf, the 100-fathom line, by about ten miles at the southern end to about 40 miles in the north. This depth contour bends more sharply than the American coast line and the Gulf Stream correspondingly flows at different distances from the coast. North of Cape Hatteras the Gulf Stream begins to turn east, deflected offshore by the shelving of the ocean. After the tail of the Grand Banks the northern branch becomes the North Atlantic Current. From around 45°N the flow widens and weakens and becomes more wind driven.

The location of the Gulf Stream varies by season. The greatest variation—up to two degrees of latitude—is in the north where it closes the Grand Banks. The variation here is due to the Labrador Current pushing its cold waters down the Davis Strait.

After it leaves the Florida Strait the Gulf Stream is noted for its deep blueness, warmth and high salinity. It lacks phosphorescence and can be so clear than you can see down to a great depth. The Stream keeps its blue color all the way to the Grand Banks and contrasts sharply with the green of the Labrador Current. The inner edge of the Current can often be seen from a line of ripples stretching from one horizon to the other. But the seaward, eastern edge of the Stream, is less marked. Beware, however: the eastern edge of the current is where you will find weed and large logs and other dangerous debris.

In several places along its length, but probably most markedly on either side of Cape Hatteras where it is about 150 miles wide, the Gulf Stream breaks into several distinct bands as warm waters run separate from cold. The warm waters create their own warm air so that its clouds may be seen miles away. It is the high, billowing clouds that carry the strongest wind.

One of the earliest charts of the Gulf Stream was commissioned by Benjamin Franklin (statesman, wit, drafter of the Constitution and one of America's greatest ever scientists) in 1770 when he was in charge of the (then) colonial post office. The Board of Customs in Boston had complained to the Lords of the Treasury in London that mail packets from Falmouth, England to New York were taking two weeks longer than American merchantmen sailing from London to Providence, Rhode Island. The Falmouth packets took a direct route and did not seem to realize they were stemming the Gulf Stream. Nantucket whalers tried to tell them but these English were "too wise to be counseled by simple American fishermen."

It was long assumed that the strongest currents ran with the warmest water but today's infra-red imaging suggests that this isn't so. Navigators on the Newport to Bermuda Race are now downloading data on these eddies and counter currents and offshoots at hourly intervals and changing course to benefit from them. They are looking for eddies within the 80 mile or so width of the main flow. The western or north wall of a cold water eddy might give as much as a favorable three-knot current and much smoother sailing conditions. An up-to-date satellite image just before you set off could give you a fine lift.

> The American yacht had left Norfolk, Virginia on a rhumb line for the Azores. They were traveling fast at six to seven knots in the strong winds until they caught the Gulf Stream, at which point their speed increased by another four knots over the ground. They did the first seven hundred miles of the journey in four days and the remaining four hundred miles in a week. They would have taken longer but they got tired of traveling so slowly and motored instead.

Labrador tails and tongues

The Labrador Current brings cold water, pack ice and icebergs down through the Davis Strait between Newfoundland and Greenland to join its annual battle for position with the Gulf Stream.

Thanks to the Labrador Current the northern "Cold Wall" of the warm, salty Gulf Stream is sharply delineated. At the tail of the Grand Banks water temperatures can vary by 2°F within 100 yards of one another along the Cold Wall.

As the Labrador Current travels south it recurves to the east to parallel the line of the Gulf Stream and converge with it, so that the two gradually mix and merge in a lumpy sort of way. As this happens the warm water tongues of the Gulf Stream push into the cold water of the Labrador Current, and *vice versa*, and back eddies form until finally the two are one. However, the term Cold Wall is used even just a little way north of the Florida Strait to describe the coastal edge of the Gulf Stream, and even though the axis of the Stream may well be 40 miles wide in the area from the Florida Strait to Cape Hatteras.

South of Cape Hatteras the eddies branch east and then run clockwise, lasting up to three or four days and giving useful south and southwest currents in the predominantly north-running Stream. North of Hatteras the number of contrary flows increases. Back eddies of up to one knot can be found even in the main axis of the current, and not just in the northern edge where the Stream converges with the Labrador Current.

The 45' Jeanneau left Annapolis in early July and headed SE to find the Gulf Stream. After a day they could clearly see the eddies between the Labrador Current and the Gulf Stream. Over the next few days they tried to stay with the main flow of the Gulf Stream to catch its one to two knot lift but found the center of the Stream very unstable. This was moving rapidly north or south to create eddies of ten to 50 miles across. They listened to NOAA's broadcasts of the position of the Stream but their main source of information was their own GPS. Using standard GPS functions they could measure the sideways, front and rear currents. The Stream gave them a ride north to the 40th parallel and from there they went straight to Horta. They had an uneventful passage of 17 days.

Raising seas in the Stream

The predominant summer wind on the Eastern Seaboard is from the southwest with an average strength of Force 3 to 4 from April to August. The chance of gales decreases the further south you are. Below 35°N there is less than 1% chance of a gale in mid-summer compared to 1% to 5% chance of a gale north of that line. When summer winds run with the Gulf Stream they produce coastal currents in the same direction as the Stream although not driven so fast, giving smooth water sailing.

Sailing in the Gulf Stream can get rough when dry cold air blows off the continental United States. In a hard north or northeasterly, with wind over current, you will be slamming into the short seas, the deck will run with water and for a small yacht life can rapidly shift from being uncomfortable to being dangerous, even bringing you to the point of survival conditions. Start with a good forecast and don't be afraid to let your engine help you get clear of the Stream before the wind turns against you.

It isn't just the current you must watch but the changes in depth. The area where the continental shelf begins has a reputation for confused, dangerous seas in bad weather. The continental shelf is wide and shallow, ranging from less than 50 miles offshore and 100 feet deep before dropping suddenly to ocean depths of 10,000 feet or so. Aim to get clear of the drop off with good weather.

The Gulf Stream is monitored by the US Coast Guard and information broadcast at 1600 and 2200 UTC from NMN in Virginia. You can get information on www.nws.noaa.gov or www.opc.ncep.noaa.gov.

Unexpected waves

As if this weren't bad enough, oceanographers are finding more frightening stuff for us sailors all the time. A few years ago they identified "dynamic fetch" as a contributor to the dreaded rogue wave and wave convergence, and put it forward as a reason for greater wave development in conditions when waves should be getting smaller. The Gulf Stream provides the classic conditions for this.

Dynamic fetch is when wave heights rise much more rapidly than expected. It has been noted in several oceans and usually occurs for two main reasons:

- surface winds traveling at the same speed as the waves are very efficient at passing energy into the wave train
- a rapidly intensifying storm which accelerates its forward speed to stay with the wave train acts like a bulldozer to continually increase wave heights.

Some experts think that the oceans' highest waves are due to dynamic fetch.

> The Agulhas Current off the coast of southern Africa is infamous. The opposing flows of warm water from the Indian Ocean and the colder Atlantic, the strong southwesterly winds and a south flowing current sometimes running at six knots, can create waves of 65 feet and deep troughs along the 100-fathom continental shelf. Big ships have been swallowed by these conditions, or had their backs broken.

The Gulf Stream isn't exactly the Agulhas Current but conditions here can create unpleasant seas. Waves can be higher and get up faster than you would expect just from the weather conditions.

A freaky digression

The rogue wave and wave convergence related to "dynamic fetch" is not the same as a freak wave. A freak wave is something the height of an office block, twice what a commercial ship is designed to ride over. They are a huge breaking wall of water that comes out of the blue. Not a tsunami or tidal wave. Not something I expect anyone to meet on their Atlantic crossing. So don't get frightened. What follows is just a frisson of fear to entertain you.

Freak waves were a bit of a maritime myth until 1978 when the loss of the cargo ship MÜNCHEN during its December crossing triggered some scientific investigations. The huge search found some wreckage but no ship or crew. One piece of wreckage, the unlaunched lifeboat stowed 65 feet above the water line, had clearly been hit by extreme force.

The linear model used by oceanographers and meteorologists to predict wave height assumes that waves vary in a regular way around the average or significant wave height. The model calculates that in a storm producing significant wave heights of 40 feet, a wave higher than 50 feet would be extremely rare. A wave of 100 feet is reckoned to be a once in ten thousand years event. In linear modeling terms, freak waves shouldn't exist.

In the real world freak waves happen with startling frequency. Since 1990, 20 vessels have been struck by monstrous waves on the edge of the Agulhas Current. For a while this seemed to explain the monster waves. Not freaks but current-driven waves whose intersection at some ocean fault enabled them to grow well beyond the predictions of the oceanographic model.

The 85-foot wave that hit an oil rig in the North Sea off Norway in 1985 was not current driven. Nor were the waves in 2001 that crippled two tourist liners in the South Atlantic. One, the BREMEN, was hit by a massive wall of water that left the ship helpless without power in a tumultuous sea. The other, the CALEDONIAN STAR, was hit a few days later. The First Officer saw the 100-foot wave that smashed over the ship, flooding the bridge.

Linear modeling wasn't capturing reality. A new mathematics was needed to explain these waves. Oceanographer Al Osborne applied a modified Schrödinger Equation from quantum physics, the science of strange and complex things. His idea was that in certain unstable conditions waves take energy from their neighbors. The shrinking waves donate energy to the chosen wave, allowing it to grow to an enormous size. Data from the MaxWave project, a remote sensing satellite radar surveillance project funded by six European Union countries in December 2000, supported the new theory. Over a three-week period 3,000 radar images were gathered of sea areas each of 120 square miles. Mathematical analysis revealed ten massive waves, some nearly 100 feet high. No one had suspected there could be so many.

If Al Osborne and the MaxWave data are correct we must re-think our ideas of waves. The revised theory says there are two kinds of waves out at sea:

- the classical undulating type we know and love, adequately described by the linear model
- an unstable monster that at any time can start sucking energy from its neighbors to become a towering freak.

A freak wave is not only big. It is so steep as to be almost breaking. Nothing can ride over this near-vertical wall of water. It just breaks over the ship. This rather than the conventional excuse of bad weather is now being put forward as the explanation for the loss of more than 200 super-carriers in the last 20 years.

There are even eyewitness reports that the high and violent walls of water that sunk some of these ships rose up out of calm seas.

WaveAtlas, the research that follows on from the MaxWave project, will use two years of radar images to create a worldwide atlas of freak waves. Scientists hope to discover how these strange cataclysmic waves are generated and which parts of the oceans are most at risk. However, there is hard evidence that one cataclysmic event can lead to another.

Ivan in the Gulf

Hurricane Ivan, the fearful storm of 2004 that devastated several Caribbean islands and part of the United States, triggered Naval Research Laboratory water pressure sensors on the ocean floor of the Gulf of Mexico. Scientists using the data calculated that extreme waves under the eye of Hurricane Ivan were more than 90 feet high. These are thought to be the tallest and most intense waves ever measured. Even so, scientists suspect that the instruments missed some even taller waves that might have risen to 130 feet. Fortunately, none of these monsters made it to land.

Naval Research Laboratory scientists conclude from this data that previous estimates for extreme waves are too low, that waves in excess of 90 feet are not rogue waves but may be fairly common during hurricanes, and that theoretical models of wave generation during hurricanes may need to be revised. With hurricane activity already at record breaking levels in 2005 and predicted to worsen over the next decade, more research on the matter seems vital.

Mixing highs and lows

The northern half of the Eastern Seaboard from about 32°N upwards is exposed to the variable Westerlies and rapid weather changes from passing depressions. The weather is largely determined by two features of the North Atlantic: the Azores High and the Icelandic Low.

The High, centered on the Azores archipelago but usually to the south or southwest of the islands, generates a ridge of high pressure westwards towards the American coast roughly along 30°N. This ridge moves north and south with the seasons, beginning to move north in February and being furthest north in October when it can reach to 38°N. This ridge tends to dominate the whole of the Eastern Seaboard but the area under its northern flank, between the high pressure zone and the low pressure of the Icelandic Low, is most subject to middle-latitude lows or sub-tropical depressions.

These depressions cross the region from southwest to northeast. Some are already intense as they come off the interior and are at gale force as they cross the coast. Others of lesser intensity may still deepen as they reach the sea and bring gales behind them. The steep sea-temperature gradient on the landward side of the Gulf Stream helps trigger or deepen the depression. The sea area to the north of Cape Hatteras is subject to depressions coming northwards across the sea from Florida and the Carolinas as well as off the continental landmass from Virginia northwards.

Mid-May, in latitude 36°N, the small yacht experienced rapid changes in the weather as different fronts came through. It was making five knots in a gentle southwesterly when the wind slammed round to the north. The skipper dropped the jib and hoisted the storm jib, triple reefed the main then hove-to. Waves driven by the new wind made sailing to windward too uncomfortable, even dangerous. A few days later he passed through the clearly defined center of a storm. Circular with no rain, blue skies, confused seas and a clear demarcation between the windy and windless zones. He made a lot of sail changes as the wind veered, backed, rose and died.

Guides to weather en route

Pilot Charts and ocean passages

Ships at sea are themselves a wonderful source of weather information. Reports from commercial ships over many years have been collated and published by the Hydrographic Center of the US Defense Mapping Agency and the British Admiralty respectively as Pilot Charts and Routeing Charts to give the average conditions likely to be met at sea.

Charts are published for each month of the year. You will need the charts for April, May and June for the trip to the Azores, from July through to October for the onward journey to Europe, and from November to January or February for the return trip. You might as well buy the full set for the year.

Each chart shows:

- wind roses and arrows of the strength, direction and probabilities of wind
- curves of the speed and direction of ocean currents
- lines of storm tracks and the seasonal limits of the Trade Winds
- tables of expected barometric pressures.

I love using Pilot Charts to help my strategic choice of route but I recognize their limitations. They show typical and average conditions whereas it is probably true that the most constant feature of winds and ocean currents in any part of the world and at any time of year is variability. Sad to say, using a pilot chart to derive a route can be little better than checking the tea leaves.

> **PETRONELLA log**
> As we came through the Horse Latitudes we spent hours each day staring at the Pilot Charts. I looked at charts for the month before and the month after. I moved our position north a bit and south a bit, east a bit and west a bit, trying to find circles of weather that matched ours. We could so easily have suffered from data overload if it hadn't been obvious that in no month, within a hundred or more miles of our position, would we find a decent wind. That's why we didn't have a decent wind.

In preparation for leaving the Caribbean G and I studied the Pilot Charts for April, May and June and read all we could about yacht experiences on different routes from the Caribbean to the Azores, as they sail from 18°N to 38°N.

The classic sailing route given in that classic volume *Ocean Passages for the World* (first published in 1895 by the British Hydrographer of the Navy but still a standard work for all ocean sailors) is to head north to Bermuda to clear the Horse Latitudes as directly as possible and keep going north till you pick up the strong westerly winds. By heading north you take advantage of the tendency for southerly winds once you leave the Trade Wind belt. The problem is that you might have to sail west of north to keep a breeze before you can lay your final destination to the east.

Yachts still take this route. Indeed, it is the classic route for those wanting a fast sail in predictable winds with a favorable current before the permanent high pressure system over the Azores robs you of wind and you must motor or drift.

I looked at the wind arrows on the Pilot Chart and wondered how we would get north to Bermuda and beyond. Then I looked at the arrows along 40°N and wondered why I wanted to go there anyway. Up around 40°N the good winds come with a higher chance of gales. The old commercial sailing ships that went that way were, of course, biggish vessels of about 2,000 tons, with Cape Horn crews and skippers who said challenging things through clenched teeth, like: "I put the sail up. Only God takes it down." Such vessels, able to make more than ten knots, would think nothing of the 600- to 700-mile detour that the north-about route to Bermuda involves.

Perhaps we little yachts grown used to the Caribbean are better suited to the vagaries of the Horse Latitudes. Perhaps the generally fair weather with little rain or cloud was thought too much like a vacation for the paid crew of windjammers.

I decided, as Her Majesty's Hydrographer of the Navy might have said in 1895, to follow a more expeditious route of my own devising, expressing my preference for shorter distances and gentler ocean breezes.

Little sailing boats and novice crews have increasingly taken the rhumb line, modifying it by heading east of north after the Trade Winds in the hope of finding some wind. They go northwards to clear the Horse Latitudes but track northeastwards to keep close to the direct line to the Azores. The rhumb route is best suited to yachts that can sail in light winds or have the double blessing of a reliable diesel engine and big tanks.

Pilot Charts show variable and light winds north of the Trade Wind belt and occasionally the promise of a good breeze. Not strong, seldom more than Force 4, but from the east or southeast coming south and southwest after the latitude of Bermuda. It looked like we could manage a track northeast direct for the Azores so the plan was to head in this direction and see what came, favoring a tack to the north over one to the east whenever we couldn't actually sail northeast. We would travel on port tack and let the windvane follow the breeze from east to southeast and then to southwest to west. Lucky the man in our port berth. No need for his soft flesh to suffer the hard timber of our lee-board.

Tracking northward had three advantages:

- it modified our rhumb line into a better approximation of a great circle route
- it got us up to the stronger winds faster
- it took us across the adverse current at something close to a right angle rather than head on.

If the wind forced us to sail a little west of north I would mind this less than if it had us sailing a little south of east. It never occurred to me that I might have to make the choice between going west or going south, but in the Horse Latitudes these things happen.

PETRONELLA log
Even I was hoping for stronger winds. Not much stronger, but stronger and more reliable and able to drive us at better than two knots. Our noon-to-noon runs are a disgrace and not improving. If we want the stronger winds to the north we have to point ourselves at Florida.

Following the Pilot

The Pilot Charts show that in May, the main month to set out for the Azores, ocean currents sweep northwest through the sea area from the Caribbean to 30°N at half a knot. Above 30°N they become variable, part of an inner circle that swings round to the east near Bermuda but is not reliably heading east till about 38°N, roughly on the latitude of Delaware.

The Eastern Seaboard has much stronger currents from the Gulf Stream. After its rush through the Florida Strait the Stream curves northeast to Cape Hatteras at one and a half knots. Winds in summer here are predominantly with the current, blowing south to southwest at Force 4 to 6.

> The 28-foot sloop left Port Salerno, Florida in mid-May, bound for Bermuda, the Azores and then to Spain. In her first 24 hours the current gave her a lift of 30 miles northwards.

The Trade Winds are distinctly easterly in the north Caribbean and on both the Bermuda route and the rhumb line become more southeasterly and lighter the further you travel from the Caribbean. The Bermuda route holds out more promise of east and southeast winds, possibly up to a Force 4, while the Pilot Chart shows the rhumb line route is plagued with winds from every direction, but without much in them.

Coming off the Eastern Seaboard, once clear of the main Gulf Stream current, the current south of Cape Hatteras and west of Bermuda will push you north to northeast, the rate of flow declining as you close Bermuda.

Stronger southerlies are to be found about 70 miles due east of Bermuda rather than at the island itself. Further east on the latitude of Bermuda you have more chance of Force 5 and 6 winds from the southwest. This suggests that a modified rhumb line route should aim to cross the latitude of Bermuda 70 miles or more to the east of the island to increase the chances of a strong sailing breeze. At around 35°N winds are mainly Force 5 and 6 anywhere from the west, north round to south. They may occasionally touch near gale and full gale.

> The British yacht had left Antigua about a week after us and took the route due north to Bermuda. They took six days to cover the 900 miles to Bermuda and then 12 days to sail the 1,700 miles from there to the Azores. They found the good winds they wanted. Sometimes more than they wanted. They spent some time under storm

canvas, but they were a strong crew used to offshore racing. They listened to weather router Herb Hilgenberg whenever the SSB signal was propagating, which was a little better than on our route much further south. Herb advised all vessels to stay south of 35°N to avoid the series of low pressure depressions coming through every three or four days. The British yacht only went below 35°N when blown there by the strong winds. Even if they had heard Herb more clearly they would still have stayed up north and risked the gales.

Boats leaving the coast north of Hatteras cross the Labrador Current running southwest at half a knot and pick up the Gulf Stream running northeasterly at one knot. From almost anywhere north of Hatteras, but certainly from as far north as New York, boats will struggle to reach Bermuda against the usual adverse currents and light southerly winds. They might prefer to slip into the favorable current and winds on the direct route to the Azores but if they do this as early as April or May they will run more chance of meeting gales. By June they may find themselves up around 40°N hunting a decent breeze, taking their chances with the occasional Force 7 from the south or southwest.

At a boat on the modified rhumb route from the Caribbean will meet stronger winds as it moves north and east and closer to the Azores. A boat coming due east on the Bermuda route along latitude 38°N meeting the same winds will regard them as weakening.

At the Azores the winds in May come almost equally from any direction except southeast. There are no recorded hurricanes on the Pilot Charts for May along the latitudes of the Azores. There is a 5% chance of Force 7 at this latitude but just south of this the probability drops as low as 1%.

April before May

The Pilot Chart shows April currents flowing more directly east to west up to latitude 25°N than they do in May and becoming more variable but still mainly easterly above 25°N. The inner circulation of current is now more concentrated to the north of Bermuda. You face an adverse current between Bermuda and the Azores until north of latitude 38°N.

Trade Winds are lighter than in May and tend to be northeasterly at the northern end of the Caribbean. In this month winds are lighter and more varied on both the Bermudan route and the rhumb route, and at the latitude of Bermuda are more likely to come from north or northwest.

A boat on the modified rhumb route would still seek to go well to the east of Bermuda and make a northeast track to come up to the latitude of the Azores.

A boat sailing north to latitude 38°N has a greater chance of near gales and gales until east of longitude 45°W.

Boats leaving from the Eastern Seaboard will find the Gulf Stream running parallel to the coast and strong. It runs close in to Cape Hatteras before following the continental shelf eastwards along 40°N, still running strong.

A clockwise counter current running west and north at half knot between Bermuda and 40°N would hamper boats from the Chesapeake and further north. If these boats chose to sail a direct line to the Azores they would find favorable south to northwest winds but would also face a higher chance of gales on this route. For a gentler route with less chance of a gale, ride the Labrador Current south to Norfolk and take the Gulf Stream and its sisters on the lee bow to Bermuda.

Closer to the Azores the Pilot Chart shows April winds to be similar to those in May, blowing from any quarter but less noticeably from the east.

June after May

Currents and winds fall off in June compared to May although they continue from the same directions. Currents into the northern Caribbean remain southeasterly and the inner circulation is similar. The Gulf Stream also flows less strongly than in May.

Trade Winds into the northern Caribbean are steady from east and northeast with a maximum of Force 6. North, around 22°N, winds should not rise beyond Force 4. The likelihood of calms increases.

Boats south of Hatteras will have a northerly current on their beam as they head to Bermuda and light winds predominantly from south to southwest.

Even at the latitude of Bermuda, 32°N, winds are lighter and more varied, mainly from south and southwest and seldom reaching Force 4.

The Pilot Chart shows that a vessel must go north from 32°N to 38°N to pick up stronger winds. These are mainly southwest to west but weaker than in May.

Approaching the Azores the winds are lighter than in May and more predominantly from the southwest.

Winds at the Azores are lighter than in May and more likely to be from the east. Occasional near gales may blow from southwest or west but there is only a 1% chance of this or a full gale.

June is the first month when the Pilot Charts show hurricane tracks although most of these congregate in the Gulf of Mexico. Those that curve into the open ocean typically do so well to the north of any route from the Caribbean to the Azores, although vessels starting from Miami or the Bahamas in June could find themselves on a hurricane track.

Log of STELLA, June 1998

If we had gone five days earlier we may well have been sitting under the first tropical storm of the year. Tropical waves are passing through the Caribbean quite fast so we will head out after the next one. We will make a careful assessment of conditions in the North Atlantic.

How good is a forecast?

The National Weather Service forecasts weather in three 12-hour bands of time and each has its own probabilities for being right.

Probability that the forecast will be accurate

Next twelve hours	90%
Twelve to twenty-four hours	75%
Twenty-four to thirty-six hours	66%
The next few days	33%

Anything over a two-day trip and you might as well be reading chicken innards and tea leaves.

Herb Hilgenberg of *Southbound II*, one of the best known yacht routers on the Atlantic circuit, says he can do better. His 24-hour forecast will be right about 90% of the time and his 48-hour forecast will be right about 75% of the time. This is good, but then Herb has plenty of experience and the respect of the professionals. However, the chance of a forecast being right won't be as good as this when the weather conditions are unstable and changeable, and in the vastness of the ocean there is even less chance that it will be right for just where you are.

In the old days of not so long ago ocean sailors, and the rest too, had to make their own judgments of weather. You must do the same. In the end, whatever the forecast, you have to make your own judgments of where to sail or where to stay. No forecast absolves you from your duty to keep a close watch on the three vital elements that tell you of approaching weather: barometric pressure, wind and sky. By improving your grasp of weather you can add your local knowledge to the professionals' information.

The barometer is your single most important forecasting tool. The speed and direction of change in barometric pressure is a great indicator of improving and worsening weather. You may have grown used to ignoring your barometer if you have been in the Caribbean. The closer you are to the equator, the less use the barometer because here even a small change in pressure can bring big changes in wind strength. This makes it harder to notice significant changes. In the higher latitudes a bigger, more easily observed change in barometric pressure is needed to bring wind.

Barometers need to be read continually, not just when the weather looks bad. It isn't just what is happening now that you want to know but what was happening several hours ago.

Pressure change always means a change in the wind. If the barometer isn't changing then the wind won't change even if it is blowing a 40-knot gale. Of course, if the barometer refuses to budge in a gale we need to find other information to tell us when the gale will end. In the absence of a forecast, turn to what you can see of wind speed and direction.

Clouds are a good indication of wind. Log the changes in cloud so that you can look back over eight to 12 hours to see what may be developing. Low clouds tell us about winds near the surface. High clouds tell us about winds in the upper atmosphere. High clouds rarely travel in the same direction as surface wind. These are the ones to tell us of an approaching depression.

When it comes to clouds I like simple but informative picture books. We carry Alan Watt's *Instant Weather Forecasting*. This wonderful little book helps us distinguish the two main types of cloud:

- stratiform—the layers of flat cloud
- cumulus—the more fluffy, individual type.

Unfortunately there are many types of cloud and the sky is usually more of a jumble than the photos but at least it's a start and at least we are trying.

Cumulus clouds have more defined edges and clearer vertical rise than the sheets of stratus. In the mid latitudes the thickening and lowering of stratiform clouds indicate approaching bad weather. The barometer should be falling and wind increasing, perhaps backing before steadying. The speed at which barometric pressure drops is a good indication of how strong the wind will be.

Increasing amounts and size of cumulus cloud also indicate bad weather. The higher the clouds, the greater the chance of rain. If the clouds grow into huge cumulonimbus thunderclouds then squalls of gale force are on their way.

The thinning of cloud and reducing size of cumulus indicates improving weather. The wind may still be strong since this depends on the pressure gradients around the edges of high pressure. The closer the isobars at the edge of high pressure, the stronger the winds, but you are unlikely to be surprised by other sorts of weather trouble.

Look for weather information most relevant to your circumstances, especially if planning something potentially perilous. Different barometric pressures are associated with cyclones and depressions. High pressure reduces water levels while low pressure increases it. If heading for a river with a bar or seeking shelter in tidal flats where chart depths are close to the minimum you need, this barometric effect may be very significant.

Dogged by the Horse

Our weather forecasting fell apart in the Horse Latitudes although to be honest it would have fallen apart by about day five of whatever route we had taken. That's what happened to most people, even those getting a routeing service.

By taking the rhumb line between the Caribbean and the Azores we were taking a climatic route through and deep into the heart of one of the world's great high pressure zones. We had no experience to draw on. We would have known more about our weather if we had been able to feed in day-to-day forecasts or actual reports but on PETRONELLA we were struggling to hear SSB weather forecasts and spoke to big ships too infrequently to build ourselves a synoptic chart. So we dusted off our meteorology texts and did it ourselves.

The truly wonderful thing about the Horse Latitudes is that there isn't much weather around to forecast. Our major fear was an early tropical storm, so whenever the horizon clouded over or the wind and sea rose I went through the Buys Ballot's method of finding the center of low pressure. Whatever it was I found never seemed to be the fearful vortex of a raging tropical revolving storm.

> **PETRONELLA log, Day 6.**
> We guessed we had some weather coming when long heavy squall lines were building as the sun went down yesterday. We had massive lightning in the night, so bright that it seemed to be next to us yet so far that we never heard thunder. Bad SSB reception was made

The Horse Latitudes. The thin, fluffy, high clouds tell the weather story. Not much is happening here.

worse when I disconnected the antenna in case we had a lightning strike. The new wind put us on a welcome beam reach and six knots but by morning the seas were lumpy, the boat lurched unpleasantly and when E took a wave head-on he wasted both his morning coffee and the precious fresh water he had used on washing. This could be a bad day for E. His computer has already chosen today to delete all the files on the hard disk.

I had hoped to be assisted in my weather forecasts by the top-of-the-range electronic weather station that we had brought out with us this year and had been admiring during our sail north through the Caribbean. We called it Magnus, after its previous owner. We fully expected its various measurements and its 24-hour memory to change our lives on the ocean but no matter how we changed batteries, cleaned contacts, pressed the re-set button or spoke to it nicely the high tech weather station refused to play ball. A piece of seaweed would have been more use.

2

Routes out of the West

Eastern Seaboard routes that take you close to the Azores are the furthest south you can sail with helpful westerly winds. You can start from almost anywhere on the American seaboard and still find that your natural route is through the Azores. If you want a nice round number that sums this up, remember 40°N. This, give or take 5°, is the line of latitude on which the archipelago of the Azores lies. This is roughly the line you will sail up to from Panama or the Caribbean, Miami or Norfolk, and the line you will sail down to from New York or Nova Scotia. Where you join this line depends on whether you sail towards Bermuda or not, but join it you must because this is the line between two great Atlantic weather systems. You will weave along this line, a few degrees north of it or as much as ten degrees south of it, looking for westerly winds that are neither too strong nor too weak.

The Horse Latitudes, being a large area of high pressure and calms, is not a place that sailors with a schedule want to visit. So although the direct rhumb line distance from the Caribbean to the Azores is about 2,200 miles it is usually quicker to sail the extra 400 or so miles up towards Bermuda to pick up the Westerlies. Sometimes you can pick up these good winds without having to go as far as Bermuda. Quite where you find them depends on the weather that year.

In 2003 the Azores High was being squeezed by lows coming from the west and route advisors were keeping boats well below 40°N. One fine 35-foot wooden sloop that had set out from New England stayed around 35°N and took only 16 days from Bermuda to Horta. A British singlehander on a 35-foot ketch from Anegada to Horta was told to stay south of 30°N. Even so he had a near gale with heavy rain and another Force 7 a week later. To us this was incredible. We were deep in the protection of the Horse Latitudes. Nothing could reach us there, not even the radio waves from the SSB routers.

Routes via Bermuda or any version of the rhumb line have this in common: you need to make sure the boat is set up for sailing in light airs and you should carry as much drinking water and diesel fuel as you can. For all boats sailing to the Azores the trick is to monitor the position of the Azores High and avoid sailing right into it.

You may get a gale, and you may not enjoy it, but storm force winds don't usually last long and boats usually cope. Light weather sailing is different. Most yachts spend more time in frustratingly light winds than they ever do in storms. I wish I knew the best answer to coping with it. I have tried many combinations of sails, including some bought especially for the purpose, without consistent success.

Motoring isn't the answer. The special joy of a sailing boat on passage is to make its miles quietly, day after day. Having capacious fuel tanks doesn't justify motoring or make the engine noise more pleasant.

> The experience of several yachts that sailed north of us in 2003 suggests that it might be better to wait for the wind to change than motor in calms. That year the low pressure troughs and high pressure ridges at around 30°N made for very variable winds—from calms to near gales. Light winds usually lasted less than a day, sometimes less than half an hour. The periods of good winds gave plenty of chance to make up distance. Unless you have a motorsailer or such good weather information than you can motor to good purpose, the mental readiness to use the engine to keep moving can make for frustration that takes away the pleasure of being at sea on a sailboat.

Via Bermuda and the Azores

Leaving from the Eastern Seaboard

You have a short summer window of April to June. The adverse current between Bermuda and the Eastern Seaboard lessens during May, making this your best month. In June and July the incidence of Northerlies is reduced but you have entered hurricane season. In August the west going current between the Azores and Bermuda becomes more marked and boats heading to Bermuda from the Eastern Seaboard north of Cape Hatteras will be sailing into an adverse north to northwest going current. Boats from Newport and north of there may prefer the more direct route of North through the Middle covered later.

If all is well after you clear the Gulf Stream you may decide to stay north in the westerly winds and not visit Bermuda. If you put in to Bermuda you may need to go back north to get out of the light variable and unreliable Horse Latitudes and find the fringe of the Westerlies.

Harbor authority data shows that boats arriving in the Azores leave Bermuda any time between March and September but the main months are May to July. Nearly 60% arrived in June, which means that many left in May. It looks like skippers are following the climatic plan.

Leaving from the Lesser Antilles

The classic point of departure from the Caribbean is Antigua or thereabouts, at 17°N by 62°W and the ideal time to leave is end of May or early June. Fronts coming across the US usually stall before they reach the northern Caribbean. A boat coming out of Antigua gets a good slant to reach the northern limits of the Trade Winds, usually up around 26°N to 28°N. Boats leaving from the Virgins, as we did, two degrees further west, lose this windward advantage.

The area from the northern Antilles to Bermuda, as well as the rhumb route from the Antilles to the Azores, is dominated by a strong west going current during late spring and early summer. This current weakens sometime in May and turns more to the northwest, becoming less of a problem for boats heading to Bermuda from the Antilles. Even in May the route along the line of 40°N has half to one knot of adverse current and a greater risk of gales than the direct track to the Azores along 38°N or 39°N.

By June the adverse current on the rhumb line from the northern Antilles to the Azores can still be as much as half a knot and the winds are frustratingly light and variable even as far north as Bermuda.

Over half the boats visiting Horta leave from the Caribbean, including the Virgins. The main starting places within the Caribbean are the French islands of Guadeloupe, Martinique, St Martin and St Barts, perhaps reflecting the large number of French yachts crossing the Atlantic, and the more northerly islands of St Lucia, Antigua and the BVI. These are the first boats to reach the Azores in any numbers, coming in a month ahead of boats on the Bermudan route. The data shows that there are always about 15 skippers willing to sail here in winter (October through February) but many of these are racers and Challenge Business yachts and others pitting their boats against the sea. I have never felt the need to do that pitting stuff myself. Arrivals peak in May. June is still a good month but the flow from the Caribbean stops sharply in July, when hurricanes get underway. Boats from the Caribbean typically take from 15 to 20 days. Very few take more than 25 days.

Leaving from the Virgins

Even in May you need a weather forecast that shows no norther coming down from the American coast. Cold fronts can still bring intense weather systems down between the Bahamas and the Virgins.

Leaving from the Panama Canal

There is no direct passage from Panama to Europe, nor even an easy one, so most boats will find themselves sailing into the island chain and working their way north up the Caribbean. Of the three or four direct routes you can choose it is just a matter of how much windward sailing you want to do and how best to time a weather window. Probably what you don't want to do is time your transit through the canal so that you end up waiting around Panama for months until conditions allow you to head eastwards.

The area around Panama is usually safe from hurricanes but as you head into the Caribbean Sea it is best to avoid the hurricane season. Boats heading directly northwards towards Cuba or Puerto Rico must be especially alert to both the hurricanes of summer and the winter storms. Summer winds are better for this course, being lighter and more likely to be from the southeast, but squalls will be mixed with calms and there is a danger of hurricanes. When winter northers come out of the Gulf of Mexico the conditions get increasingly dangerous the further north the boat gets. Wait for the norther to pass and go with the lighter winds which will last for several days.

The Gulf of Mexico is badly affected by hurricanes and storms that form there or in the Caribbean. These, often late season hurricanes, give less warning than the classic Cape Verde hurricanes which are tracked all the way across the Atlantic even when they are only tropical depressions.

However, it is likely that the combination of wind direction and current will not allow a boat to sail this course or even make Hispaniola or Puerto Rico. In which case, the best course may be to head for the western end of Jamaica and use the land breezes to work along the big island of Hispaniola. Take care, though. The Caribbean Sea has many shoals and banks on which the sea may break in heavy weather. Strong west running currents can set you down onto these dangers. On the direct course from Panama to Jamaica beware of New Bank and Pedro Bank, both of which can be dangerous.

Panama to the southern Caribbean

The southern Caribbean is a fine cruising area and it is wholly in keeping with the spirit of your new life on the ocean that if you get the chance to be there you should make the most of it and not hurry along. Facilities in Venezuela and Trinidad, in particular, and air links back to the US and Canada enable easy crew changes or allow crews to leave the boat to fly home if they need to. A fine balance has to be struck to time your passage between hurricane season and when Trade Winds are least boisterous. Then, depending on which route you have taken to arrive in the Caribbean, find your way north either to Antigua or the Virgins as your jumping off point for the ocean.

Head winds and contrary currents along the Venezuelan coast make a non-stop passage to Trinidad or Grenada uncomfortable, even impossible at times. This passage can be a test of rig and crew.

> Don Street, one of the main pilot book authors for the Caribbean, describes the damage he has seen on boats which were not prepared for the passage into the Caribbean. Torn sails, broken rigging, even dismasting. Don't be fooled into thinking that just because this looks like paradise it will be soft and kind.

Fortunately, you didn't come here to test your rig or your ability to sleep on a bucking bronco. There are some wonderful places to visit on the way east that can be reached in short hops taking advantage of the variable and lighter winds common at the change of seasons.

The most comfortable conditions are in late spring and early summer but this would bring you into the Caribbean too close to the start of hurricane season. Avoid this by transiting the canal in April or May and cruising the Colombian coast, the Dutch ABC Islands of Aruba, Bonaire and Curaçao and then the Venezuelan islands until it is safe to enter the Caribbean. Boats on this timetable should aim to make the last leg to Trinidad or the Windward Caribbean before the Christmas winds. These are the stronger Trade Winds, intensified by the northerly winds coming out of the Gulf of Mexico. In early winter, around November and December, the winds on this coast have more north in them compared to the northeasterlies which usually prevail. On balance, this is the best time for this trip.

The worst winds are probably January to April at the height of the winter

Trades. The summer months of the rainy season can also be unpleasant, being unsettled and squally with rough conditions if big storms or hurricanes are passing to the north and east.

Land and sea breezes are strong on this coast and need to be taken into account. The morning sea breeze comes from the northeast and moves progressively into the east from mid morning to dusk. It veers during the night to become southeast, but also moderates. Keep close inshore and take advantage of the land breeze and the tendency for the Trades to reduce overnight. Remember, the wind also affects wave heights, making for a more comfortable sea state at night and early morning.

For part of the year there is a circular current in the bay between Nicaragua and Colombia which can give you a push of half a knot to the east before you hit the strong west going Caribbean Current somewhere between Cartagena and the ABC Islands. At times this east going current is no more than a weak back eddy close in along the Colombian coast; at other times it can flow east at half a knot well offshore. Month by month variations are shown on the Pilot Charts.

From the Bahamas

The Bahamas is not a good setting off point. The prevailing winds and current run from east to west through the archipelago, against the direction you need to go. Up till May the region is subject to strong winds from cold fronts coming off America and tropical waves from the south. At least one severe storm should be expected during May. From June the Bahamas are right in the main track of hurricanes. This gives a very short window to leave the Bahamas. Most boats will be joining the Gulf Stream and taking a ride north before they can begin to head east for Bermuda. Some I know even called in at Miami.

After Bermuda

Sailing from Bermuda to the Azores is also a short season, with your best month being May. Even on the route via Bermuda you may encounter strong winds and big seas and much colder temperatures as you come up into the low pressure system. You are also losing the warmth of the Gulf Stream.

> **PETRONELLA log**
> It is getting much cooler. Sea temperature is 68°F compared to the 80°F we left behind in the Caribbean. I now wear long trousers and sleep in my sleeping bag, not on top of it. The cold north wind is tiring, sapping my energy.

Yachts from 50 to 250 miles apart may be in completely different weather systems, one getting gales from the west while the other is in 15-knot winds from the southeast.

In June 2003 the yacht WINDSONG had strong winds which dropped to Force 4 while a boat 240 miles to the east had a Force 7. WINDSONG was in a low pressure trough; the other boat was between two fronts. After motoring east for two days in search of winds the skipper realized he lacked the speed to get out of the low pressure system.

The gap between the calms of high pressure and the lows that track across the Atlantic is narrow. Use the barometer to edge north and south to keep a good wind. As you close the Azores you may find that the summer high pressure system hasn't established itself. If so, stay far enough north to pick up the Westerlies of the mid latitude lows.

Changes can happen very quickly in this region of variable winds. Also, one year may be very unlike another.

WINDFREE left Bermuda in June 1989. They got their first gale three days later at 35°N. Four days after that, in gentle rainy weather just north of 36°N, the light southwesterly suddenly flew round to a strong northerly and laid the boat over. Within an hour the wind was Force 8 gusting 9 and the skipper had hove-to under triple reefed main and storm jib. Over the next 30 hours the boat alternated between heaving-to in the gale or struggling to windward with a veering Force 7 and rough seas on the nose. When the wind died to dead calm the skipper noted swell from east, southeast and northwest, all going right at each other. After a day of light winds and yo-yoing barometer another storm hit. The wind changed from NNW gale to S7 to SSE9 but without any change in barometric pressure. The yacht spent three hours lying a-hull trailing warps until it could sail east under storm jib to escape the worst. It was another eight hours before the waves fell below 20 feet. Out of the storm the boat met strong easterly headwinds and could make no progress into lumpy seas. When the easterlies turned into another gale the skipper was forced by frighteningly giant waves to hoist more sail and move out of the danger area. It took nearly two days for the seas to settle to a more regular pattern and more survivable 25 footers. In all, this was a six-day storm that ended suddenly and left WINDFREE becalmed in cross swells for two days. The boat was now at 37°50'N. To escape a half knot adverse current the skipper worked northwards to 39°N. The storms were over. WINDFREE took another eight days of light and variable winds and flat calms to reach Horta.

Caribbean rhumb route to the Azores

At this time of year the Trade Winds blow mainly from east to southeast, making the first part of the direct route possible. With luck a boat might carry southeast winds all the way through the Horse Latitudes. Constant southeast winds through the Horse Latitudes give clear, bright weather. Other winds mean cloudy, overcast skies.

The rhumb line journey through the Horse Latitudes is a story of the strange Sargasso Sea. This two million square-mile ellipse of fabulously deep-blue water covers the western Atlantic area from about 20°N to 35°N. The Bermuda islands are up in the northwestern part of the Sargasso Sea. The precise location of the Sea varies as it ranges about with the clockwise ocean currents that define its perimeter.

These perimeter currents—the Florida, Gulf, Canary, North Equatorial, Antilles, and Caribbean—are some of the strongest in the world. They interlock to separate the Sargasso Sea from the tempestuous Atlantic. The waters within this great swirl of currents is still and warm, exceptionally clear and its surface, thanks to the rotational effects of the currents, is about three feet higher than the waters of the Atlantic Ocean.

The Horse Latitudes and their Sargasso Sea is a truly ancient place, untouched by man. It is remote from the things we do on land or even to the shallow waters of our continental shelf. For all I know this primordial wilderness is little different from the time, hundreds of millions of years ago, when life on earth settled into some of the forms familiar to us now.

The Sargasso Sea was named by Columbus and his sailors in 1492 for the brown seaweed that grows there. They gave it the ancient Portuguese word for grapes (*salgazo*) because of its berries. Some sailors claim that Sargassum weed lies in dense rafts through which no ship can hope to travel, but I think they exaggerate. Surely it is only in myths that the seaweed could be thick enough to hamper a ship from sailing through. We saw plenty of weed floating around but never saw anything that might be called a raft.

Biologists regard the Sargasso Sea as a marine desert, albeit with its own unique ecosystem. The surface waters take so long to change that they are depleted of nutrients. The organisms are specially adapted to live among the

The Wide Sargasso Sea

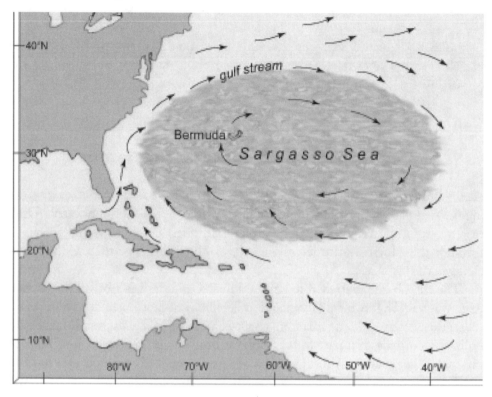

Sargassum mats. Whatever lives here has had millions of years to adapt to the biological imperatives of deep water, free of any interest from humankind.

Scientists say that anything that drifts into one of the surrounding currents eventually ends up in the Sargasso Sea. In effect this is a catch-all for the Atlantic Ocean. Things circle around until they eventually reach the middle, where they must sink or float forever. The ancient natural gifts of seaweed and dead animals will sink; man's most ubiquitous modern contribution to the natural environment, plastic bottles, float. I have read that tar balls formed from congealed oil after an oil spill are now floating in increasing numbers in the Sargasso Sea. They don't sink and they have no other place to go.

It isn't just tar balls. The Sargasso Sea is a sea of legends of lost ships and floating hulks. The Sargasso Sea overlaps the fearsome Bermuda Triangle, although the Sargasso legends are older by centuries than those for the Bermuda Triangle. There are so many reports of lost ships and lost crews from the days of sail that I have to believe that conditions here can affect ships. The perennial calms and the possible thunderstorms would certainly explain some of this. The weed might stop the propeller of a small yacht but I doubt it could stop that of a large commercial ship and nor would such a ship, with twenty different sorts of radio on board, ever stay lost for long. Yet large cargo vessels have been unaccounted for after entering this sea. It's a mystery. It's an enigma. Don't go reading over-imagined books about ghost ships while you sail on this route. Sadly the modern mind is no freer from fears of the inexplicable than those of earlier centuries and just as given to invent invisible force fields and claim "disconformity with the laws of probability."

The meteorologists and pilot books describe the Horse Latitudes as a region of clear sky, light winds and gentle weather. They should flash this message in huge letters onto the sky so that you get a sense of how unchanging and unthreatening and all together wonderful this weather is. I know it was a bit final for the horses in the great days of sail but us little yachts don't carry horses.

The Pilot Charts show adverse current on the rhumb line from the Virgins until close to the latitude of the Azores and hint at long periods of flat calm below 38°N. On our Horse Latitudes journey the light wind was compounded by a definite adverse current. It pained us that the slower our boat speed the greater the impact of the current. A one-knot current takes a massive 50% of your distance in a boat making only two knots through the water, but only 20% if you are making five knots. We got used to two knots. We only thought of using the engine when our speed dropped below one and a half knots.

Even the Horse Latitudes must come to an end. As we neared the Azores we felt the wind strengthen, which wasn't at all what we had expected. Later we discovered that for those who took the Bermuda route or even went further north than us on the rhumb route it had been a stormy season with gales pushing south of 40°N and the reliable Azores High was later than us.

A British boat we knew from Trinidad left the Virgins at about the same time as we did. He headed north to Bermuda and was getting squally Force 6s at the time we were settling into Horse Latitudes calms. A day later he was exhausting himself reefing and repairing sails while we were studying our charts to see where to look for wind. A few days later he gladly took his router's advice to head south out of the path of a gale but got a Force 7 with heavy rain anyway. We were becalmed at the time. Because of the advice he was getting from his router he took a more southerly Bermudan track (or a more northerly rhumb line than us). His 24 days from Anagada beat us by four days but he was still catching up on sleep when E and I arrived in Horta, fresh and raring to party.

Direct routes to the North

I think of those routes that take a yacht north of the Azores High and do not involve a stop over at the Azores as the northern routes. They divide into three branches:

- North by North
- North by South
- North through the Middle.

Sailors at the northern end of the Eastern Seaboard, especially if heading for Britain or Scandinavia, would see the logical route across the Atlantic as heading up to St John's, Newfoundland and across from there. This is the shortest of routes. In summer it brings long days and, if the weather is kind, the bright blue skies and good sailing breezes of high pressure systems. But you will need an ice chart to keep yourself below the likely limits of icebergs, a close eye on the weather, good oilskins and be ready to cope with gales and even severe gales when the lows come through. If you want to sail these routes, research them well.

Routes to the North

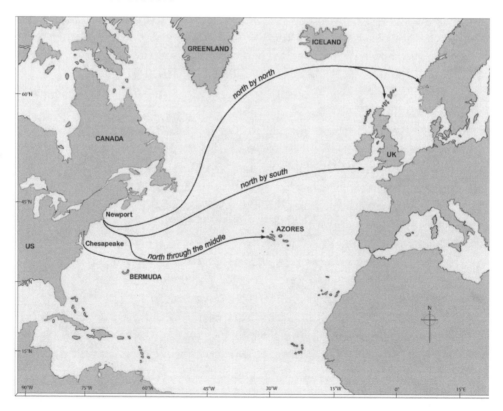

Limits of Icebergs and Fog - July

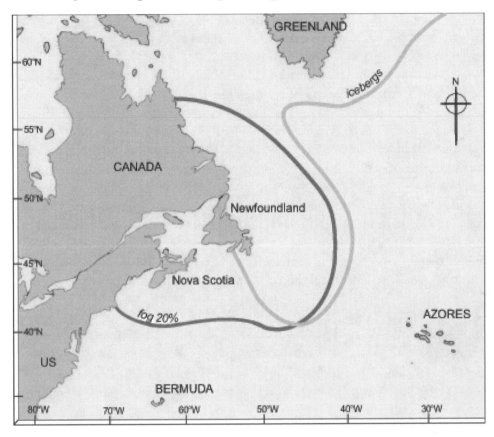

June is rather soon for any of the northern routes. There is still a danger of pack ice off Cape Race, Newfoundland, and icebergs coming out of the Davis Strait on the Labrador Current as far south as 40°N between 55°W and 40°W. The Labrador Current is also running southwest inside the Gulf Stream as far south as New York, giving boats on this route an adverse current of about half a knot. At this time of year there is an almost certain chance of a gale anywhere north of 40°N. Boats heading further north into 55°N to 60°N will certainly have gales although the risk of gales reduces as you get further east.

Even in July there is danger of icebergs down to 40°N but not usually east of 40°W. The risk of gales lessens but they must now be expected further south, down to 50°N. Boats approaching southwest Ireland need to be ready for heavy weather.

Even in August icebergs are likely south and east of the Grand Banks, along 40°N as far as 45°W, and gales must be expected down to 45°N. But boats coming north along the Eastern Seaboard will suffer less from adverse current, now found mainly close to the coast and only as far south as Delaware.

North by North

This is the shortest northernmost route across the Atlantic. It allows you to use Greenland and Iceland, the Faeroes and Shetland or Orkneys as stepping stones before reaching Norway or going into the Baltic. It is likely that Europeans had traveled to the Americas before Columbus by these stepping stones, possibly as early as the 9th century. Certainly, the Viking settlement at L'Anse aux Meadows-Vinland pre-dates Columbus by many centuries. Perhaps the Vikings also returned to Europe the same way. Your timing here is to fit in between the icebergs and bergy bits and even pack ice if you start before July, and the early season hurricanes coming north along the axis of the Gulf Stream if you leave much later.

During the sailing season the winds usually blow offshore or parallel to the coast of North America, giving you a good start. On much of this route you will have fair winds and current but the chances of gales and severe gales are higher than on other routes. That pretty feathery cirrus is bringing you an early warning of a deep depression. Have your heavy weather sails close to hand.

> HB said that from St John's, Newfoundland to Iceland he had to keep a close eye on the tracks of the lows, since this route is north of their track. He couldn't sail in a straight line. He had to dodge the worst of the weather. With proper clothing and his diesel heater he stayed comfortable.

The great circle route from the northeastern seaboard passes close to Nova Scotia and well inside Sable Island, to Cape Race, Newfoundland. The shallow Nantucket Shoals extending 30 miles southeast of Nantucket Island have strong tides over them and breaking seas in bad weather. Strong currents and shoal waters made Sable Island off Nova Scotia a graveyard for ships in the past. Cape Race is also noted for strong currents and bad visibility.

Careful watch is needed crossing the "iceberg alley" of the Labrador Current after Cape Race. Ice can be found southeast of Newfoundland as far south as 40°N. You don't really clear the danger of ice until you cross east of 40°W at some point around 50°N. From early spring the Canadian and US Coast Guard monitor ice on this route as soon as it starts to come south along the eastern edge of the Grand Banks. Information is broadcast daily. Get a report before sailing.

Ice Patrol reports will tell you the position of the bergs but the danger of hitting one is a real possibility. The Ice Patrol say that there is no better way to be aware of ice than by eye or radar and at night or in fog it is essential to be vigilant and to travel at an appropriate speed. Sailors we know who have sailed in bad ice have virtually stopped their boat at night or in fog. You must be ready and able to stop or sheer away if a berg comes up ahead of you.

Most of an iceberg is underwater, hence the movement of a berg is mainly due to sea current rather than wind. Bergs may sneak up and surprise sailing yachts, which not only normally travel with the wind while sailing but also travel with the wind when drifting hove-to.

This is a foggy region in summer. South or southwest winds over the coast of Maine or the Grand Banks carry warm moisture-laden air across the cold Labrador Current to bring frequent dense sea fog above 40°N. Fog, which is technically defined as less than 1,000 meters visibility, may be accompanied by near gale force winds. There is considerable commercial shipping, fishing boats and oil rigs on this coast to add to your problems so boats choosing this route should have radar. But beware, sailing in fog and ice is a hard pastime and ice does not always show on radar. In some weather conditions sub-refraction can reduce the usual useful radar range. Also, even big bergs can give a poor echo depending on the slope of their reflecting surface. This can be as important to the echo as the size of the berg. Bergy-bits and small "growlers" can be the most dangerous. Worn smooth, they tumble like transparent rocks in the water or bob about just below the surface, giving little or no radar echo and being taken for sea-clutter. Remember: just because the radar isn't showing an echo doesn't mean the ice isn't out there. Vigilant watchkeeping is the essence of your safety.

> "For the whole week . . . we have been in fog. The ice-watch routine has become robotic: up on the wave crest—search forward; down in the valley—look side-to-side. We look to the sides . . . because it will warn us that there is ice in the neighborhood. Each seven or eight seconds we repeat the monotonous motion: look forward, look to the sides, look forward . . ."
>
> Rolf Bjelke, NORTHERN LIGHT, the account of a 33,000 mile passage from the Arctic to Antarctic.

When bergs reach the Gulf Stream they may crack and calve. Sharp gun-sounds may be your first warning of ice.

North by South

Yachts sailing from Newport, Rhode Island can avoid the worst of the ice and fog by this southern route, sailing east along 40°N till they reach 50°W and then taking the great circle route towards Lands End, England and either going into the English Channel or striking north to Ireland and Scotland or Scandinavia. Boats leaving Halifax, Nova Scotia would sail southeast to this same point before picking up the great circle route.

The northeast current runs with you, becoming more easterly as it reaches the other side of the Atlantic. Winds will be westerly except when a low pressure system passes and the winds follow it round.

The weather on the northern routes is determined by the relationship between the Azores High pressure system and the Icelandic Low. The isobars of pressure are squeezed between these two systems and define the main storm track from west-to-east. Sailing up to Greenland and Iceland inevitably brings you into the main storm track but in summer you may also encounter hard weather on this more southerly route as the axis of the storm track is pulled south.

North through the Middle

North through the Middle is masquerading as a northern route. It is a more southern route than going North by South. It is an Azorean route, and the middle referred to is the middle latitudes of the ocean. North through the Middle misses out Bermuda.

Yachts leaving the Eastern Seaboard from Chesapeake or Newport or indeed anywhere north of Cape Hatteras might prefer to miss out the southerly leg to Bermuda. They can more or less sail a line from Cape Cod to the Azores. Stay roughly on 40°N or a little south of it and carry this route all the way to the Azores. By the time you get to 50°W you will be joining yachts that went to Bermuda and then sailed northwards to pick up the Westerlies.

Yachts from Nova Scotia can more or less parallel this route to the Azores.

Yachts starting out from Newfoundland would go through the Azores if they were heading to Spain or southern Europe, or if they were heading anywhere in Europe but wanted to see the Azores first. Head southwards to about 45°W on 40°N and then sail eastwards to the Azores.

It isn't just North Americans who sail to the Azores directly from the Eastern Seaboard. The data shows large numbers of French and British yachts on this route, as well as most other nations of Europe. Interestingly, in the years 2003 and 2004 the data shows that only Canadians sail to the Azores from Canada and Nova Scotia. Most boats on this route arrive in the Azores in June but small numbers of late arrivals are still coming in August and September. Our Canadian friend André was an early arrival. He landed on January 8, 2002 after 20 days singlehanded from Iles de la Madeleine in the St

Lawrence, Quebec. The other boats made a great fuss of him. The local newspapers fêted him as a sailor who had braved the Atlantic winter to visit them. Clearly they didn't know the frozen extremes of André's hometown Chicoutimi, due north of Québec City. The records show he was the first boat in that year, which surprised me less than it appeared to surprise him. Perhaps it's hard to tell the seasons in Chicoutimi.

If sailing in a year when the winds around the Azores are weak, yachts on these routes might miss out the islands and continue along 40°N or higher to Bayona or Biscay or take the Portuguese Current and Trades down to Cape St Vincent for the Mediterranean.

Southerners also go North

Northern routes are not only for sailors based in New England. Vessels from Miami to Delaware can also take the northern route. Those from Miami would head up to Charleston, working their way in south and southwest winds to the north of Bermuda and then riding these winds east as they increase in strength. Currents push boats north to the latitude of Delaware then due east at half a knot and more.

The Canadian couple on the 49-foot Oyster had spent two years in the Caribbean then sailed north up the coast to spend winter in Nova Scotia. We met them in Cádiz, Spain, after their crossing via the Azores. They liked the Azores but only spent a couple of weeks there. We suggested they winter there instead of the Mediterranean but they were determined that the next two years would be in the Mediterranean. They had no fierce storms or worrying calms to report. Summer 2005 seemed like a good year for the ocean.

3

Routes from mid ocean to Europe and Madeira

From the Azores your west-to-east ocean crossing to mainland Europe has three main points of arrival:

- the English Channel (La Manche as the French call it)
- the Iberian Peninsula of Spain and Portugal
- the Mediterranean.

You could also cross to Madeira if you lack the time to visit mainland Europe or had to revise your plans after reaching the Azores.

There are good reasons for choosing these three mainland landfalls. Each opens you to a very different region of Europe:

- the English Channel is the gateway to northwestern Europe, the great cities of London, Paris, Amsterdam, Hamburg and then through the Baltic to Copenhagen, Stockholm, Berlin and the cities of Russia and eastern Europe
- the Iberian Peninsula of North West Spain and western Portugal is not just the nearest landfall from the Azores, it is also a fine coast to explore with remarkable cultures. Of course, the nearest land is not a bad thing to aim at
- the Mediterranean is where many west-to-east crossers want to go, as well as many of the boats that come south out of northern Europe. All that dawn of civilization, sunshine and islands. Goodness me, it's almost the Caribbean with red wine and amphitheatres.

The Iberian Peninsula and Mediterranean are easy hops of 800 to 1,000 miles, to Lisbon on 38°N or Gibraltar on 35°N. The English Channel on 49°N is a more taxing 1,000 to 1,200 miles with the possibility of fog and gales and

Mid-ocean to Europe

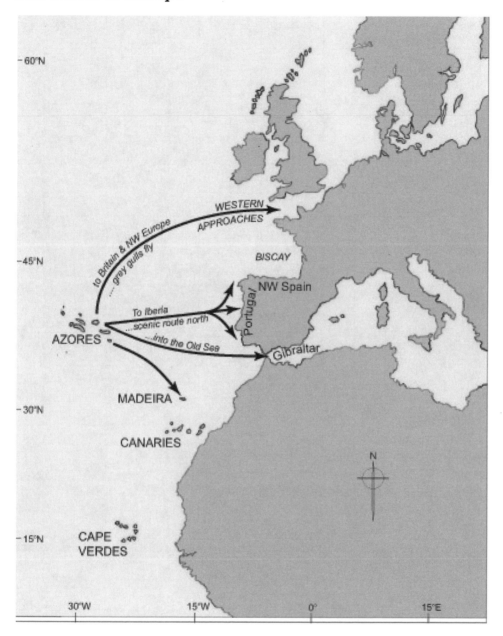

the busiest shipping lanes in the world. Your passage to the English Channel is also the most seasonally restricted of the three but don't be put off by this. The rewards of going there are great and it can't be so very difficult to sail there. All those British and German and Dutch and Scandinavian boats, and half the French ones too, that you see in the Azores or the Iberian Peninsula are heading this way.

Cruising seasons

	J	F	M	A	M	J	J	A	S	O	N	D
Scandinavia and Baltic						■	■	■				
Britain and northwest Europe					■	■	■	■				
Iberian Atlantic coast				■	■	■	■	■	■			
Algarve coast			■	■	■	■	■	■	■	■		
Western Mediterranean			■	■	■	■	■	■	■	■		
Eastern Mediterranean				■	■	■	■	■	■	■		
Azores and mid latitudes					■	■	■	■	■			
Atlantic islands	■	■	■	■	■	■	■	■	■	■	■	■
Caribbean islands	■	■	■	■	■	■					■	■

In many ways the passages to the Iberian coast and Gibraltar are similar. The main difference isn't the extra 150 miles but the tricky entry through the Straits of Gibraltar where you might be forced to wait for the Levanter and its rough seas and dust storms to pass before you can enter the Mediterranean.

You can make passage from the Azores to the Iberian coast and Gibraltar at almost any time of the year if you get your weather right but since winter in the mid-Atlantic is less kind to sailors, you will probably make this passage in summer through to late fall.

Whichever route you choose you must beware the danger of a hurricane coming across as an extra-tropical storm. These can still be very active depressions.

Azores to Britain and northwest Europe

The cruising season for Britain and France is roughly May to early October. It is shorter for Scandinavia and northern Europe and longer as you move south into Biscay and then to Spain and Portugal.

Two choices appeal to sailors leaving the Azores:

- to go direct for the Western Approaches to the English Channel
- to make this a journey of hops by first going to North West Spain and then working across Biscay and touching south or north Brittany as the weather dictates, before entering the English Channel.

Between the Azores and Europe. The happy crew relax in conditions almost as benign as the Horse Latitudes. The clothing is obviously from the same store.

Boats making direct for Scandinavia may not bother with the Channel but go round the north of Scotland. Boats heading for Ireland will take a route similar to the one for the English Channel but usually head further north before turning eastwards.

As the grey gulls fly

Boats leaving the Azores for the English Channel usually head north out of the Azores High until they pick up the Westerlies. You may need to go as far as 45°N to clear the area of calms normal in the Azores and get a reliable west wind. You may even have to sail west of north before you get your good wind. It depends where the High is that year.

Going north will put you into the helpful east-going tail of the Gulf Stream but beware of not going far enough north into the Western Approaches to the English Channel. Part of the North Atlantic Current turns southeast somewhere about 45°N/20°W to carry boats towards the Bay of Biscay, before later turning southwards down the Iberian coast. By keeping north of the rhumb line you get an eastward push from the current and avoid being pressed into Biscay.

The Westerlies should give you a beam reach or close reach most of the way, and good average speeds. Bishop Rock lighthouse in the Scillies is the traditional landmark if visibility is good, and many yachts then head for the west country harbors of Falmouth or Plymouth.

This direct route is good from May to September but most boats, unless driven by hardened delivery skippers and other forms of sea-going ogres, will not be approaching northern Europe much before June or later than August. The later you leave this route the greater your chances of cold, wet and windy weather and gales:

- in June, as you head north from the Azores to the latitude of the Western Approaches, the winds have plenty of west in them.
- by August the winds are more varied, coming from south and from north, and the North Atlantic Current has moved north and will give you a southwest running current. Thunderstorms are not uncommon, bringing sudden squalls and days of strong winds.
- by September the winds are mainly Force 4 to Force 6 but the likelihood of a gale increases. My experience of the last couple of decades is that September has become a strange, unreliable month, subject to more deep depressions than indicated on the Pilot Charts. Watch your barometer carefully for signs of a depression. A fall of 6 millibars in three hours shows bad weather is coming. A fall of 9 millibars is almost certainly a gale.
- October is late enough for this passage. For cruising hedonists November is too late, with gales crowding in to the Western Approaches and

sea and air temperatures falling fast. Cold weather adds no pleasure to a late season gale.

For most of us this 1,000 miles plus passage of at least seven days takes us outside the reliable part of the five-day forecast we got in the Azores. Even in summer you must be prepared to meet at least one gale on this route, as depressions run across the Atlantic from Cape Sable to Ushant (Ouessant), dying as they go but not dying fast enough. Try not to be caught by a gale as you come into soundings and onto the continental shelf, about 200 miles west of the approaches to the Channel. Gale force seas are bad enough without the additional excitement of catching them here. The sudden rise of the seabed from miles deep to a few hundred feet deep can cause heavy seas in a gale. You have plenty of sea-room and should use it.

You may find heaving-to a better option than running before the weather, so make sure you know how best to make your boat do this. And beware not to relax your guard too soon. After the strong wind passes you may experience uncontrollable seas, uncomfortable at best but potentially dangerous too. In 2003 a yacht was caught right on the edge of the continental shelf, off the Irish coast. The yacht was swamped and sunk by monstrous breaking waves.

When approaching the English Channel beware of the high level of commercial traffic. Ships must keep to shipping lanes on both the British and French coasts and yachts arriving in the area need up-to-date charts to show where these and other separation zones are. Both sides of the Channel are busy but I find the area around Ushant and Brittany to be the most worrying. It is here that the big ships must turn to enter or leave the Channel. Tides run strong on this coast and fog is not unusual. In bad visibility keep offshore and outside the Ushant shipping lanes.

A skipper from Montana told me that the English Channel lived up to all expectations for fog and mist, cold temperatures, strong currents, fluky winds and thousands of freighters. They were not using their radar when they arrived in the Channel. That first night the skipper came up on watch to see what looked like a city on collision course. They had thought visibility was good but this enormous freighter had come from nowhere. They panic-turned and passed up the side of ship less than 100 feet away. After that it was radar and two people on watch for the three nights it took them to clear the Channel and make the North Sea. During this whole time visibility was so bad that all they saw of England were the lights from the city of Southampton, and that only for about an hour during the night.

Both the Channel and the North Sea are busy with commercial shipping. There are traffic separation schemes (TSS) off the English coast at Land's End and the French coast off Ushant. Midway up Channel there is another TSS off the Casquets at the end of the Normandy peninsula. Channel traffic then bottlenecks into the TSS for the Dover Strait, where the problems of dense traffic are made worse by the sandbanks and shallows of the 20-mile wide Strait. The Dover Strait TSS continues northeasterly into the North Sea with a major branch coming off into Europort at the Hook of Holland. The *British Admiralty Routeing Guide*—English Channel and Southern North Sea (chart number 5500) is a great help getting through this area.

The English coast is the easier one for a passage maker. It saves you being caught in the busy lanes of Ushant, the huge tides of Brittany, or bumping into the peninsula of Normandy. Even so, once in the Channel you will need to work the tides. These are most problematic for yachts working up the Channel close to the coast and least of a problem for boats that stay offshore and have a commanding wind. You will soon learn the meaning of "tidal gate" as you struggle to pass the great headlands of southern England. The flood tide will sweep a yacht eastwards past each headland but the ebb tide combined with a head wind will stop you dead, as though a gate had just been slammed shut in your face. Respect the headlands. With wind over tide the overfalls can be rough several miles offshore and you should refer to a Channel Pilot book to help you along this coast. For a cruising yacht exploring the south coast of England a good strategy in persistent head winds is to sail to the nearest pub and have a few days ashore.

If heading straight to the North Sea my preference is to run down the middle of the Channel. Then the main problem becomes the narrowing at Dover,

English Channel Tides and Headlands - HW Dover

where tides run hard, shipping converges and ferries cross at high speed. It probably sounds worse than it is. I have made this journey many times, even crossing the entrance to Dover Harbor singlehanded in thick fog without radar, suffering no more than heart palpitations and abject fear.

In summer small yachts sail everywhere on the English coast. Many rivers and harbors are available at all states of the tide and many more are good but dry at low water. Once you reach the Solent you have arrived in one of the world's main yachting areas, with every facility you can dream of.

The scenic route north

An alternative slower route to northern Europe is to head to Portugal or North West Spain and cruise up the coast in easy stages as breaks in the prevailing north winds allow, to cross the Bay of Biscay when you have a good forecast or explore the French Biscay coast and islands. The Rias of North West Spain and the little harbors along northern Spain are worth a full summer but the coast from La Rochelle to Brest, with the Îles de Glénan, is a real sailor's paradise. Boats wanting to see northern Europe before winter should avoid this route, as should sailors who cannot resist temptation. This is such a slow route to the Channel that you may never arrive, preferring to spend the rest of your cruise right here.

To the Iberian Peninsula

You can make a good landfall anywhere between the Rias of North West Spain and the southern end of Atlantic Portugal.

The Rias are the deep drowned river valleys at the top corner of Spain, running from the prime harbors of La Coruña in the north to Bayona in the south. There are about seven rias. Each has its own character. In summer they are popular with visiting yachts from Britain, France and northern Europe but they are never crowded. Most tourism here is local, reinforcing the Spanish or Portuguese feel to the area.

Facilities for yachts have improved in the last decade, with more marinas and pontoon berths being laid for the summer, but there are many good anchorages and shelter can be found whatever the weather.

Bayona is the last major yachting harbor in Iberian Spain for boats heading south on the Milk Run to the Caribbean, as well as being the furthest destination for many British and other yachts on a Spanish cruise before turning for home and Biscay. You can meet a fleet full of interesting sailing stories here.

South from Bayona you have the choice of harbor hopping down the Portuguese coast on your way to the Mediterranean or going offshore direct to the islands of Madeira and the Canaries. The harbors of Portugal are well placed for day hops, are pretty and welcoming. They too have changed in the last few years, with small marinas appearing where once there were only fishing harbors and anchorages.

Expect two different sailing regimes on this passage from the Azores. You will probably start out with a belt of calms close to the Azores but once through the Azores High you should be into strong steady northerly winds and a fast beam reach. Since you need to head east to find your winds you will probably motor through the Azorean calms. The barometer will show the change from Azores High to the low pressure system off the Portuguese coast.

> The yacht WINDFREE left the Azores towards Cádiz in July expecting a fast reach with good northerlies. Instead, the skipper said, they had wind like molten lead and seas the same. The wind rose on the July pilot chart shows a 5% chance of easterlies and a 2% chance of calm. WINDFREE felt like the exception that proves the rule.

Once into the good winds stay north of your line to counter the south setting, half knot or more Portuguese Current, and leeway from the prevailing northerly winds.

> The unlucky WINDFREE didn't get the expected winds but did get the perennial current. She was carried south 30 miles in a single day of being becalmed.

Also take care with shipping. There are traffic separation zones off Cape Finisterre in North West Spain and off Cape Carvoeiro and Cape Raso running north from the approaches to Lisbon.

> As PETRONELLA came in towards Bayona we crossed a stream of southbound traffic about 50 miles offshore and soon after that came up on the northbound ships. Continuous lines of ships swept by, seldom more than two miles between them.

You will meet ships outside these lanes. There are major commercial ports on this coast and it is a major shipping route to northern Europe.

Conditions en route

The currents around the Azores at this time run from north to south. The winds are almost always favorable, coming usually from the west or southwest through north and sometimes as far round as northeast. From June through till August you can expect winds of Force 4 to 6 with only a slight chance of a Force 7. The north wind lightens in September and October and anything over a Force 6 will be unusual then.

If leaving in November you should be prepared for gales during the first half of your passage but as you close the Iberian Peninsula you will probably get nothing more than a Force 6 from the north. A Force 7 would be rare. Winds increase in strength noticeably in December and you have more chance of a gale or near gale closer to the coast. Sea temperatures are falling too, getting close to 60° F. Not cold but an indication of winter.

From early summer to late fall a low pressure system over the Iberian Peninsula determines the weather patterns on the coast. The northerly Portuguese Trades are on the western edge of this low pressure. They blow parallel to the Iberian coast usually up to 100 miles offshore but sometimes as far as 350 miles, and are usually steady from July to September. They can be strong and when enhanced by the sea breeze can blow at gale force with a touch of west in them at times in the late afternoon close inshore.

The Portuguese Trades are the prevailing summer wind but they don't always arrive.

> We sat in Bayona in North West Spain with the rest of the southbound yachts. One by one they left, motoring south to stay on the cruise program. We enjoyed August but by September even we felt the need to move on. We motored south. The Portuguese Trades didn't arrive that year.

The weather from December through to February still allows a relatively comfortable passage to the mainland although sea temperatures continue to fall. In these months you must listen more carefully to the weather forecasts. This is a five- to seven-day passage for most of us, taking us outside the reliable part of a five-day forecast.

The Iberian Peninsula is subject to ocean swell even in summer but especially when a big gale blows to the northwest. The swell from mid-Atlantic storms ten or 15 degrees further north is carried down onto this coast by the Coriolis force. The drag effect of the land turns the swell onshore. The continental shelf is very close to the coast here, only ten to 30 miles off, allowing heavy breakers in the mouths of the rivers and an uncomfortable refraction sea off the high cliffs. In bad storms some of the harbors will be closed. This is rare in summer months but if making this passage from November onwards be prepared in case the river mouth or harbor of your choice is unsafe to approach or even closed by the swell and gales. Have an alternative in mind or be ready to stay at sea for a few days till the weather settles.

To the Mediterranean

Gibraltar lies about 900 miles southeast of the Azores. The conditions for your route to the Mediterranean are not so very different from those for the passage to the west coast of the Iberian Peninsula. It should be an easy sail in warm weather.

If making landfall at Cape St Vincent keep north of the rhumb line from the Azores. This keeps you clear of two dangerous ocean ridges. The Josephine Seamount about 250 miles west southwest of Cape St Vincent rises to within 500 feet of the surface but the Ormonde and Gettysburg seamounts of the Gorringe Ridge, about 100 miles west southwest of the Cape, rise from a seabed depth of 16,000 feet to within 60 feet of the surface in less than 15 miles. Strong winds make for rough seas here.

Beware the shipping and traffic separation zones around Cape St Vincent. Traffic separation starts about six miles west of the Cape and extends about 15 miles offshore. Cross to the coast when north of the Cape and go round the headland in the inshore zone. Be vigilant. On this route you will meet more and more ships heading to or from the Mediterranean.

The McConnells on their "First Crossing" were nearly run down en route from North America to Europe when they thought they were still a few miles west of the shipping lane here. It was 3 a.m. and both Malcolm and Carol were in the cockpit to keep watch. They had been busy with two vessels passing ahead on their portside. They didn't see the ship coming up from behind till it was 500 yards away. The McConnells had all their navigation lights on, had been flashing a masthead light and shining a flashlight on their sails, all for the benefit of the ships ahead but these lights should have been visible to the ship astern too. The ship passed doing 20 knots and less than 70 yards away. They could tell this was a brand new ship. It had several radomes, all turning. Everything was in apple-pie order except no one on board was keeping sufficient watch to see the lights and radar echo of the brave little yacht MATATA.

Conditions change as you round Cape St Vincent to run along the Algarve coast. Now you are in touch with the Mediterranean and North Africa. You lose much of the ocean swell and come into a region of land and sea breezes. Usually this means you have fine sailing breezes and broad reaches as you head east towards the Straits. However, even in mid-summer you might experience headwinds and hazy visibility.

There is much to see on the Algarve and many easy harbors to enter. Yachting has developed rapidly on this coast in the last few years, mainly for northern Europeans rather than local sailors, and the new marinas are large and well equipped. There are also easy anchorages but beware that some of the rivers have bars and as with all such places are best entered on a rising tide and not when there is a strong onshore breeze.

Gibraltar is one of those ports steeped in history that every sailor must visit. It is also a good place to provision or have work done and rumored to have the cheapest diesel in the region.

Into the Old Sea: through the Straits of Gibraltar

The Straits of Gibraltar is a windy place and the currents are strong. Getting through the Straits, the Pillars of Hercules as it was known in the ancient world, requires some forward planning and I would recommend *The Straits Sailing Handbook* by Colin Thomas, available in the Algarve, for all the information you need.

The wind here, though varying every few days, blows most of the time from either due east or due west, straight in or straight out of the Straits. The winds often blow at Force 4 to 5 at one end of the straits but, usually briefly, up to Force 7 at the other end.

When the strong easterly wind, the Levanter, is blowing it is best not to force your way through. This wind can carry dust and sand and, especially in summer months, can bring fog. Worst, though, is that this strong wind over the prevailing east-going current will kick up short steep seas and make life unpleasant. Put into an Algarve harbor and wait for the Levanter to blow itself away.

The high rate of evaporation in the Mediterranean Sea is greater than the flow of fresh water from its surrounding rivers, hence the continuous flow of surface water into the Mediterranean from the Atlantic. There is also a lower level movement of the denser water flowing back into the Atlantic, but this need not bother you unless you are unlucky enough to be sailing 1,000 feet or so below the surface. When there is no Levanter blowing this steady surface current helps give you an easy sail through the Straits.

Tidal flow in the Straits is vital to your passage. There are three separate tidal flows in this narrow neck of water. The central flow runs counter to the north and south flows for part of the time. In the center the tide flows east from high to low water at Gibraltar and west from low to high water. On the Spanish side the tide flows east from half flood to half ebb and the southern side flows east from four hours before high water till two hours after high water. This means that if you can manage the trick of changing from one flow to the other you can carry a favorable tide for about nine hours. This is useful since the tide is strong and the rule of thumb is to go through the Straits only when you can carry the tide.

The Straits is a busy area for ships. The east/west shipping lane runs through the center of the Straits. Once through the Straits watch out for the fast moving ferries crossing from north and south.

Weather in the Mediterranean is highly seasonal. The hot dry summers of moderate winds give way to mild rainy winters with a higher chance of gales than you might have expected. The Mediterranean Sea is surrounded by land—much of it either mountainous or desert—with great valleys running into it along the north coast. These valleys can funnel ferocious winter storms. This is a region where winds are so well defined and predictable that more than thirty have been given local names. How many of your local winds have names? In Britain there is only one that I know of.

A bad breath

The Aeolian Islands off the northwest tip of Sicily are named after Aeolius, the god of wind. Aeolius, like Huracan in the Caribbean, is a mean character. In the area around the Aeolian Islands, from Ustica to the Straits of Messina, winter winds are uncommonly fierce and unpredictable. Friends familiar with the area talk of being caught in unforecast gales blowing over 50 knots. Yet in spring the light winds and slight seas can give you sailing as good as it ever gets.

Gales are more likely in the western Mediterranean than the east, but I have no love for the meltemi.

The Meltemi

Scourge of the Greek and Turkish waters in the eastern Mediterranean, the meltemi is the prevailing summer northerly and can blow hard in the main sailing season. The meltemi results when the big high pressure system sitting over the Balkans meets the big low pressure system over Turkey's Anatolian plateau, in part brought about by the Asian monsoon. Now the wind blowing from high to low pressure is squeezed by the mountains into bad tempered turbulence. It swirls around the islands kicking up short unpleasant seas. The meltemi regularly blows at Force 5 to Force 6 and often at Force 7 to gale 8. It can blow for three to five days but sometimes up to two weeks. Expect it between June and October, with the greatest chance of a strong meltemi during July and August. The only compensation is that the air is clear and dry and you can probably find a good harbor close to some worthwhile cultural sightseeing.

January is the stormiest month. Near gales can be expected in the western Mediterranean on about 15 of the 31 days, usually from north and west. Across the Mediterranean as a whole the winter weather can change very rapidly and with little warning.

The Bora

A rush of cold air from the mountains of Croatia, bringing strong winds to the northern Adriatic with almost no warning. Local fishermen foretell the bora by watching the sea level in this relatively tideless area. When sea levels are high, there is no chance of a bora. When the water levels drop, beware.

Some winds may greet your arrival in the Mediterranean.

The Tramontana—Down hill racer

Some sailors call Cabo Creus the Cape Horn of Spain. It is the headland on the French and Spanish border and subject to a terror of a wind that blows in downhill accelerating gusts from the high mountains of the Pyrenees. The warning sight is the build up of lenticular clouds over the inland mountains on what till then had been a bright, clear and windless morning. These layered clouds lengthen and stay on the peaks till the tramontana is over, which might be anything from one to five days. There is no change in barometric pressure to warn you. Just the clouds. And the wind arrives like a great punch in mid morning.

They are Europe too

Military strategists say that no plan survives contact with the enemy. The same is true with sailing. You need a contingency plan if, for whatever reason that you may or may not at this stage be able to imagine, you have to cut short your Atlantic crossing. Not all is lost. One possibility would be not to sail to mainland Europe from the Azores but instead go south to the other Atlantic islands of Madeira and the Canaries. Park the boat in a marina if you need to fly home, otherwise cruise the summer away. Then, with the pressure off, decide whether to join the Caribbean Milk Run or sail to Europe next spring.

Sailing the 500 miles from the Azores to Madeira is one of the classic first stages in a transatlantic crossing for many European sailors. The sailing is usually good, in warm weather, northerly winds and favorable current. From Madeira to the Canaries is about 250 miles, also in easy conditions.

4

Homeward bound

It may seem a little early to be thinking of your return but I think it greatly adds to a sailor's comfort when setting out on a great adventure to know that the journey home is an easier one than the journey out. Isn't that what they told Ulysses?

You will be coming home on a variant of the route known as the Milk Run. This is the Trade Wind passage to the Caribbean which you start anywhere between Madeira and Senegal. It's called the Milk Run because it is about as easy as any ocean sailing passage can be. Hot sun, blue skies, fluffy white clouds, following seas and hardly a danger of a gale. Dolphin, flying fish and whales to keep you amused. Skies as clear as any you have ever seen. Now isn't that what you wanted to hear? Let ocean racers discuss the merits of the northern route and the intermediate route from the English Channel to the East Coast of the US. Neither have any merits for most cruisers. The westerly winds guarantee head winds and the easterly current will rob you of miles. On the Trade Wind route it is as though Nature laid out the seasons to make it as easy as possible to sail from Europe to the Americas.

It is a strange truth that sailors always think their home patch is safer and easier to cope with than any place they may sail to. This is what makes setting out on a journey such a long drawn out and painful experience for most of us. We really don't want to go in case the strange new place turns out to be more than we can handle. And one of the tributaries to this erroneous way of thinking is to believe that the journey from home to away is much easier than the journey back. "What if we get there and then find we can't get back?" Surely this way of thinking, deeply embedded in the human psyche, runs counter to our folk memories as nomads and hunter-gatherers, never mind our modern understanding of geography. Whatever the reason, this isn't a problem for you on your Atlantic adventure so don't let the thought delay you for a moment.

Homeward Bound - Milk Run Routes

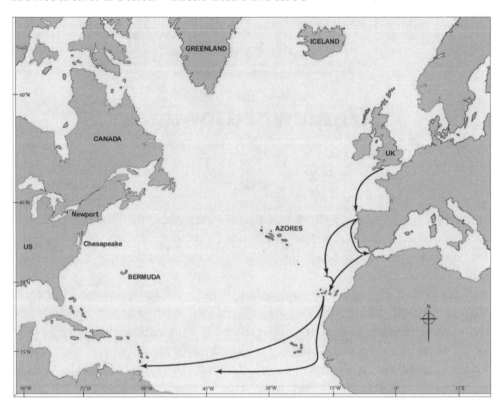

Seasoning your sailing

Getting to the casting off place for your return crossing is not difficult. It is just a matter of staying in touch with the seasons:

- get out of the English Channel as early in summer as you like but aim to be across Biscay before the first of the winter gales. All yachts coming out of Scandinavia or Germany, Holland, Luxembourg or Belgium, northern France or Britain need to cross the Bay before summer fades into fall. August is good. September may bring bad weather. November and December would be a good test of your thermal underwear. The likelihood of being caught by waves of twelve feet or over is slight in August but a scary certainty in October.
- after Biscay your timetable has less urgency. From now till your departure point you will be picking up the ever strengthening Portuguese Current and Portuguese Trades to carry you south. The Westerlies which troubled

you in Biscay give way to helpful northerlies once you pass Cape Finisterre on the Spanish coast.

- you can explore the Iberian Peninsula or the Atlantic islands, decide whether to leave from the Canaries or go further south off the beaten track to the Cape Verde islands, Senegal, Gambia or even Guinea Bissau.
- if you have been in the Mediterranean you will probably join the other ocean crossers in the Canaries and make your final preparations for the ocean there. Unless of course you too decide to check out the places off the beaten track.
- when you are sure that the hurricane season is over in November or even now December, head south with the Canaries Current until you meet the true North East Trades and take them all the way across. Old timers used to say the way to pick up the Trades was to "head south till the butter melts and then turn right." In these days of cholesterol watching perhaps we should say "head south to the Margarine Latitudes."
- many sailors make their Caribbean landfall at Barbados, because it is the first island they reach, or St Lucia or Antigua because these are much publicized yachting centers. I would aim for either Tobago or Trinidad at the far southern end of the island chain. They have much to offer and when you leave you only have to make a one-way trip to see the rest of the islands.

One of the joys of ocean cruising, which you will by now have mastered, is modifying your plans. I hope you did it on the journey over. I hope you are inclined to do it on the journey back. People who live land lives want us sailors to appear well organized and prepared. Essential to this view is that we show them a detailed timetable and list of itineraries. But the mind-set of sea rovers is the reverse. The longer they have been bluewater sailing, the more they seem open to major shifts of plan. There is much to be gained from this. On our crossing from west-to-east we modified our plans to spend a whole winter in the Azores. On our crossing from east-to-west we modified our plans to visit West Africa. These sudden whims were the highlights of our crossings, and happened as we took on board the experiences of other long-term cruising sailors.

When wind and current are going your way, as they should be for the Milk Run, navigation and life aboard is surprisingly easy. Even if you were late crossing Biscay you have at least two months to sail the 2,000 or so miles to your preferred jumping off point to return westwards. There is no rush. Really, there is no rush.

Two things determine the timing and location of your departure.

First, to avoid the hurricanes that used to come out of the Caribbean as late as November but these days might still be coming out in December.

Second, to hitch a ride on the Trade Winds as they move north and grow more reliable after November.

> The more places you visit south of the Canaries, the closer you get to the Trades. The longer you take to explore Senegal and Gambia, the better the Trades will be for you. There is no good weather reason why you should not cross in February or even later.

The plan is simple. Some time during November and January, anywhere from Madeira to West Africa, you will turn right from your southern course to bring the winds of the Trade belt astern. The magic carpet of current under your keel moves you westwards at half a knot. The magic breath of the Trades drives you at full hull speed. The Milk Run almost guarantees the quickest crossing a boat can manage under sail.

The Trade Wind crossing is the ultimate test of your downwind sails. Mine failed the test on my first crossing. Whatever your Trade Wind rig, design and test it before you use it in anger. Talk to other sailors about the gear you see on their boats. Things have moved a long way since the good old days when twin foresails were essential because they allowed the boat to steer itself downwind. If your solution involves booming out make sure you have a good pole and fittings and can handle it in worsening conditions.

I never learned to love my twin foresails. Unfortunately, twins are costly and demand a lot of expensive and space consuming gear that only gets very occasional use. And anyway, vane steering or autopilot steers the boat better than twins. I discovered that I preferred to go downwind with my main prevented and genoa boomed out on the same side because this gave greater hull stability and reduced that awful rhythmic rolling. It also meant I used gear I was familiar with and which was in regular use. Some may argue with this but I'm pleased to know that one of the great English small boat sailing heroes, Humphrey Barton, also preferred main and genoa for his downwind sailing.

> Even leaving in January gives you time to visit the Caribbean and still be in the office by May. If you're still planning to be in the office by May.

SECTION TWO

Life on the other side

5

Europe from a sailing boat

Europe is a densely populated and culturally rich continent with the linguistic diversity to prove it. Its coastline ranges from Nordic fjordic intensity to the gentle ways of the Mediterranean. How could anyone be so foolish to think of capturing this in a series of thumbnail sketches? Fortunately for you and your pre-passage planning, I am prepared to have a go. When you leave the western side of the Atlantic it is best to have decided on a more precise landfall than "just Europe."

Where you are headed is largely a matter of what you want to do for the next year or ten and in what order you want to do it. The whole of Europe is worth seeing and your sailing boat can be the ideal base. Don't be put off by the cold and snow of northern winters or the fearful local winds of the Mediterranean. Most of all, don't be put off by my shameful prejudices. Here is a sailing guide to Europe in a nutshell, with my apologies to places I have missed out and, even more, to the places I have wronged.

I have sailed much of the coast of Europe but not all of it, not by any means. I have even sailed inland, on the waterways of Holland, and seen some of the great German and French rivers and canals from trains and cars. I have watched ice flowing down the Danube, but only from a bridge in Budapest. I will only tell you about the bits I have experienced under sail but it's a start.

If you have a tidy mind that likes things to proceed in order, and you want to see northern Europe, then you should go there first. Sailing south down the long Atlantic coast of Spain and Portugal is easier than heading north. The summer wind and the ocean current pull you naturally south. In most years the best advice for yachts in the Algarve or Mediterranean who want to sail to Britain and northern Europe is to go to the Azores on your first tack. So heed this warning and sail north-about from the Azores. After that you can go south whenever you choose.

I have given relatively more information on the Atlantic islands for two main reasons:

- I can't be sure where you will go in mainland Europe but I am sure you will visit at least one of the island groups

- you may feel that these island groups are nothing more than stopovers and not worth visiting except briefly. They deserve more than that. They are cruising grounds in their own right. Also, being surrounded by sea they are the natural element for sailors, like you.

Almanacs and pilot books

A number of nautical almanacs and sailing handbooks give pilotage information over wide areas of the European coast. With up-to-date charts these are often enough to get you into the major harbors and ports but for more details of what you can expect to find there and for information on smaller harbors, yacht marinas and clubs, as well as a wealth of information on places to eat and drink, you need local pilot books. Really, there are too many to list so this is just a taster. When you arrive somewhere on the way to somewhere else, ask around the anchorage for advice on the next pilot book.

The *Sailing Directions* published by the US Defense Mapping Agency and the Canadian Hydrographic Service are in separate volumes for particular areas. They give comprehensive information including dangers to shipping and detailed descriptions of harbors but only as relevant to commercial vessels. I think they are wonderful but we only carry them because we inherited them. For most yachts they are probably too expensive and lack the information needed by small boat sailors.

Ocean Passages for the World published by the British Admiralty Hydrographic Department in 2004 covers a much greater area than the Atlantic. Full of information for all ocean voyagers.

Pilots specifically for yachts are available for the whole of Atlantic Europe and the Mediterranean. Unlike the *Sailing Directions* they are privately published and researched. They can vary considerably in quality and range. Not all still sold are still up-to-date. We carry many on PETRONELLA. The ones we usually end up using most are those produced under the aegis of the Royal Cruising Club (RCC) Pilotage Foundation. Their excellent website is www.rcc.org.uk.

World Cruising Routes by Jimmy Cornell is a useful and classic work covering all oceans, not just the Atlantic.

We also carry and use *The Atlantic Crossing Guide* by Anne Hammick & G McLaren, an RCC Pilotage Foundation publication.

Regional Pilot books

Atlantic Europe

Reeds OKI Nautical Almanac covers a large part of Atlantic Europe, from the tip of Denmark to Gibraltar, the Mediterranean as well as the Atlantic islands. It is an annual publication with information on navigation, radio aids, communication and weather, tides, harbors and marinas. The harbor and passage making information is organized in 25 coastal regions. It is well researched and up-to-date You can check it on the website www.reedsalmanac.co.uk.

The Cruising Almanac published by Imray Laurie Norie and Wilson for the London-based Cruising Association meets the needs of the Association's members. Published annually it is thoroughly researched and a magnificent destination-planner and reference. It covers the approaches to the Baltic Sea in the north to Gibraltar in the south and includes the coast of Great Britain. It contains pilotage and tide information. You might also think of joining the Cruising Association. Although headquartered in London the Cruising Association has regional sections and over 500 Honorary Local Representatives around the world, most in Europe but some also in the US. They advise members about local conditions and offer support to members with problems.

The Mediterranean

There are books on sailing in the Mediterranean for all tastes and purposes but if one person can be said to have a monopoly on pilots for the Mediterranean it has to be New Zealander Rod Heikell, whose first book was on the Greek waters back in 1982. He has written several local pilots. His *Mediterranean Almanac* gives harbor information, lights, waypoints, navigation, berthing, shelter and facilities and more. It is an invaluable cruise planning reference. His *Mediterranean Cruising Handbook* is the sister volume to the *Mediterranean Almanac*.

The Atlantic islands

We use the *RCC Atlantic Islands* by Anne Hammick. This is the only single volume to cover the four archipelagos. It is well laid out, comprehensive and very easy to use.

Local pilot books

Local pilot books are the heart of your cruising library. There are more of these than it is possible to imagine or list here. I have listed these few English language ones just to give you an idea of how many there are. You will probably end up using the ones you just happened to find. The RCC Pilotage Foundation is a good source of local pilots.

Faeroe, Iceland and Greenland, W Ker, RCC
Norwegian Cruising Guide, John Armitage and Mark Brackenbury
The Baltic Sea, Anne Hammick, RCC
The Channel Islands, N Heath, RCC
The Isles of Scilly, R Brandon & J&F Garey, RCC
North Biscay, Mike and Gill Baron, RCC
South Biscay, Robin Brandon and J Lawson, RCC
Atlantic Spain & Portugal, A Hammick and O Robinson, RCC
Straits of Gibraltar Handbook, Colin Thomas
Balearic Islands, J Marchment, RCC
Greek Waters Pilot, Mediterranean France and Corsica Pilot, Rod Heikell
Turkish Waters and Cyprus Pilot, Rod Heikell
Black Sea Cruising Guide, Rick and Sheila Nelson
Inland Waterways of Europe, Euromapping

The Irish Cruising Club produces sailing directions for several parts of Ireland and the Clyde Cruising Club does the same for Scotland.

At the dreaming or early planning stage I find useful pilotage information in articles in sailing magazines. Don't give up just because an author is detailing every tack and gibe up some endless narrow channel. There is always valuable information for you. The time they were in the area. The good and bad weather. What little things failed or worked. What to have in your medicine cabinet if you are as accident prone as they were.

Sea Charts

Up-to-date sea charts are vital wherever you sail. There is no excuse for not having the right charts for Europe. This must be one of the best surveyed areas of the world. You can buy American charts or charts from any of the European countries. I use a range of paper charts, some bought second hand and too old to boast about. Most of these, even now in the 21st century, are based on surveys done in the 19th century. Bear in mind that the survey methods and position fixing of a couple of centuries ago, and even a couple of decades ago, cannot match the accuracy of GPS. Your GPS plot will be exactly right in terms of the earth's surface but may be badly out in terms of your position on the chart.

I like paper charts, but I also like the wonderful things that can be done with the electronic chart package on our laptop computer. This allows us to play all sorts of "what if" games as we plan a passage. Using tidal information, currents, navigational dangers, aerial views and rapid zooming in and out, we end up with a much better feel for how long a passage will take, obstacles on the way and how the destination will appear from different distances off. And all this can be done faster than it takes to finger back and forward through half a dozen paper charts. Also, the electronic charts we have are so much more up-to-date than most of our paper ones. This shouldn't be the case but I suspect it is what happens over time for most sailors.

Many sailors we meet rely almost solely on their electronic charts. Some, dare I whisper it, may not even bother to have all the paper charts for the area they are sailing if it is well covered by their electronic library. One friend has a sort of electronic/paper compromise. He uses his electronic charts to arrive at the navigation views he will need at key points in a passage and then prints them off. He doesn't then need to refer to his computer screen since he has the information in hard copy and if the paper gets soaked and obliterated all he has lost is a print-out, not the vital chart itself.

Electronic charts are not exactly new. We have used one version dating from 1985 and I doubt if this is the first that came to market. But despite its lineage, this is not yet a mature technology. There are too many systems out there with different approaches to their base data and too many pros and cons and sometimes what seems like built-in scope for bad navigation errors for me to believe that all the wrinkles have yet been ironed out. Fortunately the basic systems all have good things to offer, so waiting for perfection to arrive is not a good enough reason to resist them.

Having experienced electronic charts I would never want not to have them, and at some point there will be further innovations in information content or display technology or even in bringing us such reliable communications that we will always be able to upload new charts or chart corrections, even at sea, and these things will swing the balance more completely in favor of electronic charts. However, till then I think the prudent sailor will only use electronic charts for passage planning and switch to paper charts for passage making, when they are involved in practical matters such as plotting positions or just meditating on depth contours and danger marks. This is what we do and I suspect will continue doing for some while yet.

If you are using elderly paper charts bear these important points in mind:

- check what depth measurements are used. Feet, fathoms and meters are all possible.
- make sure you know which way round the buoyage runs. Europe and the

Atlantic islands are in the IALA A region. You have probably come from an IALA B region.

- even in Europe don't assume that buoys will be where you expect to find them. In 2004, during one of the major yacht races in Britain—the Round the Island Race in the Solent—navigation buoys were actually being raised and removed for inspection while half the fleet was still trying to tack round them.

And of course, anywhere in the world, you might find that charted buoys and navigation lights may not be working or may have succumbed to external influences.

> When we came into the rock strewn waters by Bayona harbor at night, ten days out from the Azores, we were looking for leading lights to tell us when to make our final turn. What the chart showed so clearly had been obliterated by the brighter lights of the resort ashore.

Uncharted winds of change

When I attempt to excuse the age and provenance of our charts I fall back on the old adage that the rocks don't change. Well, of course the sandbanks and break-waters and navigation lights do, so it isn't what you might call a clinching argument. And now there is a new obstacle for us sailors: the wind and wave generators.

Europe is rapidly developing alternatives to fossil fuel. Wind farms have been common in northern Europe for decades. Now they are being erected along the coasts of many countries. Some, such as the Thames Array in the estuary of Britain's busiest river, are huge and have necessitated new navigation routes for commercial shipping along the east coast of England. Take care. Some farms may be too new to be shown on your charts.

Tidal and wave generators are also being expanded. Tides have powered machinery in Europe since the Middle Ages, possibly since the Romans, but this is now on a huge scale and affecting major rivers and estuaries.

Offshore wave generators are much newer, only now getting the attention of engineers to make them commercially viable. Small scale test sites will be set up in many parts of northern Europe but the first major site is likely to be off the Atlantic coast of Portugal, where the Atlantic waves can be harnessed. The second major site is likely to be somewhere in the Bay of Biscay. At the time of writing in early 2006 there is no information on the site or scale or even the technology of these wave farms, but you don't want to be sailing into them when they happen. A good source of information is the Cruising Association. Try their website on www.cruising.org.uk.

Sailing by region

There is nothing definitive about organizing Atlantic Europe into eight distinct regions. The coasts and the cultures overlap, rather like the migration of European tribes over the last few thousand years. But you need some way to simplify your cruise planning and this is how I have learned to think of Europe after years of sailing and exploring it from the sea.

I have given more attention to the Atlantic coast of Spain and Portugal and the four archipelagos of the Azores, Madeira, Canaries and Cape Verdes since these are such an intrinsic part of crossing to Europe and returning to North America.

Scandinavia and the Baltic

Scandinavians returning home from America or the Caribbean might take the northerly route around Ireland and Scotland but then, they are in a hurry and have already seen the North Sea coasts and the English Channel. They don't want to get stuck in adverse tides up the English Channel or through the Dover Strait. You haven't done this scenic route and I would suggest you do. For one thing, it gives you more scope to shelter if storms are brewing and in this period of increasing chaotic weather G and I have noticed how severe the lows are around the top of the British Isles even in mid summer.

The west coasts of Norway and Sweden are more protected than you might think. A line of islands, the Skerries, give good protection from the rough Atlantic seas but still lets the sailing breeze through. As you push through into the western Baltic you enter a world of weak tides and narrow rocky passages. You will sail through rock-bound channels that seem too narrow for your beam, and if you meet another boat coming the other way one of you might need to pull the boom in. In an area of fierce tides, like Brittany, such pilotage would be madness, but here in the Baltic it is a joy. The passages are well marked and the scenery wonderful. You will learn to anchor close in to little islets or largish rocks and take a bowline ashore.

The snag to the Scandinavian west coast is the rain. Even in summer the cloud can hang thick and low and grey for days at a time, but when it lifts you have wonderful sailing. Further into the Baltic you will get long periods of absolutely clear blue weather and light but sufficient sailing breezes. I haven't been as far as the Stockholm archipelago but it sounds like a sailor's dream. It's on my list.

The North Sea islands and the Netherlands

Off the coast of western Germany and the Netherlands are the Friesian Islands, a curving sandbank broken into low lying islands. You should think of visiting them when you come south from Scandinavia or are in the Netherlands. Some are busy summer resorts but others are protected nature reserves and idyllic. They have a special physical environment as well as an important cultural link for English speakers. Linguists believe that the language spoken here is the nearest surviving precursor of what has developed into modern English.

The fun of sailing here is the need to play the tidal streams. The channels are well marked but each has a watershed at some point along its length, where the flooding or ebbing tide chooses to go in opposite directions to find its way around the nearby island. It helps to be shallow draft in these drying channels. Anyone sailing these islands should take along the classic sailing thriller *Riddle of the Sands*, written by Irishman Erskine Childers more than ten years before World War I to alert the British government to the possible build up of a German invasion force. Childers was a great sailor who knew the area well and makes the sailing background to the political and military intrigue come alive.

The Dutch say that God made the sea but the Dutch made the land. The coast of the modern Netherlands is a tribute to massive civil engineering. Wide estuaries have been dammed to make inland seas. Deep water channels with bridges and dams link these seas and along these channels and through the seas go all sorts of vessels, from massive, deeply loaded pusher barges to little camping yachts. Little islands remain in the seas themselves, giving anchorages and moorings everywhere. And best of all, the towns and villages of the seas are forgotten places, beautifully maintained as they were when the dams came and their reason for existing ceased. Once they were major sea ports for the Dutch empire or huge fishing harbors. Now they may still have fishing fleets, but on a smaller scale, and they are quiet places for visitors to see what the Dutch world once looked like.

We love sailing in the Netherlands. Summers can be finer and hotter than we are used to in Britain. We can sail from one delightful town to another in an hour or so. If we fancy a thrash, we can cross one of the inland seas in the full majesty of a Force 5.

The Netherlands is a good base from which to explore other countries of northern Europe. The rivers and canals and inland seas allow you to push a long way inland even on an ocean going yacht, and there is no shortage of marinas or yacht harbors to leave your boat while traveling on land. Also, English is widely spoken.

The British Isles

The British Isles are an immensely varied sailing area but for the North American visitor with only a single season you must limit yourself to a part. This could be the Scottish and Irish coasts, wonderfully rugged and dramatic but demanding a closer eye on the weather. Better, though, would be to stay a little longer, explore the west and south coasts of England and come up to London or sail further east to the classical music festival at Aldeburgh on the Suffolk coast.

The southern coast of England and the protected waters of the Solent in particular are the prime sailing grounds of the British Isles. The south coast with the Isle of Wight and the Solent is a good place to find shelter and do some exploring but it is busy and expensive unless you tuck into places off the main track.

The rivers of the English West Country—Cornwall and Devon—are some of the prettiest you will find and there are good safe anchorages in among the thick woods of their upper reaches. Falmouth and Plymouth are protected river-based harbors popular with boats arriving in or leaving Britain.

Still, my preference is for the lonely shallow estuaries of eastern England. No visit to Britain would be complete without piloting through the sandbanks of the Thames estuary and working your way up one of the little creeks of Essex or Suffolk to anchor in lonely silence where the old barges and the smugglers used to come, but nothing comes now.

The Thames is London's river and there are now marinas close to the City of London itself where you can spend time in the metropolis and base yourself while exploring inland Britain. All roads lead to London, and all railway lines and airlines too. London is the center of cheap flights to Europe and North America. This is a good base to explore from or return home to see the family.

Britain has strong resonance for many North Americans. So much in our histories are shared. Just a glance at a list of place names in one country brings echoes of the same names in the other.

Brittany and Biscay coasts

The French coast of Brittany is more rugged and tide-driven than the Devon and Cornish coast on the other side of the Channel, but it is a wonderful cruising ground. Harbors lie up the little rivers or are found by meandering through tightly marked rocky passages. You find more open waters in the Rade de Brest once you have gone south through the potentially fearful rock-strewn passage and tidal race of the Raz de Sein. Brittany is like Cornwall—the less developed western arm of its nation, strongly independent and proud of its separate identity.

The Bretons and the Cornish share a Celtic language as well as much that is common in their myths and culture.

Southern Brittany opens the way for the magical islands of the French Biscay coast and wonderful old harbors like La Rochelle. You could cruise a whole season here, discovering the waters inside the Baie de Quiberon, which in turn guards the entrance to the inland sea of the Golfe du Morbihan. Biscay weather can be stormy and the combination of wind and current setting the old unhandy square riggers into the Bay made this a graveyard for ships. But islands like Belle-Ile, Ile de Groix and Ile de Ré give you shelter from the west, the mainland harbors like Lorient and La Rochelle give you shelter from the east, and your reliable diesel engine does the rest.

If you have the draft for it you might even think of going up the river Gironde to Bordeaux, entering the French canal system and the Canal des Deux Mers and coming out into the Mediterranean through the Canal du Midi. But then, if you have the draft for it you might think of the rest of the European canal system, allowing you to range from the Baltic to the Mediterranean, overwintering in some charming little German or French town to learn the language or test the cuisine. What about winter in Paris and then down the Rhône to the Mediterranean? Now that's what I would call changing a plan!

> The countries of Europe are connected by a truly vast and well maintained network of inland waterways. Rivers and canals have been used for centuries to go from the Atlantic and northern seas to the Mediterranean and other inland seas. Some of these waterways are constrained by draft and air draft but I know that a boat like PETRONELLA with a draft of about six feet and her masts down could find a pleasant route from the Baltic to the Mediterranean that touched on Germany and France and didn't have to follow the bigger commercial canals. How do I know this? Because G and I plan to make that trip. Amaze yourself and check out the network. Hush. It is a secret most sailboat sailors don't know.

North West Spain and Portugal

Many sailors go misty eyed when they speak of sailing in the Rias of North West Spain. These wide and often deep drowned river valleys, some with little islands offshore, are less visited by foreign tourists than other parts of Spain. Most visitors from abroad are sailors and pilgrims. The Rias are resorts but mainly for the Spanish, and there is an unadulterated Spanish feel to the region.

After being away from Spain or Portugal for any length of time we have to re-adjust to two things in particular. First, dinner is late. Often restaurants don't open till 8 or 9 p.m. Second, people promenade. These are family-oriented cultures and much of life is lived on the streets. This means that in the vacation season in the resort towns the evening streets are filled with families of three or four generations strolling and chatting and pausing for entertainment. Small children take pride of place. Teenagers, even macho young men inclined to rank sullenness, think it perfectly natural to take care of the baby or walk arm-in-arm sharing a joke with Grandma.

I love the Rias of Spain and like the Portuguese coast too but yachts approaching the land must beware. The coast is freer of outlying rocks and has weaker tides than the Brittany and Channel coasts but it is subject to summer fog, ocean swell and heavy shipping. Northerly gales are not uncommon in summer and can arrive with little warning. Northwesterly gales are fierce in winter. In onshore winds do not attempt to enter harbors with a bar. The breaking seas should be enough to warn you of the danger.

The old rules always apply, no matter where you are. Don't try to enter harbor in strong onshore winds and seas. In these times of disordered weather the European coasts at the back end of the year (October through to December) now seem to suffer more storms as a greater number of tropical hurricanes come off the Caribbean and Eastern Seaboard. A 35 footer doing Yachtmaster training was lost in November 2005 when their weather forecast got it wrong. The expected northerly 5 became an unexpected northwesterly gale as they hopped down the Portuguese coast. They changed plan and headed to a safer harbor but were knocked down in the entrance by a breaking wave. The boat was totally lost when she hit the beach. The investigation by the British Marine Accident Investigation Branch (MAIB), whose Digest is a wonderful source for improving our seamanship, commented that too many yachts are lost on lee-shores when they would have survived by staying out at sea. It's a hard call for a skipper to make. Harden your heart and make it. Stay out at sea.

The Rias of North West Spain

These fjord-like drowned river valleys make for a fascinating and charming cruising ground. The dense coastline allows yachts to cruise at their whim and find shelter almost without thinking about it.

La Coruña

La Coruña at the northern end of the Rias is strategically placed for a crossing of the Bay of Biscay. The yacht harbor is on the eastern, inner side of the bay and well protected by a long east-west breakwater. The yacht club is welcoming and the town is charming.

Bayona

Most yachts sailing this coast will come to Bayona, the last major yachting harbor in Iberian Spain for boats heading south to the Algarve, Mediterranean or Caribbean.

Bayona yacht harbor is protected by a long breakwater on its northern side, making the bay almost land locked. There are now two marinas in the bay. The old anchorage is to the east of the yacht club marina and to the north of the commercial marina. The yacht club also provides mooring buoys. The club has good facilities and its helpful staff is used to catering for overseas yachts.

The town is well connected to the rest of Galicia and a good base to explore inland.

The Atlantic coast of Portugal

The west coast of Portugal is a long, low lying, mainly sandy affair with good harbors and marinas in some very pretty old towns. The distances between harbors mean that you must plan your passages and watch the weather more deliberately. The list below follows on from Bayona to Cape St Vincent where the Atlantic coast turns into the Algarve.

Viana do Castelo

A small very sheltered marina a mile and a half up the River Lima. The marina entrance is to port, just before a low road/rail bridge. Call the harbor master to guide you in and help you moor Mediterranean style. There is no anchoring in the river.

Povoa de Varzim

A new marina with good shelter in all winds, although the entrance is rough when there is a heavy swell running.

Oporto, Portugal. The azulejo wall tiles such as these in Oporto are a feature of Portuguese architecture.

Viana

Good facilities.

Leixoes

The marina of the river Duoro, the center of the port wine trade. A bar at the river entrance makes for dangerous seas in strong winds or heavy swell but the commercial port where the marina is can be entered under most conditions. Since the destruction of the floating pontoon in Gaia on the south bank of the river, it is no longer possible to dock in the city of Porto itself. However, most yachting facilities are in the marina. The marina is busy so check first that a visitor's berth is available. Porto and Gaia and their port lodges, where you can taste this fine and ancient wine, are not to be missed.

Figueira da Foz

The marina is in the middle of the city and well-protected but if a large sea is running at low tide entrance to the river can be difficult. Conditions over the river bar are broadcast on VHF channel 11.

Nazare

The marina is a mile and a half south of the town. This is an artificial harbor with all-weather access and very good shelter. No anchoring in the outer harbor

Lisbon, Portugal. Lisbon is a charming city and very much a city of the sea.

Peniche

A small marina inside the port on the south side of the peninsula. This is an all-weather harbor but subject to swell and wash from ferries. There are mooring buoys and anchoring is permitted in the SE part of the harbor. The ground is possibly foul.

Cascais

A large, modern marina at the mouth of the Tagus River with 125 visitors berths. Famous as the most expensive marina on this coast. Yachts anchor in the bay north of the port but this is subject to swell and open to the south. We rose and fell on huge swells in milky blue water in an impossibly gentle manner. Cascais may be a better base from which to explore Lisbon than the Lisbon marinas themselves.

Lisbon

Do not miss Lisbon, even if you have to go there by bus. A wonderful city. The approaches to the River Tagus (Rio Tejo) are straightforward and well marked. Yachts are required to listen out on VHF channels 12, 13 and 16. The working channel for port control is VHF 64.

Four different basins on the north bank of the river are used by yachts. The main marina for visitors is Doca de Alcantara, just over one mile upstream of the Lisbon bridge. Officially the swing bridge at the entrance opens on request (Channel 12) but word is that it is now permanently open.

The Doca do Bom Succeso and Doca de Belém, down river from Doca de Alcantara, are mainly for local craft. The Doca de Santo Amaro is used by naval craft and harbor launches. Expo Marina, built for Expo'98, is six miles upriver and was closed when we visited Lisbon in 2004. We heard of plans to make a new marina at Doca dos Olivais, north of Expo.

Sines

A useful stop, being halfway between Lisbon and Cape St Vincent. Sines is a pleasant old town. Its small marina is inside the Porto Pesca (fishing harbor), itself in the NE corner of the large commercial harbor. Anchoring is possible off the beach.

The Algarve

Cape St Vincent (Cabo de São Vicente) is a grand cape. We came around in wonderfully calm weather. The cape has a bad reputation for big seas and I wouldn't want to be here in an onshore gale. The Algarve showed itself as lines of stunning cliffs interrupted by small beaches, some of which have large resort developments presumably fed by the international airport at Faro. At first sight we found the coast oddly off-putting. The cliffs are grand but the land is dry and barren, lacking trees or vegetation. Further east the cliffs give way to a low-lying

Cape St Vincent, Portugal. The Atlantic coast of Iberia turns into the Algarve and brings the first sense of the Mediterranean. Best not to be here when the great storms blow.

coast with mudflats and lagoons. Watch out for tunny nets. They are well marked with large yellow buoys and lights, and often have a guard boat to shoo you round them, but these nets can reach several miles offshore and may not have a safe inside passage.

Lagos

The marina is one mile up river from the harbor entrance and appears very sheltered, although we heard that bad swell runs up the canalized river and breaking waves can make the arrival pontoon untenable. The arrival pontoon is on the eastern side next to the fuel dock and just before the lifting bridge connecting the new marina to the old town. Like other marinas on the Algarve, facilities are of a high standard and the marina is much larger than most on the Atlantic side. It is part of a shopping, commercial, residential and leisure development and a popular long-term base for yachts from northern Europe.

The old town of Lagos is a mixture of charming old Portuguese buildings, some of very fine architecture and on a grand scale, and the bars and restaurants and shops of mass international tourism.

Portimão

The marina is on the west side of the river, just beyond the entrance through the breakwaters at the beach resort of Praia de Rocha. Portimão Town is another two miles further up river where the low road and rail bridges stop yacht navigation. The flood and ebb streams run in the marina. Swell coming into the River Arade can be felt and there is wash from fishing boats.

Anchoring is common inside the east mole or by the small creek on the eastern side of the river a mile or so from the river mouth. Beware of shoaling.

Boatyards and hard standing are on a spur of land by the fishing harbor close to Portimão Town. The yards serve the fishing fleet but there is little problem hauling out or finding repair and engineering services for a yacht and there are chandlers, GRP repair services, sail making and the like.

Vilamoura

The largest and longest established marina on the Algarve. The entrance between the breakwaters can be very rolly even in light onshore winds. The reception pontoon and yacht club is on the western side of the marina entrance and curiously cut off from the marina berths. We thought the yacht club would be busier if sailors didn't have to walk a mile or more round the perimeter of the marina to get there.

The commercial and hotel development around the marina here makes Lagos seem almost rural.

The Portuguese Algarve coast becomes less developed east of these three major marinas. Starting at the Ria Formosa, with the towns of Faro and Olhão, the land becomes more low-lying and the coast is a series of shallow lagoons fed by rivers and protected by off-lying sandbanks. Working the tides and identifying channel markers is now the key to your navigation. Care should be taken entering these rivers and lagoons. Onshore wind over an ebbing tide can create dangerous conditions at the entrances and the tides can run fast. It is, however, a wonderful cruising ground and yachts heading for the Mediterranean or down to the Canaries often stay for years.

The Spanish Algarve is more built-up than the Portuguese and the rivers become larger after the Guadiana, the river that separates the two countries. Spain also has some major cities on this coast. Seville, at the head of the Guadalquivir River, is a large and exciting old city. Cádiz is an ancient city with Roman, Moorish and Spanish architecture, good marinas and a fine bay for sailing. Neither city should be missed.

The Mediterranean

If anywhere defies being described in a nutshell it is the Mediterranean. This inland sea is 2,000 miles long, making it almost as big a trip as the Atlantic itself. It isn't even a single sea. The long peninsulas from the north such as Italy and Greece, and the island chain of Corsica and Sardinia, create the Ligurian Sea, Tyrrhenian Sea, Adriatic Sea, Ionian Sea and Aegean Sea, just to name a few. And then there is the mighty Black Sea reached through the Sea of Marmara and the narrow Bosphorus.

The peoples and cultures and inventions of this region have been the driving force of our western way of life. Nowhere has contributed more. Europe, Asia and Africa come together here. Agriculture was developed in the golden triangle at the eastern end of the Mediterranean 10,000 years ago. Major empires followed. Philosophies and cultures from the last three to five thousand years underlie our mindsets and technologies. The mathematical tools we use in our small boat navigation developed here. Revolutions in thought and the arts in the last millennium are prime influences on today's Europe and America. Yet the nature of the countries and cultures around the Mediterranean basin, their moral values and social organization, are intensely different from those of Northern Europe or North America.

There is a distinct difference between western and eastern Mediterranean cultures. The west is the culture of Roman Catholicism, its various schisms and then the Enlightenment and the Renaissance, those radical changes in culture largely originating in Italy from the 14th to the 16th centuries that ended the medieval and brought the mindset of scientific inquiry and secular values of the modern age. The eastern Mediterranean is the culture of Orthodox Christianity and the huge and rich and diverse empire of Islam.

Frankly, I have to admit defeat. I cannot describe the Mediterranean in a nutshell, but I can get you started and give you a few hints.

The region has given its name to a climate zone noted for light and warmth and good agricultural conditions. Summers are settled and relatively dry. Weather here is local, generated by the sea and the land. Winter is the rainy season, when depressions to the north can force their way into the region. Winter winds can be violent as they funnel through the mountains. In winter in particular the weather can change much more rapidly than elsewhere in Europe, with big variations in local conditions. As in other parts of the world, the Mediterranean weather also seems to become more unsettled.

Summer months in the eastern Mediterranean are often times of very light winds interspersed by a few days of strong winds. Usually these stronger winds come with plenty of warning as the usual signs of a depression come across the sky. But keep an eye on the barometer and keep in touch with sources of local information. Locals can tell you what the danger signs are. In the Ionian Islands, for example, a dense cloud lying low on the top of the islands usually warns of strong wind.

The high land temperatures in summer can cause strong sea and land breezes. We used to find that the light winds we had motored through during the day suddenly gave way to a Force 6 and a short chop. It wasn't frightening but until we got used to it we might find our sails taken hard aback or the boat suddenly accelerating off course towards a passing rock. Often these winds blow like clockwork, being strongest during the afternoon. I found the Aegean summer winds would die off around 8 p.m., just after I had battled my way into harbor.

The Mediterranean is a populous region and crowded with sailing boats yet it is still possible to escape the crowds and the high costs by sailing off the beaten track and out of the main summer season. Like other popular sailing destinations, you just have to try a little harder to escape the crowds.

The last couple of decades have seen the arrival of large charter fleets from Spain through to Turkey. This is most marked at the western end of the Mediterranean, which is probably the region you will come to first. Here you can, if you wish, enter the domain of luxury super-yachts, but you don't have to. Many yachts prefer the islands to the mainland and find they can escape the worst of busy marinas. The highly indented coastlines mean that you can find deserted bays if you wish. The beautiful Balearics and the big islands of Corsica and Sardinia still have relatively empty anchorages. Croatia is being discovered now. You might still have time.

Croatia, on the eastern side of the Adriatic Sea across from Italy, was a popular tourist region till the break up of Yugoslavia in the

1990s and the vicious Balkan Wars. Now it is recovering and has turned its attention to sailing as well as land-based tourism. The coast has beautiful historic towns and enough islands to make it a sailor's paradise. The close proximity of the islands makes for easy passages. Swimming is good although I was often surprised by icy cold currents in what was otherwise warm water.

Cruisers who have spent years in the Mediterranean say that the further east you go the better it gets. Yachting is less developed here although Greece has catered for charter yachts since the 1970s and Turkey since the 1980s. Turkey is becoming a base for liveaboards. Good air-links, service standards are high and costs are still low. The local people are very welcoming.

The coast of Turkey is reputed to be stunning, with its islands, mountains and fjord-like bays. As in Italy and Greece, ancient history is only a scratch below the surface. After the Hittites and seafaring Greeks founded their great cities, the Persians and the Romans, Crusaders and Turks came along. I have sailed the nearby Greek islands of the Aegean and the harbors of the Peloponnese and when I next sail the eastern Mediterranean I will be exploring Turkey. But not before I stop off in the Balearics and check out Sardinia.

The Atlantic islands

The Azores are just one of the four groups I think of as the Atlantic islands on the eastern side of the Atlantic and which you can build into your itinerary. You will see the Azores as you sail to Europe if you take the southern route across the Atlantic. Flores is popular with American yachts, being the first one they reach, and it is no hardship to spend a few weeks or even months exploring the remaining and very different islands in the archipelago. It is unlikely that you will see the Azores when you head back home. The route to the East Coast of America is more or less impossible from there. The currents are against you until you get south perhaps as far as 35°N and the winds are likely to have so much west in them that the only part of the east coast you can aim at is Nova Scotia. If going west from the Azores expect to see Madeira before you can head south for the Trades.

The islands of Madeira, the Canaries and the Cape Verde can be visited on an east-to-west Trade Wind crossing. Each in turn helps sailors escape the cold winters of northern Europe. You could have a fine year just touring the Atlantic islands themselves, without ever reaching mainland Europe. With the development of the Canaries as a resort more and more sailors from northern Europe are wintering there and in the summer months they leisurely sail out to the

Azores for the mid-summer races and parties, sail over to Madeira and Porto Santo before the Milk Run rush starts, and then perhaps cross to Spain and Portugal for some metropolitan culture before picking up their marina berth in the Canaries for the winter again.

The Azores, Madeira and the Canaries are rapidly developing their yacht facilities. Perhaps this is most marked in the Azores, where every island aims to have a marina for visiting yachts and the existing harbors are being much improved. Be alert for changes since even the latest pilot books may not have kept up-to-date.

The best weather to cruise the Azores is May to September. Madeira, the Canaries and the Cape Verde can be cruised throughout the year.

The Azores

This archipelago of nine vastly different islands is spread over 300 miles of ocean. The islands are the peaks of some of the tallest mountains on earth, if measured from the seabed. There is no continental shelf. The islands rise steeply straight from the ocean bed. Depths are irregular near the surface and can vary considerably just short distances from shore.

All islands are of volcanic origin, thrust up by the immense pressures generated by the African, American and Eurasian tectonic plates along the Mid-Atlantic Trench. Pico is the only mountain to have retained its original cone but the rest all have ancient caldeiras (craters) and some have mud geysers and hot water springs. Volcanoes still occasionally erupt. The last eruption was the Capelinhos Volcano on Faial in 1957. Earthquakes are common and the last major one in 1998 caused widespread damage in the central group of islands.

There are many social, economic and political dimensions to the geographical remoteness of the Azores, all of which give it a very special charm for visiting sailors. Their mid-Atlantic location gives them a moderate climate and a unique eco-system.

The Azores have been Portuguese since discovered by Europeans in 1427. Colonization began in 1439 with people from the Algarve and Alentejo regions. In later centuries people also came from Northern France and the Low Countries, and their legacies can still be seen.

The nine islands are divided into three groups:

- the Western Group (Grupo Ocidental) of Flores and Corvo
- the Central Group (Grupo Central) of Terceira, Graciosa, São Jorge, Pico and Faial
- the Eastern Group (Grupo Oriental) of São Miguel, Santa Maria and the tiny Formigas Islets (The Ants)

The Azores Achipelago

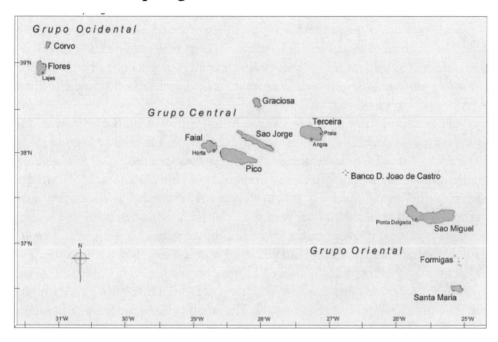

The Azores are an autonomous region of Portugal. This means that they have a locally elected regional parliament running regional departments of government but they have budgets set by Lisbon and obtain funds from the European Union. Despite long conversations with local Azoreans and people in government I never managed to pin down the precise, practical meaning of autonomous but Portuguese. It seems like a continuation of the historical, arm's-length relation the islands have always had with the metropolitan power. In the 16th century, for example, they were the last part of Portugal to resist Philip II of Spain's rule over Portugal. Then in the 1820s, during the Portuguese civil war, they stood out against the changes on the mainland.

The islands must have been vital and busy during Portugal's 15th and 16th century heyday as a world power, but the 18th and 19th centuries, with the earthquake destruction of Lisbon in 1755, the Napoleonic conquest of Iberia, the civil war and the independence of Brazil from Portugal in 1822, were not good times for the country. Nor has Portugal had a good 20th century. For much of the period since the monarchy was deposed in 1910 Portugal had repressive governments. Parliamentary institutions worked poorly. Corruption and economic mismanagement were widespread. Salazar, almost the last of Western Europe's 20th century dictators, ran the country from 1932 until 1968. Like other autocrats he depended on an efficient secret police. Censorship was strict. The politically suspect were closely watched, opponents were jailed or exiled, and sometimes murdered. Salazar's corporatist state was continued by his supporters until the non-violent socialist *coup d'état* known as The Carnation Revolution of 1974.

1974 was a deep seated rebellion against half a century of dictatorship, isolation, and backwardness. As well as political change from top to bottom, there was also a profound societal transformation far beyond what happened elsewhere in Western Europe during the 1960s.

Salazar, a university professor of economics, left Portugal the poorest nation of Western Europe, and the Azores as the even poorer offshoot of Portugal. The 1974 government introduced far reaching democratic reforms, which included giving independence to Portugal's remaining African colonies of Angola, Mozambique, and Guinea-Bissau, but the country remained politically and militarily unsettled until the Assembly of the Republic was elected in 1976. In 1986, Portugal became a member of the EU and modern times began. It qualified for the European Monetary Union in 1998 and became a member of the Euro-Zone in January 2002 along with 11 other EU members.

The transition to democracy was highly successful. Portugal is politically stable. The press is free. For much of the EU period economic growth has been above the EU average. Economic growth has solved many social problems.

The economic base of the Azores is a tribute to economic Darwinism. It finds a niche that other economies don't want and clings to it until the changing environment of technology wipes it out and it must find a new way of making a living. A few centuries ago the mild mid-ocean climate gave the Azores a comparative advantage in wine and fruit. Its produce supplied the royal houses of Europe, including Russia. But no longer. In the 20th century its location in mid-Atlantic made it a vital half-way fuel-stop for the flying boats between America and Europe. But no longer. Also in the 20th century it was a major base for the transatlantic cables connecting America and Europe. But no longer. It was a major location for the 19th and 20th century whaling fleets. Whaling is over but the effects continue. Many Azoreans recruited as whalers left ship in New England for a better life. The annual summer vacation of the large expatriate Portuguese communities in New England and the northern states of the US are probably the islands' main source of tourist revenue.

The mild climate and the high rainfall that make the landscape so green and lush supports large dairy herds. Their wonderful cheese and butter are major exports to Europe. Fields are prettily hedged by blue hydrangeas, growing tall and bushy. I have never seen this anywhere else. Bananas, oranges, lemons and other sub-tropical fruit grow everywhere all through the year. Wine is still made from local grapes. The Azores are like a well kept and well stocked garden.

There are few good natural harbors. The best bays are often relatively shallow indentations on the protected side of an island, a little too naturally open to summer storms and winter gales. Today's Azorean harbors are a tribute to the power of breakwaters. Without these simple but huge structures the harbors would be more rolly in the summer season than modern yachts would accept, and untenable in the winter. The main Azorean marinas at Horta and São Miguel shelter behind massive outer breakwaters and smaller inner breakwaters. But the sea, being the sea, has the power to make even these structures seem puny and temporary when great storms blow.

> Monte da Guia, a 500-foot volcanic peak, and its almost perfectly circular *caldeira do inferno*, is on the southeast corner of Faial a mile from Horta. We often climbed the peak just to look at the sea. The nearest land to the southwest is Surinam or the Guyanas, about 2,000 miles away. The nearest mainland to the south, if you miss Recife on the eastern most headland of Brazil, is Antarctica, more than half the world away. Usually we looked out over a blue and flat sea but when the big winds blew from the southwest they drove heavy seas hard onto the headland. As the seas swept round the headland they would meet the water of Pico Channel moving in a different direction. Wonderful whirling wave circles would spin up from the sea, as high as ten feet, dashing half a mile or more out towards Pico until they lost their energy. We had never seen such waves.

Faial

Most yachts visit Faial and its main city of Horta has a legendary reputation as the ocean crossroads where sailors recharge their batteries. For about three months every year this is the party capital of sailing. We rate Horta as the best harbor to winter in the Azores. Ponta Delgada on São Miguel may be just as secure from winter weather but it lacks charm. Horta certainly has charm.

Most things that sailors need can be found in Horta. The marina staff is courteous and wonderfully helpful. All chandlery and equipment can be found at or obtained by Mid Atlantic Yacht Services (MAYS) near the marina, a friendly operation set up by a North American several years ago. There is a good cheap supermarket, an excellent though small daily produce market, restaurants, free and commercial Internet, cinema, theatre, concerts, art exhibitions and a wonderful but small public library. We enjoyed it all. Our cultural experiences ranged from watching England win the Rugby World Cup on TV, foolishly seeing all three parts of Lord of the Rings at the Teatro Faialense in a single week, hearing a selection of readings for Women's International Day and seeing an exhibition of watercolors by a friend. In between we heard *fado*, wonderful concerts by the Ukrainian musicians at the Music Conservatory and saw plenty of good English-language films.

Faial, Azores. Looking from Monte da Guia over to Horta town and marina one calm, bright day. It is spring and boats are already arriving in the harbor.

In most countries of Europe the convention is to tip for services like being waited on in a restaurant, as you would back home. However, this is not usually the convention in mainland Portugal (except where tourism rules) and certainly isn't the case in the Azores. Don't be tempted to break the convention, however good the service and how-ever uncomfortable you feel about not tipping. You will be insulting the person. A better way to express your pleasure and gratitude is to say thanks in Portuguese, even if you give the language a bad mauling.

As on Pico and São Jorge, much of Faial's housing stock was destroyed by the 1998 earthquake, giving it an undeserved air of poverty and neglect. The repairs will take many years but some major work was well underway by our visit in 2003/2004.

Hiking is good and the island is well worth exploring beyond the pretty harbor town of Horta. It has a deep and lush caldeira that is well worth the effort to climb into. As an antidote to this lushness, visit Capelinhos to see the weird lunar landscape of the most recent volcanic eruption. This eruption lasted 13 months and added about 1km to the length of the island. When it was over the old lighthouse was too far from the sea to be of use. Today, over 50 years later, the land remains bare and dusty, with only scrubby plants slowly colonizing it against the constant winds.

Horta is famous for its graffiti-filled "wall" where all visiting sailors leave a message. The walls have long since been filled and artists have had to make do

Faial, Azores. We struggled for inspiration and in the end our painting on the stones of Horta Harbor was inspired, though simple.

with the pavement as well. The legend is that any boat that does not leave a message is doomed never to return. Or doomed to return? One or the other, depending on your point of view. This age-old practice only started a few decades ago but it would be a miserable crew that didn't make their own contribution. You'll see PETRONELLA's work of art at the entrance to the pontoons. Deceptively simple, it took us most of a year to think of it.

Pico

Pico is the wonderful island a few miles across the strait from Faial. It has a perfect volcanic mountain, the highest in Portugal, about 7,500 feet high. It is *the* view from Horta harbor. I can't imagine a better view unless it is to see dawn from the top of the volcano. Pico is still live, but not very active. Anchorages exist but the best idea is to leave the boat in Horta and take one of the frequent ferries across.

São Jorge

São Jorge, a long narrow island, is a few hours sail from Horta. The often cloudy upland plateau is used for cattle pasture. The cliffs fall steeply away from this plateau sometimes ending in a narrow, broken coastal plain called a *faja*. The central plateau gives superb views of the neighboring islands.

The main harbor at Velas when we visited was a summer anchorage only and rolly even then but the small harbors of Urzelina and Calheta are really only good in settled weather and better visited by land. Velas has plans for a bigger breakwater and marina.

Cory's Shearwater (*Calonectris diomedea borealis*) is common in the Azores. Roughly half the Atlantic population lives there. At night, especially in Velas on São Jorge we would hear their unmistakable noisy cry as they returned from their feeding grounds. Sometimes it sounds like a twanged harp, sometimes like a strangulated cry. I'd never heard any bird like it.

São Miguel

São Miguel is the largest of the Azorean islands and Ponta Delgada is the largest city in the archipelago. Ponta Delgada is busy with more tourists than anywhere else we visited in the Azores but the marina is secure, a new one is being mooted, and the big town has excellent amenities. Best of all, though, is the variety of landscape on this volcanically active island. Nowhere can be more relaxing than the circular lake filled with volcanically heated water in the gardens of Furnas.

Terceira

The old town of Angra do Heroismo is the most beautiful Azorean town and the new marina could hardly be more scenically placed. It sits at the end of one of Angra's main streets. Anchoring in the bay can be very rolly.

We loved the classical architecture of Angra and the pride with which it is being restored rather than ripped down and turned into cheap new buildings.

Terceira has the largest and most celebrated fiesta of the Azores, São Joaninas, every June, and bull-running through the narrow residential streets of the old part of town above the harbor.

The marina at Praia is likely to be less subject to swell than Angra. Indeed, it's hard to imagine a marina more subject to swell than Angra. Praia sits in a large open bay now protected by the long arms of a breakwater. Winter storms batter holes in this from time to time. The marina is inside the outer breakwater, behind a breakwater of its own.

Graciosa

Graciosa has gentle rolling hills that can be seen from far off. Smaller than Flores but with a larger population. Quiet, unspoilt and charming. Villa do Praia is the main anchorage for yachts rather than the capital, Santa Cruz. It has good holding in sand but is exposed to southeasterlies. You can visit by plane or take a ferry from Terceira. Graciosa has an impressive caldeira. An old tower enables you to descend to the bottom to the large, beautiful underground lake.

Santa Maria

Santa Maria is the oldest of the islands and a curious geological mix. One half is flat, sunny, dry and barren, with the limestone and clays of a sedimentary period and reef growth; the other half is volcanic, mountainous, wet, cloudy and green. The main harbor at Vila do Porto is in the barren part, the main town being a steep climb uphill.

Flores/Corvo

Flores is the westernmost point of Europe and regarded by many as the most beautiful of Azorean islands. Small, with a population of about 4,000. Every year a few hundred yachts make Flores their port of entry. It is, after all, the first island you will reach if you have sailed direct from the northern end of the Eastern Seaboard. It is popular with North Americans but also with Europeans on this route.

Lajes anchorage is open to the east, often crowded in the summer and can be rolly but there is talk of a marina. The people of Flores are very friendly and the Clube Naval has a small tourist office by the anchorage to help visitors.

Tiny Corvo has a population of fewer than 400. The daily ferries from Flores, weather permitting, are probably better than taking your boat across. The

Madeira Archipelago

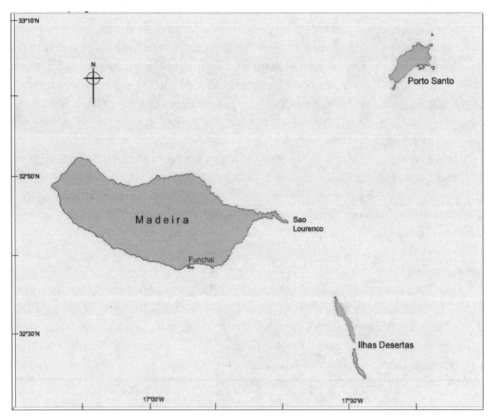

anchorage is exposed and holding poor. The weather can change very suddenly and rough seas may prevent the ferry landing or leaving for several days.

Madeira

The archipelago of Madeira is also Portuguese. It has three parts;

- the large, high and magnificently green island of Madeira itself
- the smaller, low lying and sandy island of Porto Santo
- the uninhabited stumps of the Salvagem Islands on route to the Canaries.

Madeira

Madeira lies south of the Westerly winds and on the edge of the Portuguese Trades, making a journey from the north straightforward. It has a pleasantly warm winter. The high island generates its own climate and sometimes conditions can be boisterous.

I enjoyed Madeira but I never liked the outer anchorage at Funchal, the island's capital, and when we were there the 210-berth marina was too full for us to squeeze in. I found the anchorage unsettling. On calm days boats that had been anchored on the same spot for days went dragging by. On one intensely windy morning I chatted to the neighboring crew each time our boats swung within feet of one another. We were both on anchor watch. We didn't drag but the tension was too great and we soon left for the calmer conditions of Porto Santo. Before we sailed, though, we treated ourselves to a walk in the mountains of Madeira.

I have never seen such needle sharp rocky pinnacles and ridges and steep sided cliffs as these mountains and the walking between them is stunning. Some wise far-sighted earlier generation had cut and fenced paths and stairways between the highest peaks. In places the three-feet-wide path was the mountain ridge itself. In other places it ran just below the cliffy peak at the end of a valley. In other places it tunneled through a peak of hard rock. The rain falls heavily on the mountains and the cloud sits low enough to be pierced by the needle peaks. We were lucky. We walked Madeira on a brilliantly clear day.

Funchal is a good place to get things done. In the older part of the town we found the metal stockists, welders, workshops, paint suppliers and gas stockists we craved. In the last few years three new marinas have been developed to supplement Funchal.

Caniçal, on the southeast promontory of Madeira 12 miles from Funchal, has the 242-berth marina Quinta do Lorde. On the west side Lugar de Baixo marina at Ponta do Sol and Calheta marina each have 300 berths.

Porto Santo

Porto Santo could be on a different planet from Madeira. It is dry, its mountain peaks and steep-sided valleys being too low to bring the huge rains of Madeira. Its small population and tiny main town are more relaxing than Madeira, but above all it has a huge sandy beach, secure anchorage and large harbor. The harbor has transformed Porto Santo from being a little used, rolly anchorage to a popular stopover for Atlantic sailors. The wall is beginning to look like the more famous one at Horta.

There is good holding in 30 feet off the beach close to the harbor on the south coast. The small marina inside the harbor has 75 berths.

The Salvagems

The Salvagems are tiny almost uninhabited islands on the way to the Canaries. We obtained official written permission to visit them in Madeira, to add spice to our journey south.

> **PETRONELLA log, fourth night from Madeira**
>
> We did not land at the Salvagems. We came slowly on them in a falling wind and worked through the rocky channel to the best landing place. The entry recommended in the pilot looked more difficult than our route. As we came up on the anchorage, so did the new onshore wind. We came inside the rocky approach to the anchorage but the wind drove waves at the landing place. The whole human population (both the wardens) watched us from the rocky hillside but made no move to guide us in. Perhaps they thought it too dangerous. Perhaps they were happy with the rabbits and not ready for outside company. They didn't even wave back. The wind was good for the Canaries so we hauled round and romped away.

The Canaries

The Canaries have been popular with sailors heading west since Spain and Portugal first discovered the Americas. They became an autonomous community of Spain in 1982. Now they are a stop for almost all yachts heading to the Caribbean and the departure point for the ARC. They are a cruising ground in their own right.

These seven islands in this small Spanish speaking archipelago some 50 miles off the African coast of Morocco were known as the Fortunate Islands by the ancient Greeks. Although very close to one another, each island has a distinctive flora, fauna, topography and even climate. The climate is pleasant. Weather is wetter in the western islands and desert-like in the eastern islands. The winds are mainly from the northeast and the best shelter is along the southern coasts. There are many pretty bays to anchor in and many more marinas and harbors have developed in the last few years but the increase in visiting yachts and chartering puts pressure on facilities, especially in late summer and fall. Many foreign boats spend winters or years here.

> I remember Arguiniguin with affection. Arguiniguin, at the southern end of Gran Canaria, is not quaint. It is real. It had no marina. A

small fishing fleet used the inner harbor and visiting yachts anchored in the outer bay in sand and protected by the large harbor wall. Long-stay yachts on heavy mooring weights ran stern lines to the breakwater separating inner and outer harbors. Close to the north shore is a plate of rock that looks like sand. To anchor there is to drag. I was not put off by the huge concrete plant at Porto Cementos. This wide sandy bay has good holding. When the winds shifted from north to south we went round the headland from one to the other.

The main yachting center is Las Palmas, Gran Canaria. Once the dirtiest anchorage in the Atlantic islands, now a good new marina.

I long complained about the Canaries to anyone who would listen but gradually it dawned on me that I was really just complaining about the bigger, most visited islands and being there at the wrong season. The islands are massively developed for tourism and after sailing half an ocean I just wasn't ready to share with people who had hopped on a plane that morning to escape a British, German or Scandinavian winter.

So what about the other islands? I have to admit to not having visited La Graciosa, La Palma and El Hierro, the little islands where yachts must anchor and put up with the most limited facilities. El Hierro, the westernmost island was known to the ancient Greeks as the end of the world. The island is volcanic in the south and rolling pasture in the north. Even here a marina is under construction. That should make exploration ashore easier. Perhaps you should go in early summer before the crowds roll in.

Conditions for passages between the islands are usually good and the journeys short but go with a good forecast, especially if heading north. Wind over tide and current can produce a nasty short sea.

This can be a windy sailing area normally but it is subject to locally enhanced winds. Passages between the islands have "acceleration zones" where the wind is forced to funnel between the high islands (especially Gran Canaria and Tenerife—the Teide volcano on Tenerife is the highest mountain in Spain and the world's third largest volcano). Wind may rise from almost nothing to a strong 25-knot breeze within a few hundred yards. Acceleration zones are typically found on the southeast and southwest coasts and in the afternoons. The Canaries also feel the harmattan wind from Africa. This typically carries dust up to 500 miles offshore (and even as far as the Caribbean) and will reduce visibility in the Canaries.

I was too uneasy about the anchorages to enjoy the Canaries. The light offshore wind during the day could shift into a stronger onshore wind in the

The Canary Islands

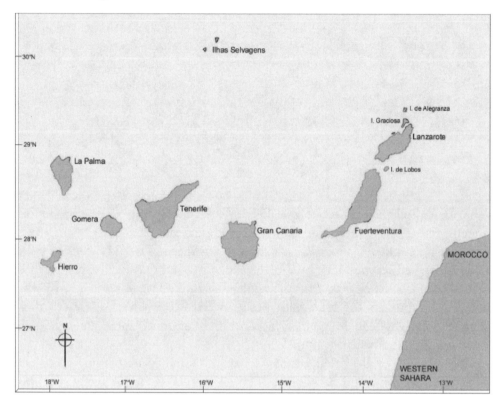

evening and if enhanced by a spell of weather can bring bad swell and put you on a lee shore. Most yachts would lie to two anchors, holding their bow into the evening wind for greater comfort. When the wind grew beyond comfort I perfected my technique of leaving the stern anchor on a buoy and coming back for it later. The new marinas should reduce the need for this.

Many anchorages are thin sand over rock and your best holding may come when your anchor slips a fluke under a rocky crevice. It happened to us once and getting the anchor free wasn't pretty. In such places I would definitely change my usual practice and consider buoying the anchor.

The other reason we went to the Canaries, and the reason many ocean crossers still do, is the quality and availability of food for stocking your boat.

Cape Verde

The Cape Verde Islands are the last frontier of Atlantic islands, more deserving than the Canaries to be called the end of the world. They are volcanic in origin and about 120 million years old, known to the great Arab explorers since at least the 12th century, part of the Portuguese empire since the 1460s, an independent republic since 1975 but still closely linked to Portugal, now petitioning to enter the EU. The islands have been subject to severe periodic droughts and famines and agricultural collapse throughout their history. Because of this it is reckoned that the Cape Verdean diaspora is greater than the population of the islands. These are economically poor, sparsely populated, much more exotic than the Canaries and closer to the Trade Wind belt.

The ten main islands and four smaller ones of the archipelago divide into the dry and barren group of windward islands to the north (the Barlaventos) and the wetter, greener leeward group to the south (Soltaventos). The climate is hot and humid and can be dusty, especially when the harmattan blows. The capital Porto da Praia is on Santiago in the Soltaventos. Fogo is still an active volcano and earthquakes are common on all the islands.

Most yachts leaving the Canaries and heading SSW to find the Trades pass close by the islands and could reach them with a simple detour, but few do this. The islands have recently developed cruise ship and land tourism and word is getting out among sailors. With luck, though, you will still find them the least developed and most natural of all the islands. Your visit here could be the highlight of your whole trip around the Atlantic.

We never visited the Cape Verde Islands. We were on our way here ten years ago but went to Senegal first instead. We could have gone to the islands after Senegal but by then it was January and we were late for the Caribbean. The islands are probably most visited by French sailors. We met many in Dakar and the Casamance who regularly sailed to and from Cape Verde, often weighing down their yachts with cargo from the mainland, and they encouraged us to go there. When the Trades are well established the anchorages here can be rough. This is a good reason to visit the islands early in November and set off for the Caribbean in December. When we flashed by it was already January and the Trades were blowing hard.

> For the first four days after leaving Senegal we flew along on a fine broad reach in strong winds from the north. There seemed no chance of making Cape Verde against those rolling waves from the north. Then the Trade Winds came to us and I was sure that if we had tightened our sheets we could have gone round with the wind and sailed straight into Praia on Santiago. But the excitement of the ocean filled us and we were done with stops.

Stopping at Cape Verde makes your main leg across the Atlantic shorter. Had we stopped there from Senegal we would have reduced the main leg of our

The Cape Verde Archipelago

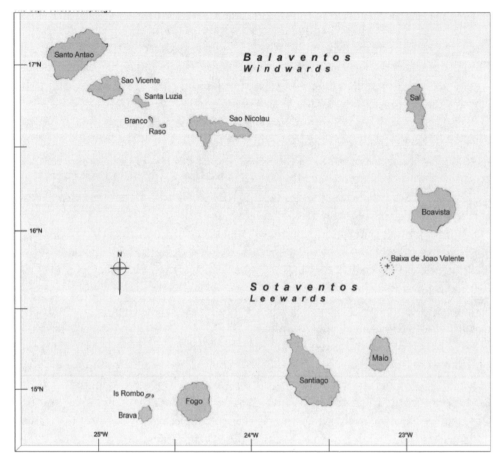

Atlantic crossing by four days. Had we sailed from the Canaries we would have reduced it by about eight days.

Mindelo on São Vicente is the only deep water harbor in the islands and the main center for commercial ships, but it does have a yacht club. Don't expect to find marinas here, not yet, although I'm told a small charter fleet has built its own dock and you may be able to get facilities there. Otherwise yachts will need to approach the commercial and fishing yards for any repairs and will expect to be spending their time at anchor. Charts and pilots are not comprehensive and you will need to discover many anchorages for yourself or by talking to other yachts you meet. Conditions will demand careful anchoring, perhaps with the palm tree techniques you have learned in the Caribbean or will practice when you get there. Be ready for wind shifts, changes from morning to evening breezes, and swell. The tidal range is small but tides enhanced by currents can be strong, sometimes running at up to three knots between the islands.

Facilities and supplies are limited. You should find water and fuel and local fresh fruit and vegetables in the wetter, greener Soltaventos but stock your boat fully in the Canaries. Like the Azores, the people of the Cape Verde Islands were recruited to American whalers during the 19th century and have formed a local community in New England. You may be lucky and find an American speaker to be your guide. Otherwise, prepare to do your best in Portuguese and, if you really want to impress, Crioulo, a mixture of Portuguese and West African languages.

People on islands like these that don't see many yachts will make you very welcome indeed but this doesn't mean that the officials won't take their immigration regulations seriously. Check with a Cape Verdean embassy before making your visit so that you know the latest regulations. Regulations vary between the islands. You will need to check in and out of each island you visit.

Pilotage information for yachts is scarce. Big ships would use the US Defense Mapping Agency's Sailing Directions for the West Coast of Europe and North West Africa and this is worth looking at. The best, most recent information for sailing boats that I have is the *RCC Atlantic Islands* by Anne Hammick.

6

Tides, weather and you

Sailing conditions on the European side of the ocean are not exactly the same as the American side, so here are some pointers to help you. You may find that in your new sailing life you have to work more with tides and manage with fog than you ever did in the past.

Tides

Tides in Europe vary hugely, from the 40-foot tides on the Brittany coast and in the Bristol Channel to the barely noticeable tides of the Baltic and Mediterranean. The significance of tides to a sailing boat changes as you move around the European coast. In the Baltic and Mediterranean the negligible rise and fall of tides allows the Mediterranean style of mooring. The massive tides of western Britain and France means that in many harbors you will adjust your lines as the boat rises or falls and get used to drying out and taking the ground at low water. In the North Sea working the tides is vital to your pilotage yet on the Netherlands side of the North Sea, where the flows from the north and south meet, the tides are neutral. In the English Channel you can really only sail along the coast and in or out of harbors according to the tides.

You will need a tidal atlas showing the flows and heights for any tide at any state of tide in any area of the Channel or North Sea. You should also learn to use the tidal diamonds on British Admiralty charts. At the very least you need a tide timetable for the areas you are sailing and become familiar with the use of primary and secondary ports to work out local tide times and heights. You can usually find this in a nautical almanac or cruising pilot of the sort I am sure you will be carrying.

The last few years have seen a number of computer programs that replicate the data from official tide tables but in a more convenient form. A good source is the British Admiralty Hydrographic Office website at www.ukho.gov.uk. This has a generous definition of Europe, ranging from the Arctic to ports in the

Western Sahara. Some commercial sites for navigation and tidal software are: www.marinecomputing.com—European and World versions; www.neptune-navigation.com—UK and Europe versions; www.tideplotter.co.uk—UK and Europe versions.

Make your own observations of tides as a way of amending the published data. Tidal predictions are made years in advance from a set of standard mathematical calculations and cannot take account of the wind that has been blowing all week or today's barometric pressure. Your observations might make the difference between a quiet night at anchor or bumping the bottom at midnight. Keep a log of when tides turn, log the depth at anchor or when entering a river and compare this with the pilot book or chart to see:

- how cautious your pilot book author has been
- whether dredging or silting has changed the channel depth since the book or chart was prepared
- what a chart datum of lowest astronomical depth really means.

Also, keep an eye on the moon. It is your best, most visible indicator of the ticking tidal clock. The pull of the sun and moon on the earth is the main cause of tides but the moon has roughly double the influence of the sun. Tides are simply the oceans washing back and forth in their basins, like water in a bowl. The moon pulls water into a bulge on the side of the earth facing it and the earth's spin causes a balancing bulge of water on the opposite side.

At full and new moon the earth, moon and sun are in a single straight line, producing the greatest pull on the earth and the most bulging tides. Spring tides, when high water is highest, low water is lowest and the greatest range occurs, come a few days after full and new moon. Neap tides, when tidal range is least, come at the first and third quarters of the moon, when the sun and moon pull at right angles to one another. The tides work on a daily cycle of about 13 hours and a lunar cycle of 28 days. The biggest spring tides occur in spring and fall, around the equinox, and since the moon's orbit also varies on a 20 plus yearly cycle there is probably a 20 plus yearly variation in tides as well. But let's not worry about that.

Tides are a mystery, whatever else people will tell you. Always seek local advice about what might or might not happen today and tomorrow if you have a particular trip that is tide-dependent. Think in terms of tidal gates, harbor bars, rules of twelfths, springs and neaps and barometric and wind effect on tidal height. There is much more to tides than the obvious one of being on a magic carpet either going with you or against you. Beating into the wind with the tide against you will be slamming into short sharp seas, with water breaking at the bows and running on deck. Even at the top end of a Force 4 or into a Force 5 you may need to reef, just to be comfortable.

Fog often adds a romantic charm to the view. But I would rather be in harbor on those days than navigating down the coast.

Through the mist to fog

For those who have cut their sailing teeth in southern or tropical waters fog may be a mystery. But while fog may not be as dense and dangerous as it habitually seems to be in summer on the Newfoundland banks, it is common place on the coasts of Europe and even through the Pillars of Hercules into the Mediterranean.

At a quiet anchorage up a non-commercial river the stillness and silence of a really dense fog is wonderful. Your ears seem to be calmed cotton wool. Your bow is the extent of your vision. Your world has shrunk to the size of a womb. How magical.

But at sea I hate fog with an intensity to match my fear of it. I have been in too many crowded sea roads when the fog has caught me. Leaving Flushing Harbour to go into the North Sea from the Westerscheldt in The Netherlands I sailed into a white bank of invisibility. The Scheldt is a narrow, busy shipping channel. The ships came by unseen, their propellers roaring and the bow wave hurling us sideways as though we were no more than 100 feet from them. As indeed we probably were. Sailing alone from the Thames Estuary to Cornwall I was sneaking past the immensely busy entrances to Dover Harbour, where high speed ferries come in and out every ten minutes, when the fog came. The coast-guard on the VHF reported visibility of 300 feet. If I had time and the nerve to give attention to my VHF radio I might have told him the visibility was more like 60 feet where I was.

I had almost forgotten what fog was like after so many years in the Caribbean. You can suffer bad visibility from heat haze and sometimes Sahara dust haze in the Caribbean, but only at a very safe distance and it isn't anything like fog. In the Azores we were troubled by low clouds blanketing the islands, but never by fog.

G and I returned to the reality that is fog one afternoon shortly after we arrived in Bayona on the final leg of our west to east Atlantic crossing. We were following another sailing boat towards a gap in the reef between Bayona and the lovely Islas Cies when the boat disappeared. The Islas had disappeared some time earlier but then they were five miles away and the boat we were following was only a few hundred feet away. We sailed back into Bayona anchorage. Discretion was the better part of our valor.

You would naturally expect fog in the English Channel and the North Sea especially in spring and fall (fortunately the BBC shipping forecast includes visibility and fog warnings) but the coast of Spain and Portugal too is subject to fog during the summer. Locals say the fog comes when the wind is from the south, which makes sense since fog is formed when warm moist air meets colder surface water and water vapor is forced to precipitate out. The wind from the south is warm. The current is from the north and the water off this coast is surprisingly cold. But from my experience I would say that sometimes the south wind brings fog and sometimes it doesn't.

Fog can be very localized along this Portuguese coast. We sat in fog for two days in Peniche with boats arriving from Cascais, 60 miles away. They had set off in bright sun and clear horizons. Also, there may be no fog five miles offshore despite dense fog on the headland.

We took a gamble. The little harbor at Sesimbra was cold and clammy and too expensive for a second night. "Once outside the breakwater we have clear sea all the way to Sines," I said to G, pointing to the chart to show her how we were crossing a wide bay and would be well offshore till we arrived at Sines 25 miles away. "No problem," I said in case she had missed the gist. Sesimbra is a small, narrow harbor with an inner and an outer breakwater. I had a clear mental picture of it. As we headed for what I thought was the outer entrance G pointed out that we were still inside the inner breakwater. Fog robs you of sense as well as sense of direction and sense of sight. We couldn't see the outer breakwater wall even though it was only 100 yards beyond the inner. Still, with G on the foredeck we negotiated both breakwaters and dodged the little fishing boats anchored outside. G stayed on the foredeck for four hours keeping watch and periodically telling me to blow the foghorn. I refused of course. You can't hear a thing with the damn foghorn going. And anyway, if I didn't watch the compass like a hawk we would go round in a circle.

Fog is rare along the Algarve coast but all too common in the Straits of Gibraltar during June to September. Cold currents flowing east through the Straits can precipitate fog from the warm air blowing out of the Mediterranean.

The little German yacht had so much humidity after Cape St Vincent that it rained inside the boat. Further along the Algarve the skipper could hear road traffic but saw nothing. It was only when preparing for a noon sight that he saw Cádiz about one mile away.

Boats without radar pray for one when they are in fog. There isn't much that makes a sailor as helpless as fog. G, from the Caribbean, wasn't used to fog on our trip from Sesimbra to Sines. Her eyes saw all sorts of dangerous forms. She leapt to attention whenever a fishing float or piece of log came into view. I didn't expect trouble but whenever I saw a float I mentally logged how far away it was and figured that this was a reasonable distance to take avoiding action. After all, one of us had to stay calm.

Even with radar, safety in fog depends on doing things the old fashioned way.

- Plot your position while you still have visibility. In the days before GPS this was absolutely vital since you relied on what you could see. Even now, with land in the offing, I feel great comfort from corroborating my chart with my field of vision. Keep a frequent GPS plot running. If it achieves nothing else at least it helps you keep a sense of the tangible world.
- Make sure your radar reflector is hoisted and you have flares and flashlights handy. A radar reflector is your first and best line of defense.

- Navigation lights are required by International Collision Regulations but don't let this lull you into thinking your lights will save you. But, since fog is often only masthead deep, your masthead lights might be seen by commercial shipping.
- Sound your foghorn every two minutes. One long blast if motoring (Morse T); one long two short if sailing (Morse D). This too is required by International Collision Regulations. Again, never assume it will save you. Foghorns may reassure your crew and may be heard by fishermen at anchor in a nearby rowing dinghy, but don't expect ocean going ships and fishing boats to hear your puny squawk over all the noise they normally make.
- Have safety gear and liferaft ready and make sure crew are clipped on. Position crew on bow and stern, if you have enough.
- Keep checking your position on the chart. If near shipping lanes, have a strategy to keep clear of the lanes. International Collision Regulations require you to keep out of separation zones.
- Leave your VHF running and if you get really anxious send out an all ships message every half hour with your speed, course and position.
- Don't bring about a GPS-induced collision. Avoid using waypoints that other yachts might use lest you meet one coming the other way.

And now do the really important things. Watch out and listen hard. The fog will fool both your eyes and your ears but they are the best you've got. If motoring, turn off your engine occasionally and listen really hard. If sailing, have the engine ready to start.

The point in fog is continuous vigilance on your part, listening and looking as hard as you can and hoping that those big cruisers with radar will not only see you on their screens but build you into their calculation for closest point of approach. But do the safety things yourself, too. If conditions and jobs on board require it, wear life jackets. If they don't, have your jacket where you can grab it. Towing a dinghy is a good idea inshore. Us ocean crossers should have a liferaft ready anyway, for any emergency, not just fog. And a liferaft means you have a grab bag ready and waiting. You might ask the grab-bag officer to chuck in a few extra biscuits and the cell phone.

Once upon a time I had an electronic device that claimed to receive warning signals from ships' radars. I was so pleased to have it, having been frightened once too often in fog. All vessels with radar are required by International Collision

Regulations to use it, so that little gizmo should have made me very safe. I sent it back to the shop. I just couldn't get the sensitivity right. I would be on deck watching passing tankers and this device claimed no shipping for miles. Or I would be staring at an empty horizon and this thing's alarm was harassing me. And that wasn't all. Not all vessels big enough to sink a yacht have radar and even if they do they might not have one in working order. I decided that the crude fact that the other ship had a working radar wasn't enough. I want a device that tells me someone is watching that screen and awake enough to know that I am a blip.

I hear that the technology of radar detectors has improved to the point of reliability. I was almost tempted to invest but thought my piggy bank money was better being turned into a radar now that they are relatively cheap, and anything left over could be spent on a training course so that G and I don't fall into the too-common trap of radar assisted collision. After all, this is more in keeping with my first principle of collision avoidance at sea. It depends on you. Don't let any mechanical aid, shining lights, noisy horns or obligations to International Collision Regulations kid you into entrusting your safety to them.

Weather forecasts

All official weather forecasts for this adventure are listed in the British Admiralty List of Radio Signals.

The English language shipping forecast provided by the British Meteorological Office covers not just the sea areas all around the British Isles but those a long way to north and south. It is ideal for yachts closing the Atlantic coasts of Europe. It does not, however, cover the Atlantic islands. It is broadcast on BBC Radio 4 long wave 1515m (198 kHz) at 0048, 0520, 1201 and 1754 (local time).

The shipping forecast gives a summary of gale warnings in force, a general synopsis and area forecasts for specified sea areas. The 0048 and 0520 bulletins also include coastal weather reports. The bulletins are based on information updated about half an hour before the broadcasts. If a gale is forecast a warning will be broadcast at the first available program break and after the next news bulletin.

These bulletins are similar to those of the American National Weather Service through its NMN station. The forecasts are read in a simple standard format.

Listen with a map of the shipping forecast areas alongside you. I have come to appreciate that the size and location of a sea area has considerable bearing on the quality of the forecast. Sea areas Fitzroy and Trafalgar, for example, are very large compared to Portland, Wight, Dover and Thames. The forecast for Fitzroy or Trafalgar will be a sort of average that may not represent any specific part of the area very well. A big depression clipping the northwest corner of Fitzroy may leave the high pressure over Galicia, Spain untouched. Also, weather in Fitzroy and Trafalgar may be re-forming under the influence of climatic factors whereas by the time a weather system reaches Plymouth it is very

BBC Shipping Forecast Areas

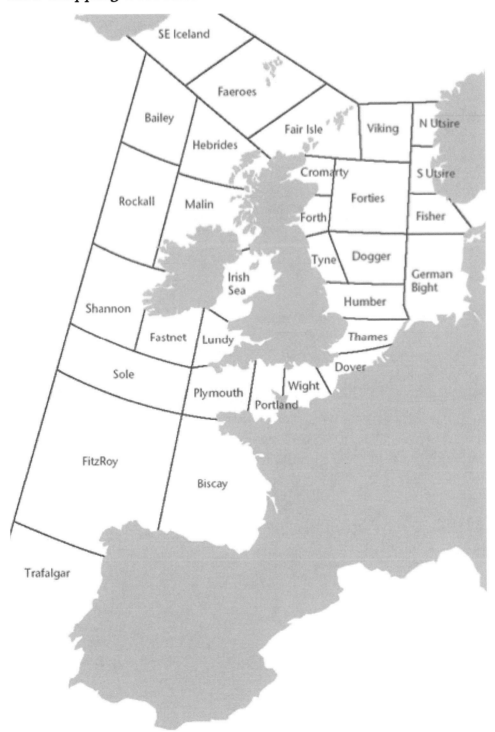

likely to run as predictably as a train through the Portland, Wight, Dover, Thames corridor between England and France.

This is how key terms in the BBC forecasts are defined:

- timing of changes
    Imminent—within the next 6 hours
    Soon—6 to 12 hours
    Later—more than 12 hours

- barometric changes
    Slowly—changing less than 1.5 millibars in 3 hours
    Rising or falling—from 1.6 to 3.5 millibars in 3 hours
    Quickly—changing 3.6 to 6 millibars in 3 hours
    Very quickly—changing more than 6 millibars in 3 hours

- visibility:
    Good—over 5 nautical miles
    Moderate—2 to 5 nautical miles
    Poor—1,000 meters to 2 nautical miles
    Fog—Less than1,000 meters

Strong wind warnings are issued for coastal waters when winds are expected to reach Force 6 and above. Remember that the expression "imminent" means that whatever is forecast could happen within the next hour or two. Depressions and secondary lows can move towards you quickly at 25 knots but sometimes the wave depression running along the line of a front can be moving at 60 knots. Either way, you might have very little time before they are on you.

You can get a very useful Marine Weather Services booklet free online from www.marinecall.co.uk or www.metoffice.com/leisuremarine/mwsbooklet.html

When in or around the Azores you can get English language storm warnings from Radionaval Horta for the sea area to the Iberian Peninsula and Madeira. Listen on SSB frequencies 2657kHz twice a day at 0935 and 2135.

For local North Sea weather the Netherlands Coastguard provide excellent forecasts in clear English for their coastal waters, estuaries and the Ijsselmeer. They broadcast on VHF channels 23 and 83 at five hourly intervals from 0805 local time.

See Appendix Five: Web sites for sailors for useful Internet sources of weather information.

SECTION THREE

Are You Ready: Boat and Crew

- Most competent modern cruising designs will cope with an Atlantic crossing. However, the nature of the average cruiser has changed rapidly in the last few decades and most noticeably in the last few years.
- Today's cruising yachts are larger, more spacious, more slippery, more luxurious, and much more dependent on electricity. They will provide a splendid base to enjoy Europe and the Atlantic islands but not all of these changes are needed to make a competent boat for a long ocean passage.
- Don't be put off if your cruising yacht is of an older, simpler age. When far offshore, different standards apply. Comfort becomes seakindliness and simplicity; security becomes robust design and rugged construction.

7

Fit to cross: the boat

Sailors setting out to cross an ocean for the first time are moving away from the known world of coastal hopping between marinas and the occasional delivery trip to another cruising area. They are moving closer to the conditions and mind set of bluewater liveaboards. For a while they may be in something like a halfway house. A boat aimed at coastal creature comforts will probably manage the long trip across the ocean but will surely benefit from some of the rugged simplifications that keep boats functioning when cruising far from home and provide security when sailing far offshore. Everything about cruising boats is a compromise and it is for you and no one else to decide which side of the balance will work best for you. In part what you decide depends on whether you are planning to come back to the coastal life or heading for a new life as an ocean cruiser. And in part it depends on what mind-set (or level of insanity) you think typifies bluewater liveaboards.

My preference is to live with as much simplicity as possible. At the deepest level, achievement of this simplicity affects not just the electronics and domestic equipment we carry but the size, design and material of the hull, the rigging and sailhandling systems and every aspect of boat handling. There is no last word on simplicity but if the complexities of your boat are making life hard for you, remember you don't have to use them. Phase them out. All boats can get back to being simpler than they are.

Whether G and I have achieved our target of simplicity is a matter of whether we have succeeded in the various compromises that come with sailing. In practice we live on a bigger boat than we need, with more complicated mechanics than we would like, with some systems that are less efficient than we want, spending more money than we can afford. We live with our heads at one end of a philosophical spectrum and our lifestyle at some point on a quite different, practical spectrum, and we watch both of these spectrums shifting step-wise as our "sailing technology environment"—a sort of space-time continuum—innovates at a faster rate than ever it did in the past.

We get by. Where are you in the equation?

What boat is best

There is no ideal bluewater boat but personally I like a bit of weight. Monohull designers say that weight is the single universal factor in producing comfortable motion. Sadly, the long keel and huge wetted area that comes with the greatest weight makes for slower hull forms. Heavy displacement Colin Archer type boats like mine need at least 10 knots of wind before they even drift. Not everyone has the patience for this, and sometimes I don't either, but it is a fault that can often be mitigated by flying bigger light weather sails. The problems of a light displacement racer meeting hard winds and hard seas are often not things that can be mitigated at all. Also, on long passages like an ocean crossing, the light weight flier may not be so quick with the extra two tons of equipments it will be carrying. This, to the heavy displacement boat, is just normal.

Light displacement, high volume designs carry much of their internal volume above the waterline. When loaded with cruising gear the waterline disappears and so does performance. Now rig, hull and rudder must cope with strains far in excess of its design. The average speeds you once used to estimate the time of a journey are now too optimistic. Even a cruising cat in full cruising weight needs to reckon on similar average speeds to a monohull.

> As a general rule a boat, whether it is a slow cruiser or a skinny racer, is most comfortable when being driven. I am a nervous sailor. Though I love the sea and being on it, I never see the point of hanging around out there without good reason. Also, I am inclined to pessimism. Making a boat sail slowly because the harbor is only ten miles away and you can't enter for another six hours is just inviting the unforecast headwind to blow you backwards in five hours time. There are times when you must slow down and times when you must stop the boat, but on any passage let your mantra be "keep her driving."

The records show that almost any sort of boat can cross the ocean. This isn't to say you should carelessly assume that your boat can too. Usually it's the fortitude and sailing skills of the crew that get the really crazy boats across. But take heart: lesser boats than yours have made the crossing. I met many lesser boats than mine all the time on my first crossing. I probably met even more lesser boats on my second crossing but by then I wasn't bothering to count. I had amazed myself. I still remember being hauled out next to a 20-foot catamaran that had sailed from Sweden to Trinidad. The cockpit was a six foot length of netting slung between the narrow hulls. The singlehanding skipper slept there. He was nearly seven feet long and couldn't fit the inside berths.

Then I met Nils Bennich-Björkman, a 67-year-old Dane who had sailed from the Mediterranean to Trinidad via Cape Verde and Brazil in his personally designed and built 21-foot ketch-rigged sailing canoe. Nils might not be the most idiosyncratic small boat sailor I have met on the oceans, but he comes very close. He had great faith in the cork principle and thought nothing of bolting down the hatches and staying below for days on end when the ocean became storm-tossed. His only moment of near loss when I met him was in harbor when he moored his little cork between two steel fishing boats. He slipped clear before they had tested his cork's abilities as a fender. Last I heard, Nils was in Brisbane, Australia, aged 75, preparing to continue his singlehanded circumnavigation after a dismasting and near sinking in mid-Pacific. The weakness of the hull after the damage forced him to handle the boat more carefully, and this in turn meant he had to learn how to sleep sitting up in the tiny cockpit. Little things like that were never likely to deter Nils from living his dream.

> It isn't just Scandinavians, honest it isn't, but we met Sebastian Naslund in Horta, a tall Swede sailing ARRANDIR, a 14-foot yawl he had built himself. His parting comments as G helped cast him off were: "I'm so happy today. I know that when I reach Sweden I shall never singlehand on such a small boat again." He was at sea a total of 195 days during his Atlantic circuit.

The early heroes of ocean sailing usually sailed boats which today's licensing authorities and Coast Guard would label too small to leave the estuary. Not that there were licensing authorities in those days. Those heroes didn't have electricity worthy of the name. They lived by the watch words of an older generation of designers.

> I still delight in what the great Nathaniel Herreshoff said: the only time you need standing headroom in a boat is if you sleep standing up.

The Hiscocks started small and eventually traded up. Their most famous boat, the 30-foot WANDERER III, is still out there, sailing the oceans with its kerosene lamps and limited supply of electricity. The Pardeys too moved up in size, in a similarly modest way. After more than a decade wandering the oceans on their

24-foot SERAFFYN they made a whole five foot leap and built their engineless 29-foot cutter TALEISIN. Tim and Pauline Carr won the Blue Water Medal of the Cruising Club of America in 1991 for 23 years of cruising in CURLEW, a 28-foot Falmouth Punt built in 1898. CURLEW had an engine when the Carrs bought her in 1968 but they took it out and never got around to replacing it. No engine, no electrics, no starter button to get you out of danger. When the McConnells chose a 30-foot Arpege for their "First Crossing" they were buying the biggest boat they could afford and a design they knew well, but I doubt that even Michel Dufour, who drew the design in the 1960s, or those brave souls who have sailed Arpeges round the world, would consider this an ideal boat for the deep ocean. English sailor Nick Skeates has been around twice in his 32-foot gaff rigged center-boarder WYLO II, and sold many copies of the design for circumnavigators and those who wish to explore extremes of north and south.

These designs of another era have covered thousands of miles under sail in all parts of the world, and yet are as far removed from what most new ocean sailors expect as the Model T is from a fuel injected air-conditioned Mercedes. They are a lesson to us all.

> William Crealock's 34 from Pacific Seacraft is a little boat with a big reputation as a solid seagoing boat that will get you there safely and without drama. I met one that had made a one year circuit from New England via England and the Atlantic islands. This is not a common design in Europe so they were greeted with enthusiasm. The boat made friends for the crew all along the south coast of England. The skipper had many reasons to conclude that this conservative design had proved right for the trip.

Sailors like bigger

The good news, for those who can't give up their creature comfort, is that a fairly indifferent large modern yacht is probably more comfortable offshore than the best of small designs, simply because stability is related more closely to size than to shape.

A recent survey of long-distance cruising yachts confirmed what I have observed over the last few years. Cruisers increasingly prefer bigger boats. The cruising couple (and most long distance boats are crewed by a couple) who three decades ago regarded 30 feet as the absolute limit of what they could handle gave way two decades ago to the couple who realized that modern design and equipment allowed them to handle a 35 footer just as easily. But since then they have given way to the cruising couple who need a 45 footer for comfort in harbor, and can handle such a boat thanks to a near revolution in electronics and mechanical aids for boat handling, sail reduction, navigation and communications. Today, coming up fast on the rails, are couples learning to cope with 50 to 55 footers.

Data from the Azores shows a remarkable range of boat sizes crossing the Atlantic. Every year there seems to be at least one boat under 20 feet. However, more than 70% of boats recorded in Horta are between 31 feet and 50 feet and the typical size is 36 to 40 feet. There are signs that bigger is preferred. More boats are between 46 and 50 feet than between 31 and 35 feet and couples (or a crew of two) seem willing to cross in most sizes from 25 to 60 feet. There doesn't seem to be much difference in the sizes sailed solo or with crews up to four people. The main difference is that singlehanders are prepared to go about the world in boats close to 20 feet long and couples are not. Bigger crews of four or more are more likely to be on boats over 50 feet.

In part, this shift in manageable boat size comes out of developments pioneered in ocean racing yachts and the increasingly dramatic singlehanded round-the-world races.

The differences between the yacht that won the first solo non-stop race, the Golden Globe, in 1968, and the yachts taking part in The Race of 2004, for example, seems to say it all. The 1968 winner, SUHAILI, was a heavily planked Colin Archer type double ender weighing 10 tons on an overall length of 32 feet, excluding the bowsprit. Today's beamy Kevlar racers weigh little more than this on twice the length. SUHAILI had a top speed of seven knots and managed to average four knots over the 10 ½ months she took to sail round the world. Today's racers can average over 20 knots in a good 24-hour period, as they must to stay in contention during the 55 to 55.5 days it now takes them to go right round the world. They don't just sail faster, they sail closer to the wind, making the journey round the world thousands of miles shorter and months quicker than the one by SUHAILI. They monitor weather systems in a way that was impossible in 1968. SUHAILI's skipper tapped his barometer and wondered what the clouds meant. Now no racer can compete without a shore team of meteorologists giving hour by hour directions on where to seek winds and how deep he or she can go into the southern ocean and still dodge the ice. That is one of the main reasons why these races of 28,000 miles end in nail-biting sprint finishes between the leading boats. Weather information, and communications as a whole, not to mention steering, winching and water making, demand masses of reliable electrical energy. Not so in 1968. By the time SUHAILI passed southern Africa she had no working electrics other than a radio receiver and no need to generate power.

Dodge Morgan broke the hair shirt mould in 1984 when his specially designed yacht AMERICAN PROMISE halved the solo round the world record time. AMERICAN PROMISE was cutting edge in hull, rig, sailhandling and electronics. She gave Dodge Morgan not just a fast time but creature comforts unlike any other boat that had attempted this record. He even managed a weekly shower using a watermaker when the norm was to top up drinking water with rain caught at the gooseneck. AMERICAN PROMISE used electronic autopilot, had radar, an SSB for phone calls home, and a host of other electronics. The boat cost Dodge Morgan $2 million back then. Not many of us are in that league. But the cutting edge of 1984 is now much less than the norm for many stock production cruisers.

Another part of the change in expectations of performance, size and comfort is down to the age and lifestyle of today's ocean cruisers. A lot of sailors looking to make their first crossing from the Americas to Europe are middle aged. After a lifetime of working and investing and saving they have considerable resources to put into their boat, equipping it with navigation and comforts almost inconceivable a generation ago. Information and comfort can make essential contributions to boat speed and safety and hence ultimately to enjoyment.

Not everyone on this journey has a lifetime of work and savings behind them. We have met many younger people taking a year or three out from work or career, buying relatively small or modest boats to go sailing. Good for them. A bigger boat is not always the practical option to take, whatever your age.

We met Roy and Carol Romine on MORNING WINGS in Trinidad. We didn't realize till we climbed into their cockpit that they were a tad unusual and heading to become icons of American sailing. They were octogenarians who had first started sailing as sprightly 66-year olds and taken their little boat from the US to South Africa. At 32 feet, MORNING WINGS is small and simple by modern American cruising standards. Why had they chosen such a small boat for such a long journey? "In case we suddenly became singlehanded," Roy said, hitting head on the question of their age and the worst fears of their children. "The he or she left on board had to be able to handle the boat." MORNING WINGS seemed very in keeping with the strong willed, pioneering character of Roy and Carol. "We tried a 38 footer but Carol just couldn't manage the weight of anchor and chain."

Don't assume that you need a bigger boat than you already have or that the biggest boat you can afford is the one to go for. Size is a balance between comfort and handiness. Every solo sailor or couple must choose this balance for themselves. Some aspects of size might just make you too uncomfortable. Bigger boats cost more, take up more time and require more effort to sail. It is quite remarkable how much bigger everything becomes. Loads don't just get heavier. At a certain point a load passes from being hard to manage to being totally unmanageable. It is all very well a husband and wife having the gear to sheet and furl big sails, but what about getting those big sails on deck, fitting them to mast and boom and hoisting them? Can you reach the tack and the clew without a hop-up? Are you comfortable with the sheet loads on those power winches and clutches when its time to jibe or take off power?

Our last trade up was from 32 feet to 40 feet. Now I suspect that I am more of a 35 footer man. On our 40 footer, all aspects of seamanship, from maneuvering in marinas to sailhandling in a rising breeze, are critical now that G and I are close to our physical limits.

> I remember with increasing fondness the 20 footer I learned on. Some aspects of collision avoidance just weren't an issue. I could physically push her off anything I bumped into. On our 40 footer I tell people not to even think of pushing off. They might hurt themselves. Use the engine, use fenders. Use lines when wind and current have her in their grip. Don't use feet or hands.

G and I change with the times too. We are open to new ideas in design. Maybe not water ballasted Kevlar skimming disks. Maybe I just mean a broad fin keel, possibly with a wing, full skeg and stunningly good performance when going to windward. Designers show that such arrangements provide comfort at sea as well as more speed and close-quarters maneuverability than Colin Archer ever dreamt of.

> An old friend philosophically opposed to almost everything I take for normal often tells me that gentlemen don't sail to windward. They may not, but if they ever go to sea their boats will. We all need a boat that will sail to windward. It doesn't need the windward performance to win races but it must be comfortable in a head sea, and comfortable when there is so much wind out there that it isn't you going to windward but windward which is passing you by. Weight, depth and length of keel are the key to this but you can do a lot with sails and seasickness remedies.

Sea time and shore time

Most boats spend 90% of their life in an anchorage or a harbor, even if they are bluewater liveaboard boats. Look at the boats in the Chesapeake or New York Harbor as you are sailing to meet the ocean. Many have the intrinsic qualities to cross an ocean or at least sail to Bermuda and back but they haven't and they aren't ready for it. The difference is that these boats are rarely sailed far from their home port or far from shelter. They are unlikely to meet the frighteningly unexpected conditions that could arise when you are a week into the ocean with another two to go before you see land. But the same 90/10 rule still applies. It is just that now, on an Atlantic crossing, you need a boat that has more seagoing qualities for the 10% of its life that is now about to happen.

The snag to increasing standards of creature comfort is that one thing leads to another. For G and me, the idea of adding radar leads to the need for more amps and battery charging. We don't have the idea of an on-board washing machine but if we did we would need bigger water tanks, a watermaker, the extra electrical power to drive the watermaker and a true sine wave inverter to provide the current for the washing machine controls. We don't even have room for the extra batteries this all implies. Comfort comes at a price that isn't just paid in money. Remember the mantra: keep it simple.

I checked a friends' specification for a modest cruising yacht he was thinking of buying. I didn't know a boat could carry so much creature comfort. Apart from the sailing equipment of radar, SSB, VHF, Loran, three GPS, weatherfax, two autopilots, electric bilge pump, navigation and other lights, bow and stern electric anchor windlasses, electric sheet winches, electric jib furling, there was the domestic equipment of refrigerator and freezer, clothes washer and drier, microwave, pressurized hot water for the two showers, heads and galley, fan driven heater and ventilation, television and DVD player, dishwasher, garbage disposal unit, and a 20 gallon per hour watermaker. To power all this they have 1,500 amps of batteries, 150-amp alternator run from the main 75hp engine, an 8kw 110volt generator, solar panels and a wind generator. They could have got all this and a separate cabin for themselves on a 45 footer but to accommodate the occasional visits from children and friends they have a high sided, beamy, spacious 50 footer. I didn't ask where they would keep their bicycles.

Your on-board equipment need not determine your comfort levels when you arrive in Europe. Europe is a continent of marinas and populous towns and cities where clothes washing can be done in the marina, fresh food can be bought daily, cinemas are a short walk away and telecommunications is in the air. If you choose, you can live and be comfortable without a boat load of domestic machinery. The simpler the systems, the less time you need to maintain them and the less power you need to run them. The simpler the systems, the smaller the boat you need. I reckon that running costs double every ten feet in size as you go from a 35 footer to a 45 footer to a 55 footer.

Preparation

It is truly amazing how much has to be done to an already well-found boat to turn her into a safe ocean-crosser and a home. I used to wonder why boats in ocean races and round-the-world events were never ready on time. Surely the corporate sponsors had put the start date in the skipper's diary. Why were they still fitting bits of electronics that they could have attached a year ago?

My first Atlantic crossing was in a boat I had owned and prepared for the previous ten years. I know people who bought a boat in April, prepared her in May and cast off in June. Surely my boat just needed to have her sweet bilges dusted and her decks painted reflective white to save our tender feet from the tropic sun. That and perhaps a few more equally simple tasks. But the list grew longer even as I worked flat out. Everything took longer than estimated. I ferried car loads of gear from my apartment at every trip I made to her. I came to know every chandler, sailmaker, rigger, steel fabricator and assorted marine and engine trades within ten miles of her berth. Fire extinguishers, screws and fastenings, timber, electronics, liferaft, charts, pilot books, propane and plumbing and food cash-and-carry are just the tip of the supply iceberg that I got to know. I should have realized that boats are happiest when you take them shopping.

> A good guide to what you will need when you go offshore is the Offshore Racing Council's regulations. Get a copy. It is a mine of distilled wisdom.

You will be hit by at least one crisis in your preparations. Try to get it in early. Try not to let it escalate into a catastrophe. Don't let it call a halt to your dream.

> I discovered a crack in my huge, barn door rudder just weeks before my first Atlantic crossing. My immediate response was relief. I could cancel this crazy plan. My second was to start ordering plywood and

epoxy. I took the stoic stance that at least one potentially terminal crisis hits everyone and if I handled this right fate would save me from others. So I re-designed the rudder to build out the weakness. While preparing for my second crossing I spent months looking at a badly worn gudgeon and pintle (the hinge thingies that connect the rudder to the hull) until I knew I could no longer persuade myself that this would last an ocean crossing. The daunting problems of getting the rudder off, finding the steel and a welder, faded away. Come the moment of resolve, come the energy to act.

Take heart. I had never made a rudder in my life. Nor a fiberglass dodger. Nor cut through a one inch stainless steel prop-shaft with a hacksaw while suspended upside down over the engine. Nor lifted 200 lbs of diesel engine out of the boat with just G, some wooden rollers and a block and tackle. We managed it when we had to. Luck and chance rule the adventure of an ocean crossing and I suppose in a Darwinian sort of way good luck has to be more common in life than bad.

The philosophy of spares

This isn't a trip around the coast. This will be a crossing of several weeks, perhaps longer at sea than you have been before. The essential qualities needed for such a passage are:

- self-sufficiency
- a sound yacht
- a capable and healthy crew
- full equipment, so that you do not run short in those places where supplies are not available.

In brief, you will be sailing a liveaboard boat, comfortable for eating, cooking and sleeping in all weathers. The average production boat is intended for short-term cruising, when supermarkets and hosepipes are never more than a short walk away. Almost all will fail in some area of preparedness for longer periods of cruising offshore.

Decks must be water-tight and able to keep the crew safe, preferably with simple and strong gear. The more unusual a ship's gear, and the more particular it is to its home port, the more sensitive or delicate, the more problems it will bring. Look hard at:

- the specialist items of sailing and deck equipment—furling gear, winches, boom preventer, anchor windlass, windvane self steering
- your main engine and generators—water pumps, gasket sets, fan belts, oil and fuel filters, thermostat, internal anodes, hoses
- your electrics—GPS, autohelm, computer, radios, radar, switches.

Make sure you have a full set of spares. When coasting you are never far from the skills, tools and materials you need to fix the boat. When riding the ocean currents or anchored in some remote little idyll, fixing things is down to you. The main obstacle won't be your skills—a desperate sailor can usually master everything from electric shock therapy and starter motors to re-building an engine-driven water pump. Nor will it be your tool kit. Usually we all carry more tools than we need, and it isn't difficult to make sure you have relevant tools. No, the main constraint on what you can fix is almost always the spare parts and materials you have on board.

Look around the boat. Do you have spares or service contacts for machinery that may be hard to source away from home? Many parts such as fuel filters can be substituted with others but take plenty of the ones you think will be hard to find abroad. Take more than you think you will need. It is the gear that will fail most, not the hull. One of our rules is: if you see something you know you will need in the future, buy now while it's within reach. It won't be so easy to find when you need it.

Think about disabling this equipment during the crossing when you will be a long way from shore power and a water hose. At the least, try to run essential equipment from a 12-volt supply so that you don't need to generate mains voltage. And remember that in Europe the standard voltage is not 110volts/60MHz. It is 220volts/50MHz. We have found it very useful that our battery charger can run on either 110volts or 220volts and that we can always have full 12-volt batteries when in harbor.

The pretty 50 footer next to us had been in the Azorean harbor for a week since crossing from Bermuda, waiting to have a part flown in. Some days we would walk into town just to get away from the noise and fumes of his diesel generator. The crew had to run the generator about six hours a day to keep their systems running. I don't know what manner of catastrophe would happen if they had to be closed down. The skipper told me, but it didn't connect to any experience of the world I have so I forgot almost immediately. The harbor only supplied 220 volts. His generator produced the 110 volts he needed. A little transformer or a battery charger that coped with 100-240volts and 50-60Hz would have allowed him to use the silent socket on the pontoon like the rest of us, but he wasn't ready for that.

Even on PETRONELLA, which seems to have more half sheets of plywood, lengths of inch teak, choices of stainless pipe, copper tubing and heavy electrical wire, sheets of neoprene, sheets of gasket paper, and nearly everything else ever made in the industrial world, we will find ourselves lacking epoxy weld or underwater cement or stainless flat bar to make up some backing plates for a deck fitting. When re-making our steering wires I discovered that we had plenty of expensive Norseman fittings but none of those little cone things that fit inside the wire. And I wish I knew where we left our Captain Tolley's Creeping Crack Cure.

> G and I have a constant tugging in our attitude to spare parts. She takes the view that we always have the special thing we need already on board, and we should use up our stocks. I take the view that we should go and buy another one while we are in walking distance of the shop, so that we still have a spare or six when we aren't.

Take a walk through the boat to see what might go wrong at sea. The forehatch gets stoved in. The bilge hose splits. The rudder is disabled. The hull gets cracked or holed. Think about the worst that can happen. Thinking the worst helps keep disaster at bay. It also gives you a better chance of being prepared when it happens. Don't kid yourself that you'll manage somehow. Now is the time to work out in detail how you will tackle these disasters.

Having done that and got the materials you will need, what conditions will help you? Where will you mount the vice? Have you a head torch and a mirror on a stick? Have you a cordless electrical drill to make the holes and drive in the screws? Have you the super-expensive drill bits to drill holes in stainless steel? That cordless drill won't do the job otherwise.

You don't need a huge workshop. It feels like we do on PETRONELLA, whenever I try to find the tool I need. We used to carry a much smaller kit and I'm not sure it was any less effective. I still think that the simple vice clamped onto the companionway step is the key to most things I do. Think "effective" when you work out your tool kit. Remember, what it has to buy you is independence.

> My friend showed me the work room on his 60-foot cat. It was huge and equipped with everything I could dream of. There wasn't a job on the boat he couldn't do. Of course, he needed the power tools, the vice, the $1000 socket set, the drawers of drill bits, etc. He didn't have such a work room at home, ashore but then he had sailed halfway round the world and this was the price to pay for

Faial, Azores. The quiet of Horta Harbor out of season was perfect for boat work. And so was the view. Pico in another mood.

total independence on a 60-foot cat. Of course he didn't have a chain saw, which was what the carpenter on deck was using to clear away a rotten mast support before rebuilding a new one. "I suppose you can't have everything," I said. My friend, who has a fine sense of humor as well as unflinching honesty, said: "Larry Pardey's 24-foot SERAFFYN carried all the tools he had used when building her. I guess that's independence."

What's in the mind

Leaving home or cutting the umbilical to the marina is an affair of the mind as much as of the body. Independence starts in the head. It is an attitude I nurture, although I also have a locker full of spares.

Once you go offshore you as well as the boat must be ready for any eventuality. One little trick I play to massage the fear and stimulate preparedness is to ask, "What would I do if. . . ." The "if" could be a sheet snapping, a rigging wire parting, a sudden heel and water flooding the cockpit, or watching a piece of gear on deck start to slide as its ties come loose. It's a game that helps remind me where the tools and spares are to fix breakages, and what alternatives we could try when our usual way of doing something isn't available.

I often wonder "What would I do if the GPS stopped working?" This isn't academic. GPS often feels the need to take five. Over a ten day passage we might lose signal three or four times. Usually we just wait for it to come back when it's ready, but it encourages us to keep a frequent plot of GPS positions on the grounds that the last one we took might be the last one we get. We have a sextant on board but I would rather be working from a good record of DR.

At the heart of this little "what if . . ." game is the idea of redundancy. Prudence should dictate that no one should go offshore dependent on a single way of doing things, whether this is navigating or checking the depth under the keel. Redundancy is a good rule. True redundancy means an independent alternative, not just some spares or a second piece of kit. I favor having a handheld GPS in case the fixed set stops working or our ship's batteries fail. But true redundancy is having a sextant for offshore position fixing and a hand bearing compass for coastal pilotage. True redundancy when going offshore means having manual systems for everything that's powered. One power failure kills everything that needs electricity. Manual winches, manual pumps, candles and oil lamps and a lead line armed with tallow, if you can still find the stuff.

The dead weight of that little philosophy

One difference between coastal cruising for a week or two compared to heading offshore for a couple of thousand miles and a year or two is the weight of extra gear you will need.

Looking around PETRONELLA I can see the gear we think vital to our independence but which would be excessive on a coastal cruiser. Some should have been thrown away long ago but sailors tend to squirrel rather than dump and the longer you travel the longer you have to gather stuff.

Just the heavy stuff

Anchors	Four	I forget where we left the 5th. Or even the 6th
Anchor warp	150 feet 1/2" chain + 150ft 1" line	
Spare chain	30 feet of 3/4"; 2 x 40ft 3/8"chain	
Diesel	125 gallons in three tanks	10 gallons in cans
Water	200 gallons in four tanks	30 gallons in cans
Kerosene	20 gallons	
Propane bottles	2 x 13kg	
Long warps	3 x 1" x 300 feet	
Other warps	About 600 feet in various lengths	
Spare halyards/sheets	About 8	
Working sails in use	4	
Spare sails carried	8	
Batteries	5	
Wind generator	1 large brute stowed below	
Liferaft	1	
Grab bag	1 locker full	
Inflatable dinghy	2	

Dinghy anchors	2	
Outboard engine	1 x 3.3hp	
Spare hull anodes	10	
Tools	8 electric machines; three tool boxes of wrenches etc; two boxes of wood-working tools; various soldering guns and gas burners	We don't but many steel boats carry a welding machine
Paint	About 4 gallons of different types in various sizes of cans	
Bosun's chairs	2	
Spare rigging wire	About 100 feet x 10mm	
Spare turnbuckles	About 6	
Engine spares	About 30 lbs weight	
Electrical wire and spares	About 30 lbs weight	
Nuts, bolts, screws etc	About 60 lbs weight	
Spare timber, steel tube, etc	About 100 lbs weight	
Other spares	About 60 lbs weight	
Two folding bikes	Regrettably, not any longer	
Charts	About 100	
Pilot books	About 20	
Books for entertainment	At least 100	
Books and magazines waiting to be disposed of	About 50 lbs weight	
National and signal flags	About 100	
Pots, pans, crocks, cutlery	Enough for a family of 10	
Laptop computers	2 plus a printer	
Sewing machine	No. We usually borrow one	

We also have our food and drink lockers fairly full most of the time. We tend to buy where we find bargains, so food and drink lockers are rarely empty, but they are filled to overflowing when we head offshore.

We also carry more clothing than we would if we had a home ashore, and that is what you will be doing when you load up for a trip to another continent. After all, this is where you now have your wardrobe. Sailing also calls for special clothing. The two survival suits we carry only weigh about 10 lbs each but they are bulky enough to take up a large locker. Also, we carry about three large travel bags for when we travel ashore, and for guests we carry three spare sleeping bags, bedding, wet weather clothes and all manner of safety harnesses.

This list is an understatement of what we carry and we don't even have the domestic equipment that many sailors consider essential. Those items come to at least three tons. Fuel and water alone come to nearly 1.75 tons, which is about 1.25 tons more than a coastal cruiser need carry.

So that's enough of that. The point is you are hauling a heavier load when you go offshore.

> Our friends in Horta lent us their sewing machine. I turned down their offer of the welding machine because (apart from not knowing how to use one) it would take them a day to dig it out of the bilges. They sail a 35 footer. They have raised their antifouling since they set out from South Africa.

Water in the tanks

Desalination is a clever trick. The ancient Chinese apparently distilled fresh water from the sea on their long voyages of discovery. Today's cheap, simple and reliable reverse osmosis watermakers have made Coleridge's Ancient Mariner *cri du coeur* out of date. "Water, water everywhere but not a drop to drink." But water is so vital to your survival on the ocean that you can't leave it to a watermaker, even though they are reputed to be among the most reliable machines on a boat and the quality of water is excellent. This is a long trip to suffer a leaking seal or failed membrane in the otherwise reliable watermaker. Also, your watermaker may rely on a small generator to power it. Small generators don't have such a good reputation for reliability.

You need old fashioned good tank habits. The old rule was to have at least two water tanks and be able to isolate them. That way, when the tank you are using runs empty you know how much you still have left. Also, if the water in one went bad you would still have good water in the other. We carry our 200 or so gallons in four tanks. The more gallons and tanks the merrier.

Here is a point I would not have needed to make even a few years ago, before commercial bottlers of water changed the way many people feel about water quality. Many travelers suspect the quality of tap water even at home, and feel that they are more likely to stay healthy if they drink bottled water when traveling. I think this is simply wrong. G and I make a point of drinking local tap water wherever we are. We fill our tanks with it and we use tank water for drinking, although we run it through two filters. This isn't simply because good water is available in most harbors we visit, though this is almost certainly the case, and nor is it because water tests sometimes show bottled water is more contaminated than tap water, though this too is true. The really important health point is that local tap water acclimatizes you to the local microscopic bugs that you will be breathing and eating as well as imbibing simply by being in that country. It isn't a matter of hygiene and killing bugs. We need bacteria in our gastrointestinal tracts to help our digestion processes. We humans have evolved to be able to acquire specific immunity to certain microbes. You don't actually want to sterilize yourself against the local conditions. You want to immunize yourself instead. Immunization is the best way of avoiding stomach upsets, and local tap water will gently prepare your system to fight the microbes. After a year or two away you may get an upset stomach when you return home. You are no longer used to the local microbes that you once knew intimately.

Of course, not all local sources of water are free of pathogens or parasites and I am not suggesting that you take a simple-minded stance to drinking local water come what may. Many countries, after all, are well known for their local versions of travelers' diarrhea striking within a day or two of our arrival. Not for nothing do we talk of Montezuma's Revenge. When visiting countries noted for problems of contamination it is wise to follow the usual precautions.

When we sailed up the Casamance River in Senegal, West Africa, we felt a long way from pure piped water. We were very careful about using local water, not least because we had to queue for an hour sometimes to get our turn at the well. We could not choose to live as though in a sanitized plastic bag while in Africa. After all, we were living on a boat. We walked in crowds, the drains looked foul and the smell of putrid cat or donkey was never far away. The African air probably nurtured a lot of bugs and we had no choice but to breath the dust of Africa, even when 100 miles offshore. Our watchword became: prevention is better than cure. We took great care to be hygienic. Not all things go to plan.

We faithfully boiled water and washed vegetables in sterilized water, as all the health books insist. We might as well not have bothered. No sooner had we got to the remote country around the Casamance River than we innocently drank a couple of pints of water from a restaurant tap. We didn't know that the tap connected to an uncovered cistern holding water that had arrived months ago during the rainy season. Dennis, the American restoring the old restaurant, reappeared when we were onto our second jug. When he realized what we were doing he grabbed the jug like it contained poison. "That probably isn't safe to wash in," he told us. If we were going to get one of those dreadful water-borne diseases it was probably right there and then. We drank more beer, to stimulate the stomach enzymes that would save us. When my crew went dancing at a wedding feast I went back onboard to stoically drink strong alcohol and save my stomach.

SOLAS rules

Very few international maritime laws apply to cruising yachts. The United Nations Convention on the Law of the Sea codifies rights of navigation in tidal waters, the International Convention for preventing Collisions at Sea (the ColRegs) sets out who is the give way vessel and what lights and shapes must be shown, and the International Convention for the Prevention of Pollution from Ships forbids us to throw garbage overboard. Now to these add the "SOLAS Five."

The first convention on the Safety of Life at Sea (SOLAS) in 1914 was in response to the sinking of the TITANIC in 1912. Its central concern was safety procedures for large ships. The relevance of SOLAS to us on our little yachts was that the big ships would have better trained personnel employed to keep a good lookout on radar sets that worked, so that they didn't run so many of us down. And that they would be listening to their VHF radios when we called them for help.

Thirty maritime nations attended that first SOLAS convention. Now 158 nations are signed up to the International Maritime Organization, the branch of the UN which has run SOLAS since 1960. In July 2002 the updated Chapter 5 regulations came into force. National governments differ on which regulations should apply to their citizens' privately owned pleasure craft but even if your government allowed every exemption this still leaves important new rules for you to follow, each one relevant to your offshore passages and your Atlantic crossing. These are not onerous rules. They should just be applied common sense to the way you already sail.

SOLAS Five/34 "Safe Navigation and avoidance of dangerous situations" concerns passage planning. It requires you to have a more formal passage plan than in the past. This plan and your prior planning should cover:

- weather forecasts and updates during the voyage
- working out relevant tides and currents
- ensuring your boat is up to the journey and suitably equipped
- that you and your crew are sufficiently experienced and fit for the journey and what might happen along the way
- examining the dangers on or close to the route and having pilot books, charts and almanacs for the journey
- having a contingency plan in case you suffer crew, radio, engine or other failures
- making sure someone back home knows your plan and will contact the emergency services if it looks like you are overdue.

SOLAS Five/19 requires an effective radar reflector, fixed so that other vessels can see you. Yachts over 50 feet (15 meters) must meet IMO requirements. Yachts under 50 feet have to fit the largest radar reflector they can. If you thought this was a straightforward matter, you may be wrong. Some currently available reflectors are so woefully inadequate that despite their makers' enthusiastic sales pitches they will have to be dumped when new specifications become law. Even the well-tried octahedral design may need to be reconsidered. New reflectors will need to reflect signals from the 3 gigahertz frequency (S-band) and 9 gigahertz frequency (X-band). Few current designs manage to reflect S-band signals at all and cannot reflect the X-band signals at the angles being specified. Radically new designs, including "active" electronic reflectors, will be introduced over the next few years. The word is that these won't need to be the oil-drum size monsters described in some recent scare-mongering magazine articles.

SOLAS Five/29 is about life saving at sea. We must all know the recognized life saving signals so that we can work with other vessels, to receive or give assistance. Carry an illustrated table of the recognized signals on board. Responding to a distress call from another vessel used to be just something we all did anyway, but now it is the law. We are also required by regulations 31, 32 and 33 to let the appropriate authority know if we come across any hazards to navigation, like a floating container or an unexploded mine. And for those X-chromosome types who can't help seeing if the thing works, SOLAS Five/35 requires us *not* to send out distress signals unless we are in distress. Don't send up flares as birthday fireworks. Don't let that little press of your EPIRB test button result in search and rescue helicopters flying over to check you out.

SOLAS Five shouldn't affect the way you prepare for a voyage and carry it out. It lays out the most basic ground rules and you and I are already practicing better standards of seamanship than that, aren't we? But if we aren't, the flag states responsible for making sure yachts comply may inspect us. This doesn't just mean that US authorities will check you out if you are a US registered vessel. It means that any IMO member country can check you if they think you are failing to comply with SOLAS while in their territorial waters. You could be detained in a foreign harbor.

> The yacht *en route* to Europe was in São Miguel, the Azores, when a passing port official noticed the liferaft was a month out of date. The nearest test station was Lisbon, Portugal. It took a week to get the raft sent and a week to get it back. But São Miguel is a pleasant place to spend an extra two weeks, so the crew weren't complaining too much.

No time for leaks

A widely held view among ocean sailors is that a boat won't sink if the water can't get in. I won't argue with that. The point, however, is to look at the danger points. I have never spent much time sailing wooden boats so I only know from repute that if they aren't leaking they soon will be. And the same can usually be said of deck hatches, windows and propeller shafts.

Ocean sailing is remarkable for the amount of water you will get over your decks, even when running or reaching. Leaks that you put up with during a day or two on a rough coastal passage will be insufferable when you go offshore for a week or three. Renew edging seals on hatches, arrange strongbacks to tighten them down, remove and re-bed with sealant. And when you have finished, carry a roll of duct tape and tape over the outside of suspect hatches before you go offshore.

> On PETRONELLA we have fine sturdy metal hatches you could bounce bullets off but the hinge arrangement of the fore hatch almost guarantees ingress of water. It takes two minutes to run some duct tape around the edge and since we discovered this little trick we don't have leaks.

Leaks from deck fittings are bad but when combined with teak decks they would tax the detective skills of Sherlock Holmes. Drips inside a cabin never come from anything directly above nor are in any logical way related to deck fittings nearby. Check the fastenings of all deck fittings and remove and re-bed them if you doubt their integrity. Bolted handrails and other fittings subject to shock loads almost always come loose enough to allow water under the base. Then, especially if the bolt is threaded its whole length, water will find its way into your ceiling. After that, it will work along an invisible line of least resistance until enough moisture gathers to begin the soul-destroying drip.

Windows and deck lights of Plexiglas or Lexan seldom have the same coefficient of expansion as the deck they sit in. They must, of necessity, move around in their frames or in their bed of sealant. Suspect them as sources of leaks. Take care to select the right sealant if you replace them. If bolting them to your hull, over-size the hole to avoid cracking the plastic and don't over-tighten the nut.

Big windows that served you well in harbor and coastal passages can be dangerous in an offshore storm. Some windows seem designed to be forced open by a passing wave. Any large expanse of Plexiglas is at risk of being broken by heavy waves. Carry storm boards to fit over the windows and have the fastening arrangements in place before you go offshore. With luck you will never meet the conditions that need it. With luck, carrying this gear is your best insurance against needing to use it.

Tighter safety

The notion of a "well corked bottle" appeals to us all in bad weather but few cultures have taken the idea of a cork as far as the classic Chinese junk vessels of the last three millenniums. These were usually built with several water tight bulkheads. Such bulkheads are common on all modern commercial ships and were first required for ocean racing in the BOC Challenge in 1986. Oddly, perhaps, they are still rare in cruising yacht designs.

I suspect that the main benefit of a water tight bulkhead in a sinking yacht is to give the crew more time to get to the liferaft. This is a worthwhile gain. On a seriously holed sinking boat time is not what you have a lot of. The more time you have, the less need you have to panic. Better still, the bulkhead might mean that the boat keeps its ability to float. Better to float badly than take to the liferaft.

There is a lot to be said in favor of water tight bulkheads. On PETRONELLA we don't have one. We have a high step between forecabin and saloon, and a bilge pump in the deep sump up there. We have to hope that it is better than nothing. That, and the inherent strength of the overlapping steel plates that make up our bow. It would have been easy to weld in a bulkhead when the boat was first built but it isn't an easy thing to do now.

If retro-fitting a water tight bulkhead the main area to protect is almost certainly the bow. If you can keep the water up there you will keep batteries and engine in working order and be able to call for help. Even one water tight door properly placed will increase your chances of remaining afloat.

G and I met a semi completed yacht in Portugal en route to the Mediterranean. The owner/builder had fitted two watertight doors to the twin forecabins. Powerful looking things when seen from the saloon. Big compression handles and lots of rubber gaskets. The doors even had ventilation so that a crew sleeping with the door shut would not suffocate. The problem was trying to open them from the inside. Almost impossible, which meant that the doors always remained wide open. Perhaps Mark II will be more successful.

A thing of wonder: stainless steel

Our boats gleam with the metal alloy we call stainless steel. There are several hundred grades of stainless but in its best known marine formula (Type 316) stainless steel has iron, chromium, nickel, manganese, molybdenum, silicon and carbon.

Molybdenum gives Type 316 its special resistance to salt water corrosion but makes it weaker than the other stainless steels. Hence Types 302 and 304 might be preferred for high strength applications like rigging, fastenings and propeller shafts.

Chromium gives stainless steel its shine and creates the protective skin of chrome oxide. Polishing helps maintain this oxide but if you deprive the metal of oxygen (by taping over or painting it or keeping it immersed in water) it can no longer "self-heal" and re-make that vital oxide layer. Chlorides, including the sodium chloride of salt water, seem able to bring about a highly localized and severe corrosion in the form of pitting and perforation that can go right through the steel. Poor welds, sharp bends and the work-hardening forces where components connect to one another can make tiny gaps or crevices of just a few micrometers, wide enough to allow salt water in but too narrow to allow it to be flushed out. So it stagnates, bringing about the ideal conditions for crevice corrosion.

Crevice corrosion is a severe form of pitting. It can occur at much lower temperatures than pitting but the two work in similar ways. Pitting is a strange and serious form of corrosion. A pit, once started, has a strong tendency to grow even though most of the steel around the pit remains untouched. It is almost as though it has an organic life of its own.

Stainless steel, like any alloy, can suffer the self-perpetuating erosion of electrolysis if the different components are not completely mixed. Higher grades of marine stainless are better mixed and have less chance of electrolysis. Even so, local concentrations of noble and less noble metals can't be ruled out. Electrolysis does not need your builder to make a bad choice of fittings and fastenings. A lump of stainless steel, with its mix of different metals, has all it needs. Erosion by electrolysis in stainless steel may not be as rapid as in aluminum but it can still be fast, unpredictable and unobserved. I am most wary of stainless steel below the waterline, whether as a whole hull or as a single bolt, because it is out the way of convenient, continuous checks. I have seen what was left of a stainless rudder after just one season. Nothing much.

To me stainless steel is a thing of wonder. I spend a lot of time wondering when the next stainless fitting will come apart in my hands.

> G was unfastening a length of timber in the aft cabin. Of four screws, two lost their heads immediately. Absolutely classic. Stainless screws and bolts in timber or where moisture is retained at the surface will often look perfect until you try to turn them, then they twist their heads off at the hidden corrosion just where they sit in the timber or whatever. If I could be bothered, I would go round the boat every 18 months and replace every screw and bolt, just so that I would never have to drill them out or waste hours with those mistakenly named "easy-out" bits.

Stainless steel is too wonderful to live without. It does away with the rust stains of mild steel. But beware of stainless steel where continued strength is vital. It cannot be trusted. Beware, too, that however much we sailors try to live by our principles and knowledge we can never be consistent enough. As I walk around marinas, passing all those bows with their anchoring systems, I have taken to pointing at pretty stainless steel anchors and chains and telling whoever is in earshot that they are not to be trusted underwater. I would never have them on our boat, I say. And it is almost true.

> I was disparaging a friend's stainless steel anchor chain, waxing almost lyrical about the weakest link, when he asked me the breaking strength of the swivel that connects our anchor to the chain. "No idea," I said, "but much greater than the chain itself because the swivel is stainless steel." I would have been grateful if he hadn't gone on about this inconsistency for the next four days.

Strong as a wire

Nearly all of us have stainless steel shrouds and stays and lovely stainless steel fittings to match. So much more pleasing to the eye and fingers than boiled-in-oil and rusting galvanized wire. Yet the salt-laden air, the high tension and repeated stressing imposed on sailing rigs means that the most obvious failings on yachts are those lovely stainless steel wires. When the wires go, so too do our masts.

At least we can keep an eye on wires, but I have learned to loath stainless steel for its sneaky ways. Riggers say that visual checks can only pick up obvious defects and even ultra-sound is not infallible. Crevices are nearly impossible to see but the fractures they produce are potentially disastrous. Let one little fitting break and that falling mast will spoil what was otherwise turning out to be a pleasant sail into the sunset.

> Not everything labeled as stainless steel is marine grade 316. Take a magnet to the wire. If it grabs at all, it isn't the stainless you want.

Time is the best indicator of when rigging needs changing. Stainless steel work hardens. All those movements the rig makes to cope with life at sea makes the wire brittle and inclined to shear off just when asked to take one more vibration. Also, it ages badly. After a certain age some molecular change occurs within the material to alter the way it behaves. Science has not yet discovered exactly when this critical aging occurs but yacht surveyors and the insurance companies they work for say that ten years is old enough to doubt the integrity of well-cared-for stainless steel rigging wires. Exactly what counts as good care? Not crossing an ocean. Not keeping a boat in the tropics. Not straining the wires by racing. Not leaving it up during a freezing winter when water wicking into the terminal ends can freeze and fracture the swage fitting. PETRONELLA failed on two out of those four and so did just about every sailor with whom we shared this new found knowledge.

> Grateful isn't the first word that springs to mind to describe how I felt when the rigger finished the job. Impoverished is closer to the truth. But I knew we were right. PETRONELLA's stays and shrouds were more than 30 years old, had five Atlantic trips to their credit and more than a decade in the tropics. Any one of those three is enough to condemn the wire, yet it still looked great. What looked less than great once we dropped the mast for a closer inspection were the cap-shrouds and hounds that fastened the wire to the

masts. The original heavy gauge stainless steel was a fine web of stress fractures. We used the traditional big hammer test. The steel buckled like cardboard. The next day, still wondering whether to replace the rigging wires or not, G and I helped a friend tension up his backstay using a beautiful, hand-crafted Highfield lever. As we raised the long lever arm to tension the backstay the gleaming deck connector split. There, just below the previously pristine stainless steel surface, was the pitting and discoloration of a crevice. "I think we'll do the whole of our rigging," I murmured to G. She had been convinced we were wasting our money changing such good looking wire. "Good idea," she said.

The riggers who see more fallen masts than you or I say that the danger areas are where wire meets terminal. Swaged ends are wonderful if the connector and wire are the right fit and if the right dies and pressures are used. Then the metal of the wire and the swage compress into a solid section that cannot be penetrated by water. Look for discoloration where wire meets the lower terminal connectors. Look for any signs of stress failure and crevicing. If a wire strand is broken, don't think twice. That wire needs to be changed.

Crevice corrosion can be exacerbated by heat. Stainless components in applications such as engine and exhaust cooling that involve the circulation of hot sea water are at high risk but temperatures as low as 30 to 40°C can speed up corrosion. This might explain why keeping a boat in the tropics can shorten the life of stainless steel rigging.

The best way to check your rigging is with the mast down. It isn't just the wire you are checking but all the toggles and pins and sheaves that your mast and sails depend on. You can get a rigger to test your wire with a tension device, and you can sit up in the bosun's chair for an hour or two, but I don't think any of this matches a long slow walk around the mast with a wrench and screwdriver and hammer in your hand. Be careful where you do your inspection though. Dragging wires over concrete can score the steel and promote corrosion. Cleaning the wires and fittings is a good idea when you have checked that all is in good shape, but beware: a chlorine-based cleaner will chemically corrode your stainless steel. Don't use steel wool to remove rust stains. It will leave tiny bits of metal that will rust and cause more corrosion. Better to use fine bronze wool or just a plastic scrubber. Don't coil the stays and shrouds too tightly. Kinking the wire can introduce permanent stress. Hold the coil together with light line, not tape. Tape will prevent air flowing over the steel. And when you have done all this just think what the price of new rigging is against the personal and financial costs of a mast failure offshore. Once at sea on a long ocean crossing you have enough to worry about without finding your eyes drawn to the mast head fittings and straining wires every time the boat heels to a sailing breeze.

PETRONELLA is a fine strong vessel not embarrassed to carry a little extra weight, and we thought it would be good for us all if we beefed up the rigging by using thicker wire. The idea could have rebounded on us. Thicker wire needs greater tension, leading to greater mast compression and greater weight aloft. If you think you need thicker wire, first get the advice of a rigger, sparmaker or surveyor so that you don't overload the mast. You don't want your precautions to bring down your mast.

A stitch in time

As I got PETRONELLA ready for my first Atlantic crossing I wouldn't have bothered with the last minute boat survey if it hadn't been required by the insurers. I don't actually have insurance, other than third party, but it was worth doing. I knew my boat intimately by then but the surveyor told me three categories of things, for which I am grateful:

- things that were fine and needed no further worry
- things I didn't know needed to be improved
- things I knew about but was ignoring.

He gave me a list and we set to work. We did all the jobs except one. The lesson I learned: do them all.

The surveyor said I should fit seacocks to all through-hull fittings. I went out and bought seacocks. I just never fitted them. That one undone job nearly caused the loss of the boat in mid-ocean months later. We were lucky but it caused a lot of fear when I was fighting off an African bug and didn't need the extra exercise.

PETRONELLA log, Day 3
The hull fitting for the bilge pump is leaking. The solution is obvious. Pull the brass junction out of the plastic pipe, clean it, smear it in lubricating detergent, warm the plastic pipe so that it becomes pliable and then whack the whole lot together. Absolutely impossible in these conditions. I tighten the jubilee clips . . . this slows but does not stop the leak. . . . I crawl out of the engine room and lie exhausted on the galley floor. . . . I am worried. This is no time to be sinking. We are a few hundred miles off Africa with a whole ocean to drift across in a second hand liferaft.

There are other reasons for a survey. It can help you through the totally unexpected things that may happen later. You may wish to sell the boat en route, renew insurance, prove seaworthiness or ownership. For more reasons that I can imagine, but will have happened to someone, you may be in a strange place, in need of a survey, without the time or local knowledge to get one.

On my first Atlantic crossing I was trying to get all the really important jobs finished before we left. This is not necessarily the right thing to do. There is a balance to be struck in how you spend your diminishing time and a cost to pay if that balance is wrong. I thought the most sensible way to timetable jobs was their relative importance. Wrong! With hindsight I would have chosen the "reverse order of universality," if you see what I mean. That is, I would have left till last the jobs I could just as easily do anywhere in the world, and done first those that I knew could only be done with the services and resources I could find at home.

Doing the jobs on your list is, of course, only part of the work they entail. When planning each job on the boat, think about where and when you will want to test this to see that it works. And then think about what you will need to fix it if it doesn't.

Breath easy

On a sailing boat the direction of air flow is counter-intuitive, or at least it is counter to my intuition. The air from your mainsail blows into the boat and travels from the stern to the bow, even though the boat is moving forward and on the outside the air is moving from bow to stern. Air can get trapped in the main cabin and forecabin. At sea this isn't likely to be lovely air to begin with. The movement of the boat in a seaway disturbs air that has lain for months in the bilges or under the engine and now it is this air that fills your lungs and nostrils. This usually happens shortly after you meet the rolling or bouncy ocean waves and before you have developed your sea-legs. If you start to think the boat smells foul, it probably does; but your enhanced sensitivity is also an early symptom of seasickness. Cleaner air may do nothing for your motion sickness, but it is a more pleasant environment to suffer in.

> On PETRONELLA we always dog hatches when sailing at night, even when conditions during the day have allowed us to crack them open. And we pull the main hatch to, even though this is usually left open during the day. I always hated the smell of foul air during night passages. When I enlarged the Dorade vent in the heads, forward of the saloon, I stopped noticing the foul air. I had given the air an escape route.

It only takes a moment with the fore hatch open to clear the foul trapped air but with the bolts dogged down, a strongback fitted and $3.25 of duct tape around the sides of the hatch your next moment won't come till you make harbor. Think about how air will escape the boat, not just how to get it flowing in.

Cooking gas

Liquid petroleum gas, propane or butane, is the common fuel on most boats even though some old salts won't have gas within a mile of them. They prefer the inherently "safer" fuels of kerosene or diesel. Unfortunately, kerosene and diesel usually need to be pre-heated by some sort of alcohol. You can tell the old salts who don't have gas on their boats. They don't have eyebrows either.

Gas bottles and their fittings differ between North America and Europe as well as between most of the continent of Europe and Britain. I have never let this worry me. We had British propane gas bottles when I sailed around the Scandinavian coasts of northern Europe and we still had them when we sailed down to Africa and across to the Caribbean. Despite being told that it would be impossible to fill them outside Britain, we managed to fill them in Denmark, Holland, France, Spain, Senegal, and again in Trinidad.

Now we have US bottles on PETRONELLA and so far have filled them in Trinidad, the Virgins, the Azores, Spain and Portugal. At some time our gas and luck will run out and we will need to change to a local supplier and their bottles but till then we just assume that every gas depot has all the fitting and tubing and pressure gauges and gas to put propane in our bottles.

A time to sit—self steering

G and I assume that in all our maneuvering and sail setting we are singlehanding. That way we cope with having just one person active at a time. We couldn't do this without self steering. This is vital gear, continuously in use. No wonder we have a love-hate relationship with Mr Aries, our windvane self steering. No equipment can reach the pitch of perfection we sometimes demand of it. We have electronic self steering too, but we expect nothing more from that than a steady compass course while we motor in flat calms. We can't work up any emotional attachment to the autohelm.

Windvane self steering is a near-living thing, sensing the wind and water around it and responding to their forces. It only performs as well as the rest of the boat allows it. Sails and course must match the wind and sea conditions. These are only right when the crew get off their deck cushions and do it. Of course, sometimes we curse Mr Aries. Self steering can be more stubborn than a mule if you treat it wrong.

Of the three ways of steering a sailing boat each is appropriate in particular circumstances. Hand steering is best in close quarters and light airs or when sailing between nearby harbors when steering gives entertainment and no one need be at the helm for more than a couple of hours. Hand steering is particularly poor at night and in a following sea, when having to steer by compass, some other instrument or the feel of the wind on the back of your neck. The inevitable loss of feel in wheel steering compared to tiller just exacerbates this. Crew deserves better treatment on long passages, and so does the boat.

The electronic autopilot has come a long way in the last decade, largely thanks to the special needs and huge budgets of super-fast, short-to-single-handed, round-the-world-or-near-as-damn-it racing yachts. Today's autopilots are not the rubber-band devices of my youth. They are computerized hydraulic ram driven machines that not only steer better but do all manner of other tricks too. They are more powerful, robust, reliable, versatile and, of course, more expensive than in the past. They are also more complicated to fit, usually needing their own rudder quadrant and hydraulic connections regardless of how the yacht is usually steered. Fitting is best thought about when the yacht is being designed. Retrofitting the quadrant, computer, pumps, reservoirs, feedback unit, compass, rams, hoses, wires and circuit breakers, not to mention the backing plates and platforms to hold the components in position, can involve a fair degree of engineering.

Ten years ago the electronic autopilot was usually just a back up to the wind-vane for cruising boats crossing oceans. Now it may be the only method of self steering. A recent survey of the ARC fleet found that half the boats relied solely on new-generation autopilots. A quarter of these experienced problems and failures during their Atlantic trip. This may not be total dependability but a much improved and impressive level of reliability, achieved in the main because these ARC boats are using units similar in specification to those on ocean racing boats. The next step is probably for the ocean cruiser to fit two or even three autopilots, as racers do.

Phillipe Jeantot carried 14 electronic autopilots on CRÉDIT AGRICOLE 4 in one of the singlehanding Globe Challenge races. He might have carried more but didn't want the extra weight. On an earlier CRÉDIT AGRICOLE he had an Aries but with CRÉDIT AGRICOLE 4 the apparent wind changes were just too fast for a windvane.

The autopilot is clever. It can talk to other members of the electronic navigation team and add to the complete system onboard. But being electronic it is working hard in an environment that could hardly be more corrosive for it. Even when its sensitive parts can be located out of the way of the crew's boots and the salt-laden air, it will still be liable to fail at sea. It is a natural choice for a boat making a one-off Atlantic crossing or circuit because being push-button and digital it is familiar technology to skipper and crew, and may already be on the boat. But it isn't the perfect solution for shorthanded crews, especially those who intend to visit remote places and aren't sailing a power generating plant.

Windvane self steering was purpose designed for long passages and remote places. Today's models derive from the sudden need for efficient, sensitive steering when the first singlehanded transatlantic races were started in the 1960s and sailors took up the challenge of non-stop, round-the-world, singlehanded record-breaking.

We forget how truly awful some of the pioneering yachts were by comparison with our modern designs. Captain Slocum seemed to have got it right with his SPRAY, which he claimed could sail herself on all points of sail. But perhaps he was gamming with us, and she sailed like a pig. One of the great achievements in the 1960s was Francis Chichester's trip around the world in GYPSY MOTH. Such a pretty boat, it is hard to believe he cursed her most of the way for being tender and uncontrollable. Chichester added extra length to the keel when he reached Australia, but by then he had sailed halfway round the globe. He used a backed mizzen to balance the boat and make her self steer. It took a knot off the speed but it was the compromise that enabled him to continue at all.

We should give thanks to Colonel "Blondie" Hasler, instigator of the transatlantic races and a pioneer designer of windvanes. Windvanes eat no volts, are reliable and don't mind seawater. They aren't perfect either, of course. They can't keep up with the speed of modern racing pedigree yachts. Modern monohulls able to sail fast in light winds and almost any fast multihull probably shouldn't even consider windvanes except as a back up or when sailing on the wind. A yacht on a fast reach or running downwind will not have enough apparent wind to drive the windvane and if it is rising and falling in deep swells the change in wind between crest and trough will confuse the poor thing. But for most of us, as we tote all our belongings and sail below our marks, windvanes are the most appropriate self steering technology for the ocean.

Nearly all the models I know (and I have had four different types so far in my sailing life) are subtle pieces of design clumsily constructed. I don't mean this as an insult. I mean it as a statement of fact. I can sit for hours watching our Aries, marveling at the offsets and angles needed to convert the swings of the air blade into the rotation and swings of the servo water paddle. And then my focus switches and I wonder why it is such a mix of unsuitable metals and needs oiling every twenty-four hours.

> Another quiet day of following winds. I am intently watching the self steering gear as the seas twist our stern and roll us about. I find it almost impossible to work out its logic. I wonder whether to adjust the tiller lines but since no one has touched vane or tiller for the last three days I won't break tradition now.

Our Aries represents the high point of 1960s windvane, servo-assisted design. In many ways it hasn't been surpassed. This is a small market without the impetus that electronic autopilots have had from the racing fleets. Unlike the fast evolving autopilots, today's windvane designs may use newer materials and have learned a few new tricks but the theory they put into practice hasn't moved on since the Aries and (with few exceptions) neither have the aesthetics. My previous windvane was more modern, a child of the 1980s with some improvements over my Aries, but it didn't steer better and it didn't look any prettier on the back of my boat.

The windvane follows the wind, just like a human helmsperson. This is really the only trick it knows. It only asks two things of you:

- set it up carefully in relation to the wind and the boat's course
- balance your sails for the course and conditions.

After you have attended to those two things the steering gear will sail your boat silently and effortlessly for days if the conditions stay the same. But come the wind shift you will need to reset it and if the wind changes strength you will need to tweak its snaffle lines, none of which is arduous or difficult but it must be done.

> It was my turn to sit on the stern and re-adjust Mr Aries. Thanks to the variability of the light winds in the last week I was pretty good at this. I set the wind blade for the wind direction then I moved the tiller chain a couple of links one way and waited for Aries to settle down. It was always two-link-sailing here in the Horse Latitudes. Aries didn't put us on course so I moved the chain another couple of links. No better result. I checked the angle of the windvane. Fine. I moved the links again. I was getting grumpy. Nothing was working. I was about to curse E or the sails or both when the penny dropped. There wasn't any wind. I apologized to Mr Aries and gave him the day off.

A boat under windvane steering will veer about a bit but that is life on the ocean. Don't try to make it steer down a compass course. Don't think that you or your crew can keep a better course. Learn to live with its foibles. The vital ability of self steering is to steer a better average than you.

> On dark nights, hand steering with no easy way of watching the wind direction, we would oscillate between wild over-corrections, ranging from gibe to broad reach, while always being off course. Not clever for a boat goosewinging with preventers. Mr Aries doesn't need a tell-tale to know which way the wind blows.

Plotting to arrive

Not so very long ago sailors heading across an ocean had to navigate by the sun and stars, a clock, a sextant and almanac and sight reduction tables. Ocean sailors regulated their life around the timing of sights. Slocum was an old hand at it. Novice ocean crossers like Malcolm and Carol McConnell rapidly became experts at snap sights and accurate calculations. You will, of course, be navigating by purpose-built satellites. Self steering may save our energy while we are making long passages, but GPS is one of the main reasons why you and I can sail oceans at all.

Sailing purists make a good point when they warn against over-reliance on an electronic gizmo that can be rendered useless by battery failure, electrical storms, a US military crisis, or even proximity to a US warship, but practice the hair-shirt alternatives after you've been hit by any of these crises.

I have owned two sextants since before the days of GPS and Decca and those radio direction finders with their Morse code signal. We carry an expensive sextant in case our GPS fails and a cheap plastic one for practice and in case we drop the first. Unfortunately, our Nautical Almanac and some of our sight tables are a little out of date which means that until we replace them our real back up to the fixed GPS is our handheld GPS. We keep plenty of spare batteries for this, and are ready to drop it in the grab-bag if we ever take to the liferaft. It should be in a lead box in case our boat gets hit by lightning. Perhaps PETRONELLA's Faraday's Cage effect will protect it.

> A surprising number of sailors learn their sextant navigation during their first ocean passage. I would be re-learning most of mine if the GPS failed. One sailor at the beginning of his crossing from Florida to

Bermuda wondered if he would ever manage to draw down a star or find the small target of Bermuda. Even sun sights were difficult. But he arrived off Flores right on target, still struggling to bring stars to the horizon in rough weather but confident that the sextant works.

It isn't difficult to master the techniques of modern GPS or to plot latitude and longitude on the chart, and most sailors will have had plenty of experience with GPS before they set out across the ocean. But you need to be scrupulous with your record keeping. If anything goes wrong, either because you have entered the wrong data or because the GPS shuts down, you need to be able to return immediately to dead reckoning before you even think of getting the celestial navigation primer off the bookshelf. Dead reckoning (DR) got Columbus across the ocean and me across the North Sea several times. DR by GPS is simply a continuous plot of your previous positions. When the GPS fails it becomes an extension of those positions by estimates of speed, direction, leeway and current. Even though you are a thousand miles offshore, the tiny hourly increments of DR are vital.

The US Capabilities Assessment Task Force warns us not to put total trust in GPS. Their main reason is fear of terrorists jamming the system but they also report an increasing number of incidents when GPS has been tens or hundreds of miles wrong in the positions reported. One of the main problems is that many old satellites are still up there in the Global Navigation Satellite System (GNSS), despite a program of replacement and upgrading. When first put into orbit these satellites had triple redundancy (i.e. essential components were triplicated so that when one failed there was instant back up) but over time this has been degraded. At one point 16 of the 30 or so satellites in the GNSS were without any redundancy. This is not as bad as it sounds. There will be no total system failure but it does mean that one satellite with component failure may give out erroneous positions until switched off, and that these rogues will be increasing in number and giving out increasing numbers of spurious fixes. A year ago ships navigating the congested 20-mile-wide Dover Strait in the English Channel were experiencing errors of 200 to 300 miles. The ship might have been at the harbor bar in Le Havre but the GPS thought they were at a wine bar in Soho, London.

Terrorism is a danger to GPS because the very weak signals used in the GNSS are easily jammed from a station on earth. One flashlight-battery powered jamming device recently offered on a US website could, if activated at a sufficient height in Manhattan, conceivably block out all the GPS receivers at New York airports.

But it doesn't need a terrorist to wipe out GPS signals. A TV antenna in an American harbor accidentally jammed GPS for months until it was discovered.

Similar cases have been reported in the Mediterranean. And once the experts start looking they find all sorts of other reasons for GNSS failure, including solar storms.

The message is clear. You will get no warning of GNSS failure unless you are actively checking the data at the time. Your GPS will not report poor satellite coverage. It will give you a latitude and longitude that might be 100 to 1000 miles wrong and you will accept it because one latitude and longitude looks much like any other until you compare the series or try to put a little x on the chart.

A different class of GPS danger is that as you close the coast you need to beware of inaccuracies in your charts and not be misled by the almost inch perfect accuracy of GPS. Today's method of surveying the seabed by side scan sonar will discover almost all the details down there, but some charts are still based on lead line surveys from 100 or more years ago. Also, thanks to the less accurate position fixing before GPS, you might know to within six feet of where you are on the surface of the earth but your charts might be out by half a mile.

As sailors build up a body of experience of GPS we can discover new information-rich ways of putting our boats in danger or, if we are lucky, of making life safer. At the simplest level I have learned from others to be wary of blindly using an out-going waypoint for the return trip.

In racing from the Solent to the Channel Islands a skipper had set his waypoint for the Casquets at the northwest of this infamous rock strewn, tide-racing area. His return had him approaching the Casquets from the south, not the north, and the earlier waypoint would take him over the rocks. When called up by the crew he heard waves breaking, saw the loom of the light right overhead and only just managed to turn to port to clear the dangers. The lesson: plot every course to a waypoint on a chart.

I have a natural inclination *not* to use the route facility of GPS, that convenient automatic linking of a series of waypoints. I have generated GPS routes when I knew some tricky navigation would coincide with having all hands busy sailing the boat and for comfort I plotted the route with great care and ran checks on it beforehand. But my fear is that my GPS will behave like a complete black box, taking in my accurate waypoints, mixing them into nonsense and instructing me to follow dangerous courses while all the time looking like its benign, omniscient usual self. As an extension of this I have not linked GPS to a computer full of electronic charts, a chart-plotter, autohelm, radar, VHF, SSB or even a blood-pressure monitor. There is just too much potential there for sophisticated black box enhanced disaster.

Something is happening in our lives which could be called "ubiquitous on-board computing," after the term coined in 1991 by computer scientist Marc Weiser. Computer chips have become so cheap, interfaces between electronic equipment have become so intelligently intuitive, that computer devices have become invisibly embedded in our everyday objects, at home and at work. And now they are with us at sea, the final frontier. We no longer need a mile of coaxial cable, skinny fingers and a degree in electronics to make connections. The machines can do it for themselves, through the air. With the advances in radio frequency identification chips (currently costing about five cents!!) we will have anywhere, anytime, always-on communication networks, within our boats and from our boats to others. Why? Because we can. I'm not sure that is a good enough reason.

Paper work—the ship's log

A ship's log has important legal status as a record of events should anything happen which calls for officials to question your journey or seek the cause of an accident. You need a good log just for that. But for most sailors the vital function of a log is to keep track of your navigation and enable other crewmembers to follow your plotted positions or report events relevant to all of you.

You can buy printed versions of log books or you can make your own, tailored to what you find from experience to be relevant. Our log book is just a hardback letter-sized notebook with lined pages. We rule the columns ourselves. The left hand page has columns about one inch wide. The right hand page is left unruled, and headed "Remarks."

We keep our left hand columns as simple as possible. They are headed: Time, Barometric pressure, Latitude, Longitude, Course, Speed, Wind (direction and force).

The remarks page can contain anything, e.g. "150 dolphins dancing at dawn," but is usually just what can fit on one line. Remarks are written at the time of the log entry. If anything is important or interesting between the agreed log intervals, they too are logged and the time entered. For example, if we sight ships when sailing far offshore we log their bearing and distance. During a long passage we also record the time and distance we have motored. Some sailors might do this to have a record of engine hours for their maintenance schedule, but we just like to know how many hours we motored on a passage.

Since we took to sailing long distances with GPS the latitude and longitude have become the most important of our entries. On an ocean passage we will log latitude and longitude every few hours but may only plot our position on the chart once or twice a day. On coastal passages we log hourly and may plot a chart position hourly too. It depends on what is happening. There is, though, an unbreakable rule: no position is ever plotted on the chart without having first been logged in the book. Errors occur all too easily in logging and plotting positions and each member of the crew should be able to query any other position or log entry. When a line on the chart looks wrong, or the latest position seems odd, the first check is whether the error is due to misreading the logged numbers.

Electrical needs—volts, amps and ohms

Electricity defines civilization. You can't appreciate that until you go into a war zone or move aboard a small ocean sailing boat. Your quality of life as a cruiser is the state of charge in your batteries. Comfort is a matter of how many amps are consumed. Choices are determined by how many volts will be left.

How much electricity you need to generate depends on what amps you use, so you need some idea of and some control over the big picture. You have the usual boaty needs of navigation and deck lights, GPS, sailing performance indicators, echo sounder and perhaps anchor windlass, autohelm and radar. Below decks you will need to power internal lights, SSB and VHF and other radios, computer, television and video, refrigeration and freezer, water heater, water pumps, air-conditioning and watermaker. Then you may want to power or recharge a whole range of electric tools. This is not an exhaustive list, but it certainly far outstrips what we run.

This table gives a guide to the power you will draw from your house batteries in a typical day during a long passage at sea. It's just a guide. Check the manufacturer's literature or the equipment itself to see what watts or amps are needed for your own equipment, and think about your own likely usage, then change the numbers to suit yourself. Just remember: actual use always exceeds expectation.

Items of equipment	Typical current draw		Coasting/ harbor usage		Bluewater/ offshore usage	
	Watts	Amps	Hours	Amp hours	Hours	Amp hours
Autopilot	20	1.67	5	8.35	0	0
Depthsounder	4	0.33	2	0.66	0	0
Instrument lamp	10	0.83	8	6.64	24	19.92
Log	2	0.17	8	1.36	24	4.08
Nav lights	80	6.67	5	33.35	0	0
Tricolor masthead	20	1.67	5	8.35	8	13.36
VHF transmit	50	4.17	0.5	2.09	0.2	0.83
VHF receive	5	0.42	8	3.36	5	2.1
Refrigerator	40	3.33	5	16.65	5	16.65
Bilge pump	50	4.17	0.1	0.42	0.05	0.21
Shower pump	50	4.17	0.5	2.09	0.3	1.25
Toilet pump				0		0
FM radio	40	3.33	3	9.99	2	6.66
12v TV	40	3.33	4	13.32	0	0
Reading lamp	15	1.25	3	3.75	3	3.75
Extras	60	5.00	5	25.00	3	15.00
Total		40.51		135.38		83.81

Modify the figures above with your own equipment and your expected practices. Will it be:

- windvane or autopilot self steering most of the time
- deck lights or masthead tricolor, or none at all
- a freezer. I have assumed much too power hungry to be run at sea
- a watermaker. If you have one, add it in
- electric winches, anchor windlass and bow thrusters. You may not need

these while in deep ocean and anyway may only be able to run these while the engine is covering their power take

- microwave and electric cooking. You probably need to be running a generator.

You will need to calculate from amps to watts and back again.

For a 12-volt system
Amps = watts/12
Watts = amps*12

Most suppliers calculate the size of battery bank by multiplying the amp hour target by three or four times. Most boats we know need a house battery bank with between 350 and 600 amp hours but some say they need 800 to 1,000 amp hours. We know one with 1,500 amp hours. Where can you best physically locate these heavy, dangerous, fragile boxes of power? Wherever you put them make sure the space can vent away the lighter than air, explosive hydrogen gas that all batteries produce. If using wet cell batteries, protect against leaking sulphuric acid. And wherever you put the batteries, make sure they are restrained so that they can't add to the mayhem of a knock-down.

A battery expert told me there are really no marine batteries, whatever the label says. The gel and AGM (Absorption Glass Mat) batteries replacing the standard flooded or wet lead acid battery are chemically still lead acid batteries. It is battery construction technology which is changing. Sealed gel and AGM batteries must still vent while charging and discharging. In sailing boats we usually want a higher charge rate than is ideal for gel or AGM, to save running our engines or generators for long periods. Fast charging takes water from the battery and if this cannot be replaced the battery life is significantly reduced.

House batteries are not cranking batteries. House batteries need to deliver power over a long period of time and be repeatedly discharged down to 20% of their full charge (80% Depth of Discharge). These "deep cycling" batteries need thick, solid lead plates. Often we compromise on quality and price by using batteries with a heavy sponge plate rather than a solid one, as we do on PETRONELLA with our golf cart batteries. Not quite the same, even if labeled "deep cycle." The only sure way of knowing if you have a deep discharge battery or not is to cut it open and look at the plates. But then you still won't have a deep discharge battery, or indeed any sort that still works.

Cranking batteries are designed to deliver the big kicks of energy needed to start an engine. This rush of energy comes from a plate with a large surface, created by a thin sponge plate. Unfortunately, such plates are destroyed by deep cycling or fast charge rates. They can survive thousands of cycles if used as starter batteries, when they are discharged only 2% to 5%, but will fail after 50 to 100 cycles if deep discharged.

The vital practical point is that different variants of lead acid batteries require different charging regimes to optimize their life. Make sure each of your sources of power generation are appropriate to the time and voltage curves of the batteries. You may be buying new charging devices, or new batteries. Technological change comes with many financial side effects.

Battery use is a dynamic rather than a static thing. My greatest anxieties come when we turn on some big power user after I know we have already taken out a lot of amps. At high levels of use a battery simply cannot produce enough electrons from its plates. Battery efficiency falls as the current increases. It is easy to run up beyond the nominal, gentle level of use specified by manufacturers and shorten the life of your house batteries. That's why I am so mean with our electrics at sea.

Now that battery condition is all important to your comfort and your safety, this table of charge levels will be invaluable. Voltage is so easy to read with a little digital voltmeter and it shows you the state of charge of your 12 volt batteries. The vital points are:

- each cell produces 2.2 volts hence a healthy 12-volt battery made up of six cells can give a reading of up to 13.2 volts
- a 12-volt battery reading 12 volts is actually discharged
- the gap between 75% charged and 25% charged is only 0.3 volts.

Charge levels

Voltage level	Charge level
12.7v	100%
12.5v	75%
12.4v	50%
12.2v	25%
12.0v	discharged

Make sure you have an accurate and sensitive voltmeter but beware that at times it might play tricks on you. Generator sets and inverters may show erroneously low readings:

- most voltmeters are lazy. They expect inverters to be giving out true sine waves. The cheaper sort of inverter giving out modified sine wave (square waves) may be under-read by a standard voltmeter by as much as 40% i.e. reading about 70 volts when the inverter is delivering 120 volts.
- the voltage from a genset may be under-read simply because gensets may deliver low voltages when running at low rpm.

Sparks of life

So how are you going to put back all those amps you draw? You may have increased your battery capacity before setting off. On a coastal cruising yacht with a marina base you might well double the capacity of your house batteries. If so, think about fitting a higher powered alternator to match the new battery capacity.

A high powered alternator enables your main engine to deliver greater charge to the batteries and you may decide that your main engine should be the fall back method of charging. Why not? The main engine and its alternator is the basic electrical generator on most yachts and it is a way of running the engine frequently enough, even when sailing, to check that it is still alive. But the main engine is a large beast to run just for amperes. Marine diesels are about 35% efficient. That is to say, only about one third of their power is used to deliver drive. Another third goes into just keeping the engine cool and another quarter of their energy goes out as noxious emissions. A 60hp engine would be wasting kilowatts of power just to run a 90 ampere alternator.

Diesel engines like to run under load. Battery charging or a refrigerator compressor are not enough load for most main engines. Running cool i.e. failing to raise the coolant to the healthy threshold of about 160°F, creates gum, varnish and carbon deposits, especially between the valve stem and its guide. Repeatedly running an engine cool is destructive. It will run rough, become hard to start and smoke excessively. If you need to run your main engine as a generator, give it load by running it in gear.

Fitting that bigger engine you've always felt the boat deserved may just add to your problems. It may provide you with the mental and emotional comfort of more horsepower or to give you a higher cruising speed or stop the boat in a maneuvering emergency, but it may mean your engine never does enough work to stay healthy. And before you decide you want more horsepower at the propeller, check whether your propeller is big enough to take the extra horsepower or whether there is clearance to fit a bigger propeller.

Propellers are not the simple things you first thought they were, even though they only have the two dimensions of diameter and pitch. Your fixed pitch propeller should have been designed to suit your engine at maximum revs and power. So what is the problem you are trying to solve? A more powerful engine will help you if your present propeller doesn't allow the engine to reach full revs with the throttle wide open. But then, you could think of reducing propeller pitch to allow the same engine to come up to full revs and deliver all its power when you most need it. If you fit a bigger engine you will probably need a bigger diameter propeller to handle the extra power without cavitation. This won't increase thrust but it may reduce the load on the propeller and help sustain better thrust in those sloppy conditions when you need to punch harder through the seas. If you don't increase the propeller diameter when you fit a bigger engine you will need to compensate by reducing the pitch.

You may decide to install a second smaller diesel engine, dedicated to running equipment and generating power. Many of us do. This gives you two diesel engines to look after instead of sailing, and you may not be putting either of them to work in a way which will prolong their lives.

Wind and solar generators produce much less power than a diesel motor but are quieter and cheaper to buy and run. Cruisers often have both. My preference is for solar. No moving parts, no sense of a jet plane landing on deck and no need to remember to switch them on. You don't need a deck load of solar panels to run the basics of GPS, VHF, navigation lights and one interior light.

On the passage from Bermuda to the Azores many boats said that generating electricity became a problem. Too many dull days for the solar panels. Too much light airs and following winds for the wind generator. The first thing to turn off was usually the refrigerator.

The paramount rule of living aboard applies on an ocean crossing: keep it simple. Boats bolstering their life afloat with mechanical and electrical systems to parallel life ashore can spend more time fixing than sailing, more time burning diesel than listening to silence. Fixing things gets harder the more remote and beautiful the cruising ground, in an exponential sort of way. Start by seeing what electrical devices you can live without.

SSB and satellite phone

The future belongs to Information Technology. Like electricity, *IT* gives us sailors the trappings of civilization.

The two forms of marine radio have very different functions. VHF radio is for short distance, line of sight communications. You might manage to signal a station 10 miles away if your combined aerial heights are sufficient. VHF is for communications to port authorities and for local nets with other cruising yachts. The portable VHF is great for communications when away from the yacht. We keep a portable VHF handy for the grab bag but it would only be useful to us in the liferaft once a search has been triggered. Offshore we only turn our VHF on when we want to communicate with another vessel or think they want to speak to us.

Short wave radio (usually known as HF or SSB) is for long range communications, capable of sending signals round the world. It is a very imperfect form of communication but most bluewater sailors and liveaboards will get round to having an SSB transceiver eventually, as they become aware of how much social life they are missing by not being able to meet up with cruising friends. We mainly use ours to catch weather forecasts. SSB has two main drawbacks. First, you must make schedules to keep in touch with other yachts and will only get weather and the like at the time it is being broadcast. Unless you can reach the ham radio community you cannot expect other stations to be listening around the clock. The second snag is that weather and astrological conditions affect the distance the signal can travel. This is random and unpredictable. On almost all SSB nets some stations will be inaudible and on some nets on some days all stations will be inaudible.

Two great benefits of SSB come when you link it to your on-board computer. With the right software program and a simple piece of kit your SSB radio and computer become a weatherfax. By adding a modem to the SSB you have on-board Internet access. In effect, we use SSB at sea for things we would get by telephone ashore. I have to tell you, the phone is almost always better.

From the BVI to the Azores we had several problems with SSB reception. So did other boats. Signals were too weak at times to allow weatherfaxes to be received. I arrived at the view that weather forecasts are a wonderful thing to have, but not one you should feel reliant on during the weeks you will be out there on your ocean crossing. The best rule of thumb remains: only go to sea in a sturdy boat and be ready for anything.

One of the big issues for the next few years is whether phone technology will overtake radio technology for the really important communications, between coast guards and yachts and for emergency messages. Perhaps the real question is no longer "whether" but "when." There are points for and against radio retaining this function, but the simple weight of numbers and its increasing functionality is already pushing phones to the fore. G and I have already learned from experience that if the local pilot book gives a phone number as well as a VHF channel for a marina, the more reliable way to be answered is by phone.

> The US yacht was hit by a gale and sick crew on its way from Bermuda to Newport, Rhode Island, and couldn't raise help on its SSB. The skipper managed to call Sea Tow on his satellite phone and through them organized a Coast Guard airlift for his crew. The phone saved the crew from the potentially lethal consequences of a ruptured appendix.

The satellite phone obviously has clear advantages over the land-based cell phone, but even these humble creatures are now playing a role in rescue at sea.

> The five men on the 60-foot Cornish fishing boat were out of VHF range and sinking when their pump broke in a storm. They set fire to the boat to attract attention but without luck. When the inevitable happened and their burning boat sank they took to the liferaft. After eight days they got a signal on their cellphone and called the British Coast Guard. The cell phone was their salvation.

Telephone technology will probably overtake radio technology because it does the less important things so much better and experience over the last decades has shown that it is only a small step for mankind to go from being a minor-user of telephones to having a major psychological dependency. When the satellite phone has proved it can reliably deliver everything a land line can, including fast Internet access, boats not already fitted with SSB transceivers, Pactors, aerial tuners, isolated backstays and ground plates on their hull may find the telephone is cheaper to install as well as more functional. And who needs to sit an exam to operate a telephone?

Since taking to living on our boat we too have become addicted to the cell phone. We don't have a satellite phone so we can only use ours when close enough to land to link to one of the commercial land-based networks. By inserting local SIM cards we can have relatively cheap telephone calls wherever we are. Perhaps the future for sailors will be satellite phones but so far there has not been the expected development and reduction in price to let us join the system.

Computing the weather

So what about computers? One yacht skipper came into Horta saying that yachts now use computers for so many essential tasks that they should carry two or even three computers. I can see his point. He only had one and it had ceased working just after he left St Martin for the Azores. Once that happened he had neither his expected weatherfax nor an SSB-Internet connection. We carry two GPSs on board because that is the basis of our navigation and navigation is not something to go light on. I can't get so worked up about weather computers but that's just because we don't have one. The weather pictures G downloads from the Internet are now so wonderful that I can even see myself craving this when at sea, but the reality of making this happen may take a little longer.

The sad news is that computers at sea are reliable until they cease to work, and ceasing to work is what all computers do sooner or later. Reliance on a computer for any essential task is like waiting in the queue for the disaster to happen. Having different computers for different tasks is just a matter of which will go first. I speak from experience. We are heavy computer users and currently have two laptops on board. One of these made a miraculous recovery from motherboard failure. The other one replaced it while it was having this "near death" experience. The miraculously resurrected computer replaced a fine little laptop I had used on land for years until it came with me to the boat. It "cooked" after two years in the tropics.

Several ocean crossers I have spoken to complain about computer failure at sea. Some failures were obviously due to age or a hardware fault. Others were due to accidents. Computers are sensitive little things. They don't like being bounced on the floor or flooded with salt water. One skipper was typing down below in bad weather when part of a wave came through the deck hatch onto his keyboard and put an end to the computer.

Nor is it the computer itself that will let you down. Most boats at some time suffer electrical problems. We had a generator problem that was only fixed when we reached harbor so at times we had to run the main engine just to get our batteries charged enough to power the computer through the inverter. I was very reluctant to do this during strong winds, when the boat was speeding along and hopping off wave tops: partly because it was a waste of increasingly precious fuel and partly because the engine doesn't like running in those conditions. Often that is just the time when you want to commune with the weather forecaster.

And then it all went dark

We had a close shave on PETRONELLA. A very minor problem with a dripping engine water pump filled the bilges high enough to nearly put water over the battery terminals. We would have been without power.

We met a fast 45 footer in the Azores that suffered 10 days of heavy winter weather on its crossing from Martinique. They took so much water on board that none of their electrics would work. That was before their batteries got flooded by sea water.

We met a sailor who recovered from being knocked unconscious to realize that his boat had been hit by lightning. Not one bit of electronics survived.

In the old days of less than 20 years ago most ocean crossing boats would have continued cheerfully on their way if their miserly battery bank of 100 amp hours failed on them. But these days even PETRONELLA is remarkably dependent on electricity. I am not likely to feel deprived if our radios cease to work or the refrigerator fails, but I would struggle without GPS and not having an engine to get me onto the dock.

We carry a sextant and enough kerosene to show a bright navigation light for a month or two. We have a lead line, and occasionally use it. We have a towed Walker log that *in extremis* could give us speed through the water and enable us to navigate by dead reckoning. We have strips of light cloth tied to the rigging as telltales to show the force and direction of the wind. We have canned food and dry stores to last weeks if not months. We don't have to pump drinking or washing or even bilge water or the toilet electrically. This isn't for emergencies. It is how we live normally. But the portable GPS with lots of spare batteries is for emergencies, as are the many flashlights and their batteries. We don't need any electricity to run our cooker and if it ran out of propane we would turn to a couple of camping stoves we keep for just such an emergency. We don't need electricity to steer the boat or drive our winches.

How would you cope if you had complete electrical failure?

It might happen. I'm sure you carry a liferaft in case you sink. The statistical chances of total electrical failure are surely greater than having to abandon ship. Work out a plan and have the equipment to put it into practice.

8

Fit to cross: the crew

Most boats making this crossing will be sailing shorthanded. More than 80% of yachts arriving in Horta have crews of four or less. One third of all arrivals are sailed by a couple and roughly one in ten yachts are crossing the ocean singlehanded.

By sailing shorthanded I mean most boats will be sailed by a couple and some couples might invite a friend along for a long trip. Not many will have half a dozen strong fit youths, always able to be roused to full energy by nothing more than the stroke of a cat's tail, or a dozen experienced Cape-Horners to share the duties of a boat at sea.

> Our friend P, a small lady who often cruises her 35 footer single-handed, e-mailed us to say she had been asked to skipper a fully crewed heavy 50 footer from the Canaries to the Caribbean. Her first plan was to let the men do all the heavy jobs. Later, when it became clear that the men were plagued by reasons to return home before the trip, she e-mailed to say that it would be down to her "and Ken." We didn't hear if Ken made the trip. Not all crewing plans make it from start to finish.

Duties at sea are the same for every boat regardless of the number, age or experience of crew onboard and a shorthanded crew of two or three or four can soon become weakened by bad management and lack of rest.

> The more adventurous your planned trip the harder it can be to find crew. This is either cause or effect of why singlehanders always seem to do the most taxing sailing. When our friend HB on the northern

route wanted to sail to some very out of the way and far-north places he just couldn't find crew to go with him. Plenty of people said it was a trip they wanted to make. But not just now. They were too busy right now.

Skippers' rule

Making a good crew matters above most other things because crossing the ocean must be fun if it is to have any point. Whether someone can sail or handle a boat before they sign on with you is largely irrelevant. They will have plenty of time to learn when the lines are cast off. Learning how to live on a small boat is not so easy, yet getting along well and having fun are vital. A crew that isn't having fun is not capable of the independence and sustained commitment to the common good that boat safety depends on. Making crew good is a long business, but it helps to have the right individuals to begin with. First, that means having the right skipper.

The skipper is responsible for the atmosphere on board the boat. There are no hard and fast rules about how many crew makes for a happy yacht. If you sail alone, it doesn't much matter. You can be as happy or sad as you please. After that I suspect that the bigger the crew, the more scope for dissent and ruffled egos. I have had happy times with just one other crew but not everyone can be so lucky.

Skippers tend to live too much in their own world, with their own worries and problems. The sailing literature is littered with skippers who score F double-minus in human awareness. There they all are, banging on about the trials of living with a spineless crew on the verge of revolt with never a thought for how they have brought normal, sturdy individuals to this crisis. That's bad practice. Unfortunately, what most of us learn from bad practice is how to do things badly.

The longer I sail, the less I want to be giving orders. I don't like telling people what to do. I don't want to be watching people all day long. It isn't what I go to sea for. But as the skipper I have to make sure we are all working to a common purpose and with sufficient common sense not to bring us past some critical point of danger. Most of the time things work out fine. But, then, I never stop listening and watching and checking everything on board. This doesn't spoil my enjoyment of being at sea. It's what I would do if I were singlehanding. With crew the only difference is how to bring them into the system and make sure we all have a good time.

Not everyone is a natural democrat or can see the benefits of team work over bull. On little offshore boats our attitudes towards authority still come from the ambient social values of the worlds we have just left. But the days of strict hierarchies are being undermined. The technology we carry with us sees to that.

The new technologies of seafaring also imply new relations on board. Consider the GPS. Prior to electronic navigation a ship's captain lived with a high degree of ignorance in vital areas. He didn't even know what time it was until Harrison invented the robust chronometer two centuries ago. Nor did he know with precision where the ship was and what course it should take to get to its planned destination. But this was the knowledge his very command depended on. So like all ignoramuses in positions of power he protected his authority by social isolation and a flog'em-and-hang'em brevity of conversation. He practiced mystification: baffle the lower ranks before they realize it's all empty pretense. Deliver indisputable orders at military volume and confusingly short intervals. Well, the world of technology has pulled the rug out from under that. Thanks to GPS, the most highly regarded information on a ship at sea is at everyone's finger tips. We are all democrats now.

Don't complicate life with daily lists and formal de-briefings and inflexible assigning of responsibilities. Get the big picture sorted early on. Manage the detail as it happens.

"This is where we are going. This is how I like to travel. This is how I like to manage the boat. These are the tasks of sailing and how we will share them. This is what equipment and stores we carry and how it will get used up or wear out during the voyage. This is what happens if our rate of using stores or breaking things goes faster. When something specific crops up, like a repair or a night watch or a storm, I'll talk you through how we will deal with it. If at any time you aren't sure what is expected, ask me. If you ever think there is a problem, don't delay in telling me. As the trip goes on and we learn more about ourselves as a crew and the nature of this voyage we will refine how we do things and communicate things."

Everyone has an aptitude or skill that will be of special use but don't over-egg this. The trained engineer should also navigate and cook and be part of general problem solving. The best cook might do an extra meal or two, but everyone should do galley service. Everyone should have a turn or be involved in the routine ship business of hand, reef and steer. With GPS, everyone can take a turn at navigating. Involve everyone by asking the crew to explain jobs to one another.

Whenever a job is done well or badly, whenever something occurs that catches you or the crew by surprise, talk it over and draw lessons from it. When something difficult is on the horizon, you can now marshal your forces according to their relative strengths rather than their professional training.

> We were coming into Bayona at night after 10 days at sea. I hate night entry into strange ports and wouldn't have done it if I had not been in and out of here a dozen times before. Except that was ten years ago. As the best helmsperson and the undisputed skipper, I of course positioned myself right up in the bows and had G and R share the tasks of steering, navigation and avoiding fishing boats. These are rock strewn waters and I was trying to kick my memory into full recovery. We motored from one pre-entered GPS waypoint to another. G and R did most of the work. I ducked below a few times to remind myself of the chart details.

We have very few hard and fast rules on PETRONELLA. One is: the cook doesn't wash up. Now that really is an important rule. Much more important than when to wear safety gear or check the engine oil level. It is a rule that applies several times a day and must never be disputed. The others are a matter of context and personal judgment or specific orders. If a crewmember wants to wear a life jacket all day, that is fine by me. If another crew doesn't want to wear one ever, that is fine too, just so long as they wear one when I decide conditions require it.

A second rule is: only the skipper is excused routine tasks like cooking and night watches. On a shorthanded boat like PETRONELLA this rule only kicks in when circumstances allow, of course, but it also involves a deeply important principle. The skipper's job is 24 hours, seven days a week. Make sure the rest of the crew carry the load so that the skipper is fit and ready when the moment of need comes. A skipper who does all the important jobs all the time just because he or she is best at them is wasting the potential energy they will need when they are faced with a task that only they can do.

The third rule is: two hard and fast rules are enough for any boat.

There can only be one skipper on a boat and when the moment of crisis comes it is the skipper who must cope with it and give the orders. Till then, let the skipper be the first among equals rather than a tin god.

> A good skipper and crew not only keep away from accidents, they also respond well when the accident happens. A time of crisis on a

sailing boat is a time for lots of jumping and running and shouting. Don't panic but get active. Do things. Of course it helps to have already worked out a plan for the emergency that has hit you, so that all this activity is done with a purpose, but one of the sharpest joys of life afloat is that Nature is more imaginative than you in finding new crises to test your mettle.

Choosing crew

Good crew is simple to define but hard to find. I like crew who forgive my foibles without expecting me to forgive theirs. After all, I'm the skipper and my job is hard enough without having to double-guess the emotional consequences of doing or not doing things. I like crew who by their own sunny nature wake up happy and start each day afresh without a grudge in their heart. Or if they can't manage that, to pretend convincingly that they can. I don't want crew who think they can kid me that they are happy, when whatever effort they might be making just blackens the all-too-visible cloud of their depression.

G and I often sail with old friends. Some are competent sailors, others are just good company. We don't always invite our old friends to come on long passages, however. We know our friends well enough to have a good idea of how those all important inter-personal relations will be shaping up as time and terrors take their toll. Sad to say, old friends can be the best of crew but sometimes also the worst of crew. You must choose carefully and as objectively as you can. This is no time to worry whether anyone will be suffering hurt feelings for not being shortlisted. Good friends can forgive that sort of test. Better to hurt a few feelings than to take the wrong people with you and suffer the double blow of hating the journey and losing fine friends.

A singlehander is spared the social tensions that come with having other people onboard, no matter how much you love them or find them easy company. But even singlehanders sometimes hear ethereal voices from the scuppers and think they have company. And what do they do then? Get into an argument, of course. The core of the problem is simple. Social harmony on a little sailing boat is down to the skipper.

One disadvantage of singlehanding caught me by surprise. Officialdom doesn't like it. One boat in the Gulf Stream but still in US waters was approached by a coast guard vessel. Instead of wishing the skipper well and passing on useful weather or navigation information they rebuked him for singlehanding and cast doubts on his sanity. He thought they would board him but was perhaps saved this indignity by being a German flagged vessel. The same skipper was later told by Customs officials in Bermuda that he was insane for singlehanding and for sailing a tiny 28-foot boat. The coast guard and Customs, of course, work to a different agenda to sailors. The British navy saluted him and gave him right of way in the channel as he came into St George's.

Since my first crossing I have learned to be more flexible than I think Nature intended me but even so I like to have a peace-maker on board. I learned from my first crossing that some people have better social skills than me, have more finely tuned social antenna, or just manage to strike a more sensitive note when expressing themselves. Get one of those in your crew and make sure you listen and use them.

Good crew is active, not forever lost in their own world or taking no interest in yours. Good crew is always looking around. Checking the horizon for dangers and changes in the weather pattern. Checking the deck, the rigging and sails. People who are busy doing practical things are building their feeling for the boat.

Emm is the sort of sailor I would like to be. He is a paid skipper, a professional who prides himself on always being professional. We first saw him taking the 60-foot yacht off its pontoon and round to the fuel dock and then hoisting sail to pop over to a neighboring island to buy some cheese. He was on his own. He had the sail up before he cleared the breakwater. We sailed with him one afternoon for fun. Emm was never still. He had his lines run out long before any maneuver. If there was chafe or a bad lead, he was onto it. He hoisted the spinnaker without any help from us. Of course he did, he sails this boat singlehanded on trips of 1,000 or 2,000 miles. He has to be able to use all his working sails including the light wind, down wind spinnaker. Emm is never ending energy but he values time to relax. On his boat if he can't cook a meal and read a book while the boat sails itself, something needs to be changed.

Not all sailors are models of excellence. I have met some who are excellent models of the opposite.

*I like to know that the mast fittings are still sound before we go offshore,
but I prefer Gloria to go up there to check.*

The two-day gale had at least one more day to go. The dirty white boat had taken a mooring buoy that put its stern too close to the bowsprit of a heavy ketch that had come in yesterday. With little else to do on these windy days we watched for the inevitable accident, increasingly wondering why the skipper of dirty white didn't just move. Surely he could see that the boats were dangerously close. He complained that he had to stay up half the night watching the boats swing and miss, swing and miss. He complained that the marina had put him on this buoy. He wondered about asking the marina if he should move. He seemed to prefer complaining and wondering to moving to one of the other vacant buoys. The skipper of the ketch clearly felt that last in, first out should be the time-honored order of the day, so he wasn't moving, and anyway, his bowsprit wasn't going to get hurt half as badly as the delicate windvane on the transom of dirty white. Thinking that dirty white skipper was on his own I offered to help him move his boat. It seemed to energize him at last. That and the fact that his Aries had just been snagged by heavy's wandering bowsprit. But when he called two crew on deck I decided he had enough hands without mine. G and I had spent the last few days re-anchoring to get better shelter, and then hauling up the anchor when it dragged in the early hours. I figured if G and I had done all that for ourselves then dirty white with three strong men could move the two hundred feet to a buoy with more swinging room on their own.

Tweaking your crew

Are you a strong crew or a weak crew? It's best to decide this early on and adjust your lifestyle to it.

Our boat usually sails with a weak crew for no other reason than we are a heavy, long keeled ketch with simple manual systems and I rarely go anywhere with more than G and one other. Actually, it's usually just G. That leaves us a lot of muscle short when the crisis comes. But then I know when we are a weak crew and when we are a strong crew and I organize my panics accordingly. The further offshore we go, the stronger we are and the more relaxed I am. Offshore, I can singlehand this boat and with G on board our sailing style is serial singlehanding. But put us at the entrance to a marina or let our anchor drag in strong winds among a pack of expensive yachts used to marina berths or with rocks down to our lee, and G and I are sometimes on the margins of what we can manage and my main aim in life is to get my panic in early, as a wise friend used to advise me.

A third pair of hands in a crisis is as good as a dozen. Better usually, since it comes with only one extra mouth and only one set of alternative opinions. But there are good and bad reasons for shipping extra hands and I think one of the worst must be to meet the conditions of an insurance policy. Singlehanders often sail uninsured because they are unable to get insurance. The insurance of couples often becomes invalid when they sail offshore. The companies pressing us to take on extra crew are twisting our arms over one of the key decisions a skipper must make and ultimately affecting his or her command of events when a crisis hits at sea. Think hard about your response to this.

Equipment can make you a stronger crew. Our reliable diesel engine is the best example of that, getting us out of trouble on more occasions than I can count. There have been times I have wished for the speed and remote control of a powered anchor windlass instead of our manual one. By giving us the equivalent of a third pair of hands it would make re-anchoring decisions as well as the re-anchoring itself just so much easier. But not all gear makes you a strong crew. Chose your gear carefully, so that it does. When gear lets you down and fails at the moment you need it, you go from being a weak crew to being a helpless crew and crisis is galloping towards catastrophe.

Good gear allows you to do things that you couldn't otherwise do. Raise heavy ground tackle in strong winds. Turn 360° in a tight marina. Haul up a big mainsail from the protection of your cockpit or reef in-mast with the pull of light line. But more than your gear it is the boat size and her design that make you a stronger crew.

For close quarters maneuvering we rely heavily on the main engine to help make the boat do what we want. Even a strong reliable main engine needs to be treated with caution. I try never to be so committed to a maneuver under engine that I am running down a dead end street with just a brick wall at the end.

Chuck was a machine man. He learned his boat handling watching marina staff parking charter yachts. Full speed ahead. Helm hard over. Full speed astern. Stop on a dime, every time. Chuck came in as usual at full blast straight for the pontoon. He put the engine astern and opened the throttle wide. The engine roared. The propeller shot off the shaft. Chuck did the only thing left to do. He put his arms in the air and screamed "Help!!"

G is good at picking up a mooring buoy but even if I am at the helm for some tricky last minute maneuvering I am still physically stronger and able to run forward to help when the weight of the boat comes on the seaweedy line and the razor sharp shells of sea creatures start to slice through the palm of your hand and you still need one last heave-to to get the line around the deck cleat.

It seems to me self evident that on most boats the man should be doing the heavy work around the deck at moments like that, but the evidence of my eyes is that it's hard to shift a man from the wheel of the boat, where the most punishing physical labor is pushing a throttle or gear lever. The most you can hope for from most "skippers" is a string of instructions delivered loud enough to carry from stern to bow. The one I love best is "Don't let go!!" yelled repeatedly as the "skipper" fails to take way off the ten ton boat and the woman on the foredeck is having her arms visibly lengthened as she hangs on to the buoy or pontoon. It doesn't have to be that way. It cannot be beyond imagination for a man-woman couple, or adults sailing with children, to organize matters so that come the crisis it's the physically weaker ones who are twiddling with the engine and wheel and the ones with the biggest muscles are doing the heavy work. In which case the "skipper," now on the foredeck, might learn that you can always go round for a second attempt.

Sailing couples have chosen to spend their lives with one another and have come to tolerate if not actually appreciate the foibles of the other. In which case, a small boat on a big ocean is as good as anywhere. But fathers and sons didn't choose one another, seldom tolerate one another, and sometime don't make compatible crew.

G and I stopped to stare at the unusual rig of the 50-foot trawler yacht in Horta harbor. "Can it go to windward?" I asked the young man on its deck and took his unprintable answer as a no. "Big engines, then?" I asked. Apparently not although 30 years ago its twin 20 horse engines were considered sufficient. "One hp per ton," the young man said, and added something about diddly squat. We met him next night in the bar and heard about crossing the Gulf Stream with 40-foot waves and worse. "Its ok for dad," the young man said. "It's his dream. I wanted off right there and coming this far hasn't been fun either. I've got a job to go back to and I'm missing it." After a while we said goodnight and wandered back round the harbor to look at the boat again. The elderly man on deck contentedly chatting to his neighbor was in exactly the place he wanted to be doing just the things he wanted to. The crossing had been fine by him, if a little lumpy at times. Father and son, different dreams, different agendas.

The litmus test—a serious shakedown cruise

You need a shakedown cruise to test that the boat and all its systems are working. You can usually do this in a day or two if pressed but think of taking a longer shakedown cruise to make sure the crew is all you want it to be. Take at least three nights to do this, seven if you can manage it. Two months continuous cruising might be nearer to the ideal. You can always make the passage to Bermuda your shakedown, dropping off anyone you aren't happy with or anyone who isn't happy with you.

> All boats with crew must run up against the question of whether some one should be put off or not. This is probably the most important decision any skipper on a first time crossing will have to make. I can tell you two things. First, it isn't easy to take. Second, if you reach that awful decision point once you will certainly find yourself there again.

Try to make this a communal decision, if you have the social skills to manage this. Not all of us have such skills, but the reason for involving everyone in such a decision is clear. Skippers live much more in their own world than they ever realize. An extra perspective on life around you inside your tiny little capsule can make or break the fun you should all be having. And anyway, this ocean crossing is a joint adventure. You must all "own" it in your own ways for it to work best. It might be you who is annoying everyone with one of your less endearing ways, but which you would be perfectly happy to change.

Even if you are sailing with old, well-known friends, you need a litmus cruise to make sure you are all happy together. After all, if this is your first ocean crossing it is likely to be theirs. And if they have already sailed an ocean, they might be fixed in ways that you are not and never likely to be. Well, there is a recipe for friction. A litmus cruise is essential if you are sailing with someone you don't know well.

> The British singlehander with the Trade Wind crossing in his sights had registered with a crew finding agency but wasn't getting results. Most of the replies were from young women, which could be good for him but also makes you wonder. The potential crew were hard to shake from their prejudices. Some insisted on the boat having a refrigerator. It already did, but that wasn't the point. One wanted to see a medical report on the skipper. I thought she was right, but

again that wasn't the point. It only made him want to see one on her. G and I weren't surprised when we bumped into him a year later, only 500 miles further down the coast and still singlehanding.

Fit to drop

The sailing life is a remarkably healthy one, which is just as well since you are only ever near to a doctor when you have one in the crew. It's a lifestyle that makes us physically stronger, have more stamina and become more tolerant of hard knocks. This is just as well since it also demands these things of us. Sometimes it also drains us of all our strength and then demands more than is humanly possible, and we still have to find it. If you have been living a sedentary life think about getting into better shape.

A skipper owner of an old Baltic trading schooner felt he had softened up in the months preparing his boat so he took a job on a road gang. He was in his mid 40s, stronger and fitter than most men his age, but the gang called him grand-dad and gave him easy jobs till he got his muscles working and hardened up.

Look in the mirror. Are you ready?

Al was a big man when I last saw him but he had put on a lot extra in the six months since then and from the way he was holding his back the weight hadn't done much for his spine. When he had lowered himself onto a seat and recovered his breath enough to ask me about getting ready to sail to Europe I could only think of two essentials. First, how to make him lose 80 pounds. Second, how to make Al's tiny wife Beth competent to recover him if he ever went overboard. I concentrated on the second one. Al would take a long time to lose weight. When he needed a recovery method, he would need it Right NOW!! And for her sake as well as his, Beth needed the competence to handle the boat without Al. In the end I suggested they did a long coastal passage. They did and I think I gave them a damn fine piece of advice. It was enough to frighten them out of making a trip to Europe that year. Except by plane.

Like any other traveler on a long trip you need to be up-to-date on all routine immunizations. You should look at the schedules approved by the Advisory Committee on Immunization Practice (ACIP) and do this early enough to allow time to get any shots you need and for them to take effect. I recommend you make sure you have in-date protection against tetanus and diphtheria, but that is something everyone should have anyway. Otherwise, in most of Western Europe you need take no more precautions than while traveling in the States. As a rule you won't be at risk of malaria or dengue fever, yellow fever or cholera and no more at risk of hepatitis than you are back home. Parts of Eastern Europe have malaria-carrying mosquitoes, but you would have to moor up and travel a long way inland to reach them.

You don't need any vaccinations to enter Europe (although you will need a certificate of yellow fever vaccination to enter the Azores, Madeira, and Malta if you have come from a South American or sub-Saharan country where yellow fever is endemic).

There are some less well known and much more localized problems and you should research this for your particular destinations by visiting the website of the US Center for Disease Control: www.cdc.gov.

For example, an unpleasant little tick carrying encephalitis is active in forest and grass lands in summer in the Baltic regions of Sweden, Norway, Finland, Germany, Estonia, Latvia, Lithuania and Poland and in the hills and meadows of Austria, Germany and Switzerland. The risks of infection are not high but this is a very serious and unpleasant viral infection of the central nervous system. Locals are well informed about the dangers and usually immunized but, of course, visitors without the local language may never even hear of it. You can't get the vaccine for the disease in the United States so do this in Europe if you are visiting risky areas. The disease is passed to humans when bitten by an infected tick so you can reduce the likelihood of this by covering up with long pants, long sleeved shirts and hats and using insect repellents. Take the same precautions you would for the tick-borne Lyme disease you may be familiar with back home.

You must be prepared for rare afflictions but they probably won't happen. For some problems, such as cuts and wounds not healing at sea, you need to take along appropriate medicine. Talk to your doctor about changing regular medication for your usual complaints so that it copes with the slightly more stubborn form they may take at sea. However, seasickness and sunstroke are always with you and the subtler forms may affect your whole crew without you or them realizing it.

Sick leave

I meet non-sailors who tell me they would go sailing if it weren't for the fear of seasickness. They are surprised when I tell them how many sailors I know get seasick.

I envy the sailor who doesn't suffer seasickness. A constant part of the sailing life is the motion of the boat. For me it is not unusual to suffer seasickness in the first 24 to 48 hours of going offshore and I used to assume that once I'd got over that I wouldn't suffer again. Since then I have come to realize that seasickness takes many forms, striking at many different times. I now recognize that seasickness is more subtle than a sweaty green complexion, serial vomiting and wishing for death. Whenever the weather gets rough after a period of easy sailing, or a major wind shift changes the motion of the boat, suspect that people will be operating at less than 100%.

Seasickness makes us tired and cold but too listless to do anything about it. We yawn more and feel sleepy. Perhaps some age-old survival instinct is kicking in to make us want to crawl under a rock and sleep. However, we become a danger to ourselves and others when we become unwilling to exert ourselves even when a task is necessary and urgent. Our minds lose the sharpness needed for accurate position fixing. The fit must keep an eye on the blighted. Once well into a passage the signs may become less acute but beware: less visible forms of seasickness may make the crew and you significantly disoriented and at risk. Ask yourself whether seasickness is causing the lassitude which makes them so irritable and irritating, triggering bad relations just when you least need it.

> The tiny Spanish yacht arrived in Tobago an hour after us after thirty two days from the Canaries. In the bar that evening the two-man crew were recovering their spirits. They lacked the English to say what they had suffered but they mimed to perfection the wild gyrations of a yacht on a Trade Wind sea. Later we heard of the darker side of their voyage. The ineluctable rolling had brought one of the men close to suicide. The other, I think, would have willingly dispatched him.

Motion sickness is a well-studied and prescribed condition. It is easy and important that each member of the crew tries out different solutions until they get one that works for them. Trouble is, there are so many on the market that clearly none of them works for everyone.

When my sailing was mainly coastal, so that I was rarely on passage for more than a few nights or outside the comfort of a weather forecast, I discarded the other medicines and came to rely on Stugeron. This is a drug originally developed for Ménière's Disease and people whose inner ear labyrinth is causing them serious problems of balance. Unlike conventional motion sickness remedies, which seem to rely on sedating the stomach, Stugeron goes direct to the heart of motion sickness and works on the inner ear. Very soon after it became available for these clinical conditions it was tried out for seasickness, possibly because some doctors recognized its potential to make their sailing lives more pleasant.

> Stugeron's generic name is Cinnarizine, an antihistamine. Antihistamines block histamine receptors. One such receptor in the brain is known as the vomiting center. By blocking this, antihistamines prevent the brain from sending nerve messages to the stomach that would normally result in vomiting. Motion can trigger vomiting. The balance mechanisms of our inner ear need time to adjust to the increased motion of sailing and while this is happening they send more signals than the brain can handle. The brain doesn't like to be overloaded so it sends a message to the stomach, one of its underling organs. "Vomit," says the brain. "All the stuff I'm getting from the ear is giving me a headache. Rather you than me."

Back in the 1970s and 1980s a British yachting magazine helped organize Stugeron trials. Sailors willing to be guinea pigs and report their experiences were put in touch with a medical researcher and given pills. Some, I don't remember, might have been given placebos in the time-honored way of double-blind tests. The results showed that Stugeron worked with minimal side effects. Since then the drug has been popular with British and European sailors as the cutting-edge cure for seasickness.

I too loved it back in my coastal sailing days. Gone was that awful seasickness, gone the side effects of other travel sickness medicines. But on my first ocean-bound passage the three-way combination of head winds, foul seas and Stugeron turned me into a zombie. It might not have been the Stugeron of course, but that is what I blamed at the time and I still cannot bring myself to take it.

> The problem with any seasickness medicine taken by mouth is that the vital ingredient may not hang around your system long enough to do its job. I don't think this was the case with me and Stugeron. In fact, given my tendency to "take it all now and get it over with" I might well have over-dosed. That's what us zombies do. You can get better control over drug quantities by the suppository method, as preferred by many nations on the continent of Europe. If you are going to try this method, first make sure you can read French in a rising gale.

Stugeron has proved such an effective antidote to seasickness that it must be one of the main remedies for you to consider. But Stugeron is a powerful clinical drug and not yet approved by the United States Food & Drug Administration for motion sickness. As with any such drug, check with your doctor that you won't suffer a bad reaction. Also, make sure you are taking the appropriate dose. Any drug can be abused. Stugeron sold over-the-counter for motion sickness in Britain comes in 15mg pills. The 75mg or even 150mg that doctors might prescribe for inner ear conditions will certainly make you sleepy or ill.

It isn't just Stugeron that can make you sleepy. Any antihistamine has the potential to do this, and becomes a real knock-out if taken with alcohol.

Fortunately, I didn't have to go back to the other drugs after I zombied on Stugeron. I discovered those little elasticized wrist bands with a hard plastic lump built into them. Position the lump on your wrist, the elastic applies acupressure, and hey presto, the motion sickness is gone. They work for me. Now I always wear them for the first few days at sea and carry spares for those who sail with us. The wonderful thing is that if they work for you they will work at any time, even when you have started to feel unwell.

> Some people won't try sea bands because it seems like a gimmick. I hate gimmicks. Nor am I susceptible to auto-suggestion since I doubt the sweeping claims made for pressure points and acupuncture. The point is that I knew sea bands really worked when I overheard one of the crew telling another sailor: "They work on the skipper and he doesn't even believe in them." I suppose we all have our foibles. Not that this rules out the placebo effect.

Other simple remedies can help with seasickness. Ginger is a traditional remedy for motion sickness and problems of balance. Chinese sailors chew up to a gram of raw ginger. This seems excessive. You can take it in whatever form you like. On PETRONELLA we eat crystallized ginger. I will happily eat this in harbor or on land. I really like crystallized ginger. Take it the day before you go sailing. Eat all you can. Chew ginger root day and night. As far as I know ginger has no side effects.

Apart from that, eat light and fat free the night before you set off and don't over-indulge in alcohol. Heavy dinners punish the hung-over, dehydrated and tired sailor starting a passage.

Once underway, seasickness usually becomes less of a problem and I have the greatest sympathy for those who never get over it. Take care though: insidious and significant effects lurk just below the surface. Continuous motion is a constant part of life at sea. On my first Atlantic crossing I didn't fully appreciate this. I didn't realize that continuous motion would stop my brain giving proper thought to the lesser events of our lives, such as just getting through each day.

> Staying up on deck breathing fresh air and looking at a steady horizon can help delay the inevitable, but the moment will come when the sufferer must go below and lie down. Don't fiddle and faff. This is not the time to straighten sheets or re-arrange the bedding. Nor is it the time to slowly undress and fold your pants. The instant you go below you must lie down. Don't delay. Relax. Breathe easily. If things improve, remove your boots and other antisocial outerwear. If they don't, leave them on. Better to sleep in your boots than be sick in them. Don't do anything which stops you lying flat with your head on a pillow in the most stable part of the boat.

Cabin fever

A small yacht at sea is the ideal laboratory to study human stress. Apart from the physical discomforts, there are the psychological ones. We are caged and unable to escape. The natural elements of sea and storm make us fearful. The social strains of living always in company and having no privacy or time to ourselves make us stressed. All animals have fears. Humans more than other animals can create stress just by thinking.

When we heighten worries into neuroses not even medical researchers know what electro-chemical stimuli are firing off in our bodies and brains. A few minutes or hours of stress is harmless. It is what our species is built for. But on an ocean voyage we face days and weeks of stress. Evolution didn't design us to be caged.

> Oh my, but it took forever for this penny to drop on my first crossing. I mean, there we all were, sardined into a little sailing boat that wouldn't keep still long enough for us to scratch in comfort. What effect did all that physical dislocation have on our emotional states? We stood watches every live-long day and never realized that when some of us were wide awake and raring for noise and action others were bitchy with tiredness and wanting to be left alone. No wonder tensions seemed to grow as land grew nearer and then dissolve as soon as our anchor dropped.

On PETRONELLA no one asks why one of us has decided to sit out on the bowsprit for a long while. When one of us retires below with a book, they are left undisturbed. Sometimes it is enough just to be as far away from others as you can be, even if the distance is less than a whisper can carry.

Domestic ritual

Few things inspire confidence and impart more comfort than the continuation of domestic rituals in worsening weather. I have had the pleasure of sailing with crew who had the skills and iron-stomachs to produce hot nutritious food regardless of the conditions.

> M called it a moussaka. But I knew we had none of the ingredients for this dish. He found alternative ways to make a white sauce and a substitute for eggplant which he refused to name. He used every saucepan and pot we had. The galley overflowed into the cockpit. I lacked the stomach to watch as M balanced in the increasingly jerky movement of the boat. Half my mind wondered how bad the new weather would be. The other half wondered who would do the washing up. When the meal was ready it was delicious and just what we needed in the hours before the rising gale, while we still had interest in eating, and M's balance in the galley had made us confident that we could cope with the coming storm.

Work at sea is at times intensely physical. Waves, wind and spray chill the body. Hot food is essential to your energy levels. When conditions deteriorate it is wise to get the hot food while you still can and prepare cold food for when you can't. On top of this, the fearful crew is psychologically strengthened by seeing that the domestic pattern is maintained even in worsening weather.

Look around your galley. Think of your little boat pounding into head seas at six knots, going through 10-foot plus waves in 30-knot winds. Do you have the hand holds to balance, a good place for your feet and a bulkhead to brace against? Just making coffee is a major task. More ambitious cooking can be truly hazardous. If the cook is lucky they will just get some impressive bruises. Rearrange everything with this in mind.

> Coming down the Caribbean at nearly eight knots we were rolling and pitching. E was in the galley chopping vegetables for the next

meal. Suddenly I saw him do a back flip out the galley and into the navigatorium, big chopping knife in hand. I was lucky. He didn't draw blood and cause me to faint. Shortly after this I fitted the bum-strap for the galley.

Making food and eating it is hard in a slamming sea. You only need ten minutes of steady downwind sailing or better still in harbor but the sea isn't offering this. Try stopping the boat. Try any direction but windward. Rough weather becomes so much more comfortable when you heave-to and stop. Do this for the other difficult jobs or when you need to sleep.

Life in the cockpit

It can be too easy to rely on electronics to sail your little ship. The real blue-water sailors, the ones you only read about because they are off where no one else dares go in some uncomfortably small and exceedingly slow vessel, often have a fine disregard for modern technology. They fear that "information overload" and full time screen-watching removes the essential natural senses sailors should cultivate. They are right in many respects. On a small sailing boat independent of the shore, life is best spent in the cockpit, in full harmony with wind and waves, where nothing restricts your view of the clouds, the various weather fronts and your instant weather picture book. Develop human skills. Don't be left feeling helpless when the machine dies on you, thanks to its unnatural diet of salt laden air. Perhaps it's a generational thing. Perhaps because I learned to sail on small yachts before GPS was invented and VHF was only for special days I agree with these bluewater sailors, even if I don't want to beat through the Magellan Straits or hack a lump off an iceberg to cool my gin.

T was a big ship captain living on the next door sailing boat. He had sailed from Miami to Horta like us but not on the same route. T had big ship weather and tide information available on his laptop, and he sailed his boat the big ship way, from the computer screen. His GPS was linked to his self-steering and all he had to do was change the waypoint to sail around a bad bit of weather and the wheel turned accordingly. He had sailed across the Gulf Stream towards Bermuda but got warning of light wind and headed north to catch the Westerlies. He went nearly to Nova Scotia but when a gale headed his way he went south. Later he went due north again to catch better winds.

He showed me the track. He must have sailed 1,000 miles more than us but he took a week less. Still, I think we had the better view.

You probably know about the "hood effect" of only ever looking out in the same direction. It is easier to look ahead than astern, easier to look to lee than up to weather. A more extreme form of "hood effect" is to spend your time navigating from the chart table console. Our navigation on passage is largely confined to recording GPS positions and occasionally plotting them. We don't spend much time on other instruments, not even getting weather information or listening to the SSB radio.

The philosopher Martin Heidegger observed that technology is the art of arranging the world so that we don't have to experience it. I sometime wonder whether gathering all that electronically derived information on weather and geography and ships over the horizon, not to mention the minutia of family and friends ashore, is displacement activity to avoid the fresh air on deck. When I sit at the chart table I am always surprised at how much time has passed playing with screens and charts and radio receivers. I lose any urgency to get back into the cockpit and take a look at the real world. But the cockpit is truly the real world of the sailor, not the e-navigatorium.

Watch out, ships about

The International Collision Regulations don't cut much slack when it comes to watchkeeping. Looking out for other vessels is a continuous requirement. I think this is absolutely right and wish that the big ships would take the message more to heart. Unfortunately too many are relying on automatic systems and putting commercial requirements over compliance with regulations. They are giving themselves a bad reputation. Clearly it isn't just singlehanded sailors who can't meet the International Collision Regulations.

The main reason you are keeping watch is that you must not rely on other vessels to see you even, and especially when, on a collision course. The sailing literature and the stories sailors tell one another are full of near collisions, averted only at the last minute by chance or desperation. On my first crossing we were 300 miles from Africa and 200 miles south of the Cape Verde islands, having seen no ships since leaving, when a large, ocean-going fishing boat bore down on us in the dark and early hours of the morning. It was less than one hundred yards away when it turned, just as we gibed the other way. It wasn't our lack of lights that was at fault. We had all our navigation and deck and mast lights on—tricolor, bicolor, steaming and spreader lights—and were shining a half-million candela megabeam straight at what I hoped was the bridge. I've lost the innocence to simply shine a flashlight on our sails as I was once taught.

> It was a fishing boat, of course, and all the action when fishing is behind you in the nets and the trawl. That was why they weren't looking out ahead to where we were. I wonder what supertankers would say to excuse their failures to look out?

Radar doesn't help as much as it should or as we expect it to. The term radar-assisted collision has not come into common use for no reason. What I have in mind is that big ships don't see us little ships on their radar but us little ships with radar can also get it badly wrong. During 2005 the sailing magazines were full of the sinking of WAHKUNA, a British yacht that misread its radar screen when trying to cross shipping lanes.

> It was May. WAHKUNA was crossing the Channel from France to the Solent. Visibility deteriorated in the early morning, around 0930, and the crew kept radar watch. When they saw they were on a collision course with a vessel two miles away they slowed and later stopped the yacht, calculating that the ship would pass a mile and a half ahead. When the huge bow of the ship came out of the fog four boat lengths to port it was too late to get out the way. The front of the yacht was pulverized and she sank quickly. The container ship had seen WAHKUNA on its radar and were confused by the yacht's decision to slow down. They had calculated that the yacht would pass ahead of them by about three quarters of a mile. At the moment of impact the ship's master had lost contact and thought the yacht was at least 1,300 feet off to port. The ship didn't feel a thing.

In its report on the incident the British Marine Accident Investigation Branch (MAIB) concluded that both vessels were in part to blame and that neither could have been keeping adequate radar watch. WAHKUNA would have been able to cross the ship and should have continued on course. By stopping she confused the deck officers of the big ship and put herself right in its path. In effect, WAHKUNA's crew needed professional competence to understand the changing plots on the radar screen as she went from two knots to stopped, and again as the now stopped yacht, without speed or steerage, began to swing. WAHKUNA's radar was showing the container ship coming up to starboard, but the ship hit her portside. Understanding this from the changing plots shown on a radar screen, when you have no visible marks to orient yourself, is not easy. Nor is it likely that any one on the yacht was still looking at the radar screen in those few minutes from stopping to being hit.

MAIB recommendations apply to us all. They call for better training for yachts using radar, and greater skill in using automatic plotting. We need to make manual plots in a gathering crisis rather than rely on visual interpretation of the screen.

MAIB criticized the container ship for assuming that a passing distance of three quarters of a mile was sufficient (the minimum is usually one mile) and for not slowing down from 25 knots as visibility worsened. The master of the container ship had been on the bridge for 14 hours. His judgment may have been clouded by fatigue and he should have ordered at least one extra crew to keep visual watch. It was also possible that the huge ship maintained its 25-knot speed because of commercial pressures. MAIB found that only one of the 19 nearby ships reduced speed, even though the dense fog at times reduced visibility to 150 feet.

Big ship officers make no bones about it. They are watching for other big ships to heave up over the horizon, not little yachts. A big ship gives a big un-cluttered radar signal that can be locked onto and monitored. Any little blips be-tween the two ships may be a yacht or just clutter, coming and going, hardly to be bothered with, too much to think about.

In July 2004 MAIB published findings from another and very inter-esting study. They had 1,647 watchkeeping incidents to choose from and choose to investigate in detail 66 accidents involving 75 vessels. The common features they found were terrifying: fatigued officers, one man on the bridge at night, missed course alterations, no watch alarms. Required standards of manning, hours of work and lookout were not effective. Small yachts were not being seen until too late, if at all. Bridge officers placed great reliance on radar and automatic radar plotting yet on 30 vessels radar was not being used properly and the ColRegs were contravened. Not that ColRegs are relevant if the approaching vessel has not been seen. Never assume that the approaching vessel has seen your little yacht. Oh yes, and two-thirds of the accidents involved fishing vessels.

Other vessels are the single main reason for us yachts to keep a good watch but what about the other things out there that we might see if we were keeping watch? Flotsam and jetsam, for example, including that most scary of jetsam, the steel deck container.

I have yet to see a big deck container at sea but I have seen plenty of large steel tanks and cylinders floating awash 1,000 miles offshore, and I wouldn't want to run into them. It doesn't have to damage your hull to damage your boat. Rudders and propellers and self steering are all vulnerable. On a day with good wind and the boat doing six knots there is enough noise and movement to prevent those at the back end of the boat feeling an impact. It might be much later in the day before you notice water rising above the floorboards.

Because I have never seen a container at sea doesn't mean I haven't been close to one. I did, after all, see that strange spiky contraption when 100 miles offshore, when it was too close for comfort. Malcolm McConnell reports a similar experience in "First Crossing." One thousand miles offshore, midway between New York and the Azores, he saw four rusting drums strapped together, one of which was ripped and lacking buoyancy. They were twenty yards away and rising on the crest of a wave. He saw the steel grid bolted under the drums. Girders had been ripped off to form a jagged trident. At ten yards the sharp fork of the girders were three feet above the water and sliding down the wave straight at the fiberglass hull of his yacht MATATA. A fluke gust of wind caused MATATA to luff up and the girders slid by a foot away instead of ripping a hole in the hull. When they crested the next wave Malcolm turned for another look at the dangerous debris but it was already invisible, lost among the waves even though less than a couple of boat lengths away.

Steel containers are the disgrace of modern commercial shipping. They are carried on deck, often up to seven tiers or fifty feet high, because that way they avoid cargo dues. Those containing light or floating goods will not sink until the waves have broken down their watertight seals or smashed the doors open and allowed the cargo to escape. One container full of computer monitors was found still floating after three years.

Nothing about containers is good news for us small boat sailors. The regulations governing their construction are to safeguard the contents of the containers. So they begin life virtually waterproof and unsinkable. The highest containers in a stack are the lightest, because that makes sense for the ship's stability, but it's the highest ones that are most likely to topple overboard. If lightness equates with floatability, these are the containers that will sweep the seas as often as Moby Dick. Ships don't carry the gear to recover lost containers, so once overboard it stays overboard. Containers are sociable. They seldom jump ship alone. And they are unloved. There is no system to track a lost container. A container might have a commercial value many times that of a yacht but no one has thought to give it one of those little radio devices that tells the shore-side organizers where their ocean racers and ARC cruisers are, night and day.

A 20-foot steel container can displace 37 tons. A 40-foot container can displace more than 70 tons. How does this compare with your yacht? A container awash is as dangerous as an unmarked rock at sea and no more likely to be spotted from your deck. The sharp corner of one of these reinforced steel boxes can pierce steel plating. The loss of a 3,000-ton bulk container ship in bad weather in the Bay of Biscay was probably due to hitting a container.

No one knows how many of these containers are adrift at any time, partly because insurers will not give out statistics and ships are not required to report their loss. A ship's master is only required to report a lost container if it contains dangerous substances. All masters are obliged to report a dangerous derelict when they come across one at sea, but apparently they can turn a blind eye if it used to be on their deck. One report estimated that in recent years around 40,000 to 50,000 containers were lost from Atlantic container ships. Some have sunk, but new ones take their place every year.

Here is the solution to the Bermuda Triangle Mystery. The currents around the Sargasso Sea, where the Bermuda Triangle lies, eternally trap flotsam and jetsam. It must float for ever or sink. With 40,000 or more containers out there no innocent ships can cross without hitting and being holed by one of these, yet they float so low they escape detection and fuel the mysterious nature of the disasters. What was there before the age of containers, you ask? Alien flying saucers that had run out of fuel trying to get sensible answers from the earthlings they had abducted, of course.

During my crossing from the BVI to the Azores I entertained myself by looking carefully for containers and big chunks of dangerous flotsam. The Horse Latitudes was ideal for this, having flat seas and a fair amount of floating rubbish and it was usually the sight of some rubbish going by that stimulated my interest. Here are the findings from my observations:

- even big lumps of stuff awash are unlikely to be seen until within a boat length
- if they are dead ahead of the boat, the foredeck obscures them
- flotsam is most visible as it passes abeam less than 40 feet away. More than that and you won't see it
- buoys with good top marks could be seen at half a mile but only if no more than a few hundred yards either side of our course. We saw most stuff on the windward side, since we were usually looking that way.

The snag is that these floating dangers are random events. You won't see them except by chance, no matter how scrupulous your night watches. Pure chance is a poor reason for keeping watches. These 20lb steel gas bottles, steel boilers the size of a garbage can, rectangular steel tanks, planks and logs of sodden wood, all of it large and only just awash, were nearly invisible even in broad and bright daylight.

> I know we hit something one night because there was a great clunk at the bow. We guessed it was a baulk of timber. It didn't strike the right note to be steel.

These floating menaces are there by accident. Other things are there by design, and with no more effort made to warn us of them.

I had never seen radar beacons so far offshore until I sailed through the Horse Latitudes. We saw the first when it was half a mile ahead of us and 100 yards off to port. It looked a simple device. The ten-foot pole had a radar reflector on one end and a float on the other. I steered closer to get a better look. I doubt if we would have seen it if we had passed by a mile away. We saw the second one a few days later. It made us wonder if there were hundreds out here or whether we had been lucky enough to find the only two in the whole ocean. The beacon wasn't large but it would have made a distinct clunk and damaged our pretty paint work if we had run into it, even at our gentle speed.

These things didn't fit the Heath-Robinson descriptions I got from marine agencies about their current meters. Current meters can be fixed to the seabed or made to drift slowly. The fixed sort dangle different instruments between their surface buoy and their seabed mooring. I'm not sure these are ever tethered in the depths of two or three miles that we were in when we saw our unidentified floating object. However, since current meters can be left in place for about a year they have plenty of time to break free and go off into the deeper ocean. The surface buoy has a radar reflector and light to help prevent collisions.

The drifting current meter monitors water movement through sock-like bags hung beneath the buoy. These bags act like a drogue to keep the buoy roughly in position, but the designer helps by giving the buoy a low profile and hence low windage. Low profile means it is harder for us to see. The buoy has a strobe light but I suppose that if the battery runs down before the mother ship returns the buoy will drift invisibly out into the ocean.

Nor were these floaters the bright yellow, space-age Argo weather buoys deployed since year 2000. About 3,000 untethered Argo weather floats are now adrift, sending back vital oceanographic information. These clever buoys hang around at different depths for about ten days monitoring drift, temperatures and salinity at different levels in a vertical column of water as they first dive and then slowly rise back to the surface to transmit their data. With only an hour at the surface and a distance of about 180 miles between buoys you would be unlucky to bump into one. If you did, the owners say, you probably wouldn't damage your yacht. That's reassuring as you surf off the gale-driven wave at double theoretical hull speed and see a glimpse of designer-yellow against the black of the night.

The job of the person on watch is not just to look for things to avoid. It is also to routinely check for damaged sails, fatigued rigging and breaking deck gear. This doesn't mean you have to do it at night, of course. If you set night watches for this or for fear of a dangerous rigging failure or a burst seacock you should have done more maintenance before you ever set out. Routine inspection is best done in good daylight when you will have more chance of telling the difference between a harmless streak of seaweed and a fatal crevice crack in a stainless steel turnbuckle. Don't waste your sleep over it.

Through the yawning gates of oblivion

The British sailing author Frank Mulville should be more widely read than he is. He has written several of those inspiring books about calamity and near calamity including *Schooner Integrity, Terschelling Sands* and *Rescue and Recovery: Iskra's ordeal in the Hebrides.* I have in mind the distinction he drew between tiredness, fatigue and exhaustion. Frank had been on a long journey to the north and was now sailing south alone, returning to his home waters. It was a hard journey of several days and nights at sea with little chance to rest. Disaster struck when he was almost home, sailing in the waters he had known all his life, an area of sand banks and shoals stretching 30 to 40 miles offshore. He knew the names and orders of the shoals like a mother knows the names and preferences of her children. He made an error and put himself on the most unforgiving bank of all, a shingle bank remote from help. In one tide his boat would be lost, sucked tight into the shingle and held in that stony grip until the waves battered it to pieces and nothing was left to be seen. He was lucky. A friend in his powerful fishing boat saw what had happened and pulled Frank clear before the shingle took its hold.

The reason for this near total loss was the difference between tiredness and exhaustion. Frank Mulville was beyond good judgment. He was almost beyond caring. He was just one more in the long line of storm-weary skippers who turned the wrong way and put their ship aground.

I don't personally know many boats that have been lost from lack of sleep, but I know a few. One friend was sailing from the Eastern Seaboard to the Azores when he sailed onto the rocks of Faial and lost his boat. He knew he was too close to land to leave the boat to the self steering for long, but he was exhausted and craving sleep. He slept with a kitchen timer close to his ear, in the time-honored way of singlehanders. Perhaps he had become immune to it, his brain registering the sound as normal. Perhaps he should have fitted an intruder alarm and wired his clock to that. All he did was sleep an hour longer than intended. When the wind shifted his self steering drove him onshore. He was lucky. He is a non-swimmer and managed to walk ashore.

It isn't always singlehanders. A very experienced sailor friend sailing with his family from Trinidad approached the Venezuelan islands of Los Testigos at night. He was on watch. He dozed off, confident that they were still ten miles from the islands but misjudging the strength of the west-running current. He woke up in the surf and it was too late to get the boat clear before she grounded. She broke up in a few days.

When G and I go sailing by ourselves or even with a third crewmember I don't just think of us being shorthanded. I think of us as being serial singlehanders. When the chips are down, or when sleep is essential, singlehanding is what you will be doing. It is no bad thing to think things through as though you were a singlehander, or to talk to singlehanders about how they manage. They have an ocean of experience for us to learn from.

Lessons from a singlehander on his first Atlantic crossing. Never allow the ocean into the boat. This is not a trivial point. Many people sail their boats so that they pound into the seas and take a lot of spray and solid water, increasing wear, tear and subsequent expense. Avoid surfing down waves, broaching or letting waves poop you. Jumping from wave to wave and going into free fall in the troughs may win races but shortens the life of a cruising hull. Always reduce sail early. Ocean-cruiser Eric Hiscock wrote that if you are thinking of putting in a reef it's already too late.

Training for sleep

We all find it easy to think about the on-board systems vital to the safe running of the boat. Often we fail to see ourselves and the rest of the crew as part of that system but watchkeeping systems should be about maintaining the human energy levels as well as keeping a lookout. The question of how long a person can stand watch is not as good a question as how long does a person need to rest and sleep to be alert and effective. Perhaps we should decide what off-watch periods are needed and then see what time is left for watches. Perhaps we should spend as much time training our sleep patterns as we do learning the rules of the road or how to repair diesel engines.

Studies into the sleep patterns of those who do extreme things, including those who race oceans and go round the world singlehanded, have produced a lot of information about the nature of sleep and how to make up in quality for the lack of quantity. Most people need about eight hours sleep a day, regardless of age. In a crewed ocean racing boat a crewmember might be getting six hours of sleep a day; a singlehander will be getting less and in a less regular or fulfilling way.

The brain's clock has evolved its circadian rhythm, that cycle of sleep and waking over a 24-hour period, over eons of time to induce sleep shortly after darkness and stimulate waking shortly after dawn. The 20th century introduction of electric light and 24-hour Internet has been too short for us to reset our clocks to new patterns of wakefulness but fortunately the body is naturally flexible enough to adapt to broken patterns of sleep. Studies show that a normal person can get by with about four hours sleep on average, taken in naps ranging from 20 minutes to an hour and that the body can adjust to new, highly disturbed patterns in as little as three days. I suppose we shorthanded and singlehanding sailors will eventually arrive at this ability to grab sleep in naps but a program of hard training in advance of passage making will get us there sooner. What you most want from training is to get to sleep as quickly as possible. Leave the rest to nature. A tired body will naturally move through the lighter stages of sleeping and into deep, slow-wave recuperative sleep.

Frank Mulville taught himself a sleeping regime to help him sail singlehanded. His training started while he and the boat were still in harbor. He restricted his sleep to an hour at a time, spreading across the 24 hours. It was hard at first but he wrote that he was soon able to fall asleep like a child and wake like a dog, ready for action. He soon realized that an hour was the wrong period for his body pattern. When he increased the sleep period to 1hour 15minutes he no longer needed an alarm.

Frank of course was just an amateur. Professional solo racers like Ellen MacArthur go into sleep training six months ahead of a race.

We can get to sleep more quickly if we fool ourselves into thinking we are at home in our rock-solid, feather-pillowed beds rather than at sea in a dangerous, bouncy environment. Follow well-established rules of eating and watchkeeping. Read, have a hot drink or do whatever you usually do to relax yourself into sleep.

The most vital element of sleep training is the same as Plato's advice: Know yourself. Nature divides us into owls and larks, night people and morning people. I am a night person. G is a lark. She is bright from the moment she wakes. I take two cups of coffee and two hours to get to what others consider a normal level of efficiency. But shortly after dusk G begins yawning heavily and soon has to be sent to bed, while my body begins to rev up for passage planning and complex if tedious arguments about the meaning of life. G is a siesta person. Her energy runs down in the afternoon and she needs to sleep. I hate siestas. I find it hard enough to drop off to sleep at night and near impossible if I have napped in the afternoon. Yet oddly, the owls are reputedly better able to adapt to fluctuating patterns of sleep than the larks. If training to optimize your rest during periods of broken sleep, decide if you are an owl or a lark and time your naps accordingly. Breaking up your total sleep allowance into a series of naps may help because the most refreshing sleep comes at the beginning of the sleep. Get in plenty of beginnings. Remember, though, that while sleep can often be made up during the day we humans get our best sleep and make our worst mistakes at night, so keep your longest periods of sleep for the dark hours.

> When the 20-minute alarm goes off, only do simple things. Take a look around the horizon. Sniff the wind. This is no time to check the rigging or plot positions. The point is to stay in that delightful half awake state so you can get back to sleep without delay. But the converse is that when the alarm sounds and you have to do something difficult and complicated, be aware that you may still be half asleep, lacking full judgment and efficiency.

Lack of sleep is as bad as being drugged. Tasks take longer. Jobs are done badly. Decisions and calculations are more likely to be wrong. Even a little tiredness can warp judgment. I value sleep above almost anything else in keeping a crew focused and happy. Too often the off-watch crew will have their rest broken by minor things. Sleep needs more respect than this. We have a rule that a sleeping person is to be left sleeping. No unnecessary noise around them. Sail the boat steadily. Reef or unreef when the watch changes. Don't wake a sleeper unless you need them. If only the others on the boat honored the rule as I do. Looking in the shaving mirror I have seen the murderous sense of injustice in the red-eyed zombie who thinks someone else is getting more sleep but needs it less.

I hate 24-hour passages. No one gets into the rhythm of the boat. No one gets proper rest. We all live off our reserves. Thank goodness a trip of five or seven nights at sea is not a nightmare extrapolation of a 24-hour passage. The wonderful thing about a long trip at sea is that you get into the sweet rhythm of the boat and the ocean. Not that this is necessarily the best exercise for the brain. If you haven't already done a week or three-week-long passage in a small sailboat you may not realize how easy it is for the brain to become dull. Add this to the tiredness of a disturbed night or the effort of clinging to your bunk in rough weather and you have massively reduced your mental capacity to cope with a crisis.

Sleep is about good management. Skipper and crew both need to be highly disciplined about resting. Make sure being off watch means you can rest. An anxious crew will fail to sleep during their time off, but won't be able to keep watch when it's their turn. Skippers whose anxiety drives them to always keep an eye on their crew are heading for exhaustion. Life must be arranged as much as possible so that everyone is able to sleep when things are tough and everyone must recognize the need to catch up on sleep when the going is easy. Put sleep in the bank for when you can't get enough of it later. Events, when they turn against you, will empty the sleep-bank faster and deeper than you would believe. It isn't possible to create a "sleep surplus" ahead of a period of deprivation, but at least you can be fully rested and fully charged before you hit the hard times.

Setting the watch

Some crews like to make sure that everyone gets their full share of day time. They slip in a shorter or longer watch to achieve this egalitarian end. However, sleep benefits from a fixed routine, so it may be better to decide fixed watches according to the owls and larks in the crew and keep the same watch routine day after day. That's how we usually work on PETRONELLA. We decide at the outset what length of watch best suits the crew numbers and weather conditions, and then stick to it.

With two or three people on board we usually set three-hour watches during the hours of darkness. This is probably the best interval for a shorthanded crew in most conditions although a hard beat or cold conditions can make an hour quite long enough. In the easy conditions of the Horse Latitudes with just E for crew, the two of us split the night into even halves. This maximized the time for sleeping. The routine worked and we stuck to it except when weather or problems gave us reason to change it. As soon as conditions allowed, we returned to this routine. Overall, we slept enough to be fully charged ahead of the difficult times when sleep was broken or had to be reduced.

> Our watches start around dusk and end around dawn. But crossing the Atlantic involves crossing time zones. When our clock time slips we reset it to fit with daylight and darkness. In this way the clock time of the boat is roughly local time and our body clocks are not very different from land time when we arrive.

Whatever watchkeeping system you start with, don't be a slave to it. Play around until you have the one that makes most efficient use of the crew, and vary it whenever circumstances change.

The point is to make the time spent looking out as effective as possible. I'm happy to have my watchkeepers take periodic looks around the horizon and otherwise spend their time resting below, even napping. I want a slow, serious, all-encompassing look right around the horizon every 20 minutes. I don't think the time someone spends in the cockpit crouched under the dodger and wishing they weren't there adds anything to the safety of the boat.

> One crew crossing from the Caribbean to the Azores timed how long it took a ship on the horizon to get close to them as 25 minutes. On average they reckoned this worked out as 20-30 minutes. They decided on the grounds of probability that a ship is unlikely to appear just after the watch goes below, so they timed their looks around the horizon for every half hour.

We don't have formal day-time watches. I think they are a luxury a small crew must do without. On PETRONELLA when the weather and sailing conditions are good there is usually always someone in the cockpit during the day and I assume they will always be looking around. That's what most people, even avid book readers, will do. If someone wants to take time off to sleep during the day, another crewmember seems naturally to make it his/her business to be on deck or keeping watch. It is different when the weather and sailing conditions are not good. Then we always have crew on watch to manage the boat.

The problem with putting people in the cockpit for two to four hours continuously every day when nothing much is happening is that your key personnel may be ineffective when the crisis arrives. Small crews need explicit strategies to prevent physical and mental exhaustion and be fully alert when needed. I take comfort from the solo sailors.

> Frank Mulville did not agree that singlehanders have a greater risk of being run down, even when there is no one else to keep lookout. He found that being alone brought an increased concentration and heightened awareness of what was around him. In practice this concentration keeps a lone sailor sensitive, strung up, mind on edge, able to see things before they happen. In short, they keep him or her alive. Moitessier and many other solo sailors said the same.

G and I are as close to being singlehanders as a crew of two ever gets and I think something of Frank Mulville's heightened awareness has rubbed off on us. It is quite surprising how often we sense the need to take a look around the horizon or the deck. Of course, there is rarely anything to see but we feel really good when there is. There are times when we get a little lax but events usually conspire to make us return to full vigilance.

> **PETRONELLA log, Horse Latitudes**
> We've seen five ships today, two of which passed within half a mile, so tonight we will be more vigilant. I jot down a calculation. At five knots and a line of sight of ten miles to its bridge, a ship on our nose doing 15 knots gives us half an hour to see it, watch it and avoid it. Such calculations running through my mind would only keep me awake so I might as well be up on watch.

Between the Azores and Europe we saw ships every other day, which is more than I had expected, but come the moment when we had a closer than comfortable encounter G sixth-sensed it instantly.

> G called R up for help and then the pair of them called me. All hands on deck. The night so dark and moonless. We in deep ocean, mid way between the Azores and Spain. A small coaster showing full deck lights was less than a mile to port. We were overtaking it so obviously it had stopped. How curious. We flashed passed on a good beam reach. Behind us a much larger vessel had come from being

hull-down and was maneuvering alongside the coaster. Even curiouser. What are they doing in mid ocean and why? G is wide-awake and clearly in tune with nature, so she might as well have another hour on watch.

My practical views may not be up to the watchkeeping requirements laid down in the International Collision Regulations. As long as I have been sailing there has been a debate about whether singlehanded sailing is safe. It is certainly true that no singlehander on a long passage could meet the requirements of the ColRegs for continuous watchkeeping and nor can a shorthanded crew of two or three. But sailing, like life, is about coping with events. With a shorthanded crew you need to balance the sleep-losses inherent with the watchkeeping requirements of the ColRegs against the need for a fully functioning crew when landfall or a storm or the unforeseen crisis arrives.

Watches and watchfulness

Watchfulness is a different matter to watchkeeping. A good clue to how watchful you are is how much wildlife and flotsam you see. On our passages we always see dolphin and jellyfish, the occasional turtle and whale, and a fair amount of flotsam. We also see wonderful skies and fascinating waves. We have met people who crossed the Atlantic and didn't see a single dolphin. Even if they had been chained to the stanchions during their watches these people could not have been keeping a worthwhile lookout. A good sailor is watchful and alert all the time. Change your lookout position. You see much more when standing compared to sitting and even more when you go forward to the mast. In windy or rainy weather, beware the "hood effect" of wearing blinkers and losing your sense of what the weather is doing.

The horizon looks so far away, but actually it isn't. If you stand up at your main mast your eye will probably be about ten feet above sea level, giving you a horizon of less than four miles. Of course, something taller than a wave will be visible further than this. Standing at your mast you will see a 30-foot-high object almost eight miles away and a 70-foot object a little over ten miles away. Sitting in the cockpit your horizon isn't much more than a couple of miles.

Watch and survive

The little oddities recorded in my log book on my second Atlantic crossing re-inforced the curious lessons I learned during my first. We see more ships at night than day. Leaving aside the times when we are close to shipping routes or separation lanes, it was not unusual to see the lights of a ship at night whereas by day it always seemed to be an accident when we saw the superstructure of a ship hull down on the horizon.

> In the fading light at dusk I glanced out and saw a dim shape dipping on the horizon. Looking carefully I realized it was a ship, almost lost in the background cloud and only visible when we rose on a swell. It was pure chance that I had spotted it. Half an hour later I could see the faint glimmer of its navigation lights, but half an hour after that, in the full darkness of night, the navigation lights shone clear and strong even though the ship was now much further off.

The significance of this day/night difference determines your watchkeeping policy and in turn your chances of survival on a long ocean crossing. On my first crossing we evolved several policies on night watches as we sailed to our African point of departure and when we cast off for the ocean we planned only to keep night watches when needed. This changed the moment we nearly got run down by a huge ocean-going fishing boat on day four. What saved us was our own watchkeeping, not the ship's. Our lights were obviously no help to us. We had every one burning brightly. Nor had they seen us on radar. Not all ships keep good radar watch or indeed run with their radar on, regardless of the International Collision Regulations.

Some of the best known sailing writers hardly bothered with night watches while in deep ocean and I doubt they felt any greater need for formal watches during the day. I mean, apart from your own greater watchfulness, there is more chance of the other ship spotting your sails in daylight than in darkness. The indomitable Beryl Smeeton said that she and her husband Miles always had a cocktail and turned in for a full night's rest. I don't have the nerve to go as far as that. Were the seas emptier in those days? Did ships travel within more strongly defined routes?

> In the days of sail the bulk of commercial shipping went where generations of experience told them the wind and currents were favorable. Even if they didn't get the breeze they wanted on a climatic

route they had no onboard information to guide them to a better route. Then came the age of steam. Ships' engines could drive vessels down the shortest line almost regardless of wind and current. Now we have arrived at the age of communications. Two forces come into play which make the route taken by a ship much less constrained and much less predictable. First, the business end. The ship owner doing deals ashore can relay new pick-ups and destinations at any time of night or day. His clients and his ships are just on the end of some telecommunications link or another. Second, the sea conditions. The ship will be plugged into some routing service which advises day by day or even hour by hour course alterations to optimize weather and sea conditions. This means that the paths taken by modern shipping bear no relation to the course lines plotted on old routing charts. They go where they are told whenever they are told. In deep ocean, on no obvious line between any A or B, a little yacht might well find itself briefly observing a commercial ship for no apparent reason.

Seeing more ships at night than day cannot be because more ships are out and near us at night. It has to be due to our watchkeeping and their visibility. At night the main reason for being in the cockpit is to lookout. We are more actively looking for ships. In daylight we have other things to do and ships often have to be quite close to be noticed. Unless taking a serious interest in the horizon, I wouldn't expect to see a ship that is three miles away. At night this is different. We easily see the lights of a ship hull down over the horizon, perhaps seven to ten miles away.

Imagine, then, if after a few days at sea we conclude that there was no shipping around and we do not need to keep night watches. Every day would confirm our view that there are no ships and every night we would be oblivious to those that passed. With good luck we would cross the ocean well rested and able to report that there was so little shipping that watches were not needed. And others like us would say the same. And with a little less luck we would have had a very bad fright one night or even been run down.

Night visions

Many sailors try to avoid night sailing. Some I know even made it down the Eastern Seaboard to the Caribbean without sailing more than a single night at a time. On an Atlantic crossing this just isn't possible, so it is best to get in a bit of practice first and concentrate on the good things about night sailing.

Nearly all my night sailing is done shorthanded, without the luxury of sharing the night watch. This, for me, makes the night watch very special. It is when I have the boat to myself, to watch the sky and sea or just let my mind drift in a way which the bright light of day does not allow. Perhaps introspection of the woken mind is as necessary to our well-being as the dreams of sleep.

I hate some night sailing. I hate night sailing in cold wet weather, when the body cries out to be below. I hate night sailing when it is only a 24-hour passage, when the body stays awake the whole time and you need match sticks to hold your gritty eyes open. But the further south I have sailed, the more I have enjoyed night sailing. To sit in the cockpit with nothing more than a light shirt for warmth, having been at sea for at least three days and fully adjusted to the rhythms of the boat. Now I can take full pleasure in the stars and the moon, the planets and shooting stars.

PETRONELLA log
The stars far offshore were wonderfully bright but better than these was the moon. When we sailed with half moons they left the night sky to the tracery of the stars. The big, blowsy full moon gave way to nothing. I had never seen such rising full moons as those around Madeira. It rose from the horizon as big and golden as the sun. A more primitive and ignorant mind than my own would have sworn that the earth had a second sun. The silver light only came when the moon was well clear of the horizon, and then it lit the whole world. It gave enough light to read by. We barely needed navigation lights and sometimes just ran with our kerosene light in the rigging.

Teach your crew and yourself to look forward to night sailing. When conditions are right, take opportunities to make longer than usual runs, turning what might easily be a series of day hops into a single three- or four-day passage. You don't even have to be sailing to be on the sea at night. When we travel down coasts where fishermen have left their pots to trap the unwary prop or fin keel, we often spend our night hove-to rather than trying to make progress. It can turn a 70-mile dash full of anxiety about whether we will reach the next harbor before dark into a relaxing time, full of that special enjoyment sailors get from just being at sea.

Watching for fun

The real entertainment at sea is the sea, the sky and all things in them. If you get bored looking at the sea then not even a thousand videos will keep you entertained. I am fascinated by all the moods of the sea. Storms are just the most dramatic of the shows it puts on, with all the concentrated force of an orchestra hitting the loud end of Wagner. I also like the gentle times when the sea is a string quartet and the astonishing stillness of the calm, like the silence of a great cathedral when the rolling organ echo ends and before the coughing starts.

Out in deep ocean, where there is no background light, the stars become as fascinating as a drama and the shooting stars are the divas. The names of the stars take us all the way back in human time and place to the desert dwelling Sumerians, the earliest of known civilizations. But stars, like phosphorescence, or even like flying fish and the ever-entertaining dolphins, lack the great corporeal scale to amaze and awe and entertain us that whales have.

I have seen the grey Atlantic whales crossing our stern in deep ocean as they headed south through high seas. I have seen pilot whales surfing down the waves behind us. I have seen the flukes of humpbacks rise and fall in the waters off Guadeloupe. And I have seen an orca, the powerfully built distinctive black and white killer whale, rise less than a boat length from our stern when we were a hundred miles or more off Mauritania, and later learned that he was one of a trouble-making pod that nearly sank a French yacht in the same location. But never have I sailed in close company with big whales until the day before we reached Faial.

E spotted the whales. It is the venting that gives them away. Their huge bodies are usually too low in the water to be seen at a distance. Three huge whales were a mile or so ahead and 10 degrees to starboard of our course. I nudged the wheel to pass them by a few hundred yards. We waved and cheered and the whales seemed not to be in the least disturbed. We watched them for about five minutes then they gracefully dived and we continued on our way. The next we saw was the leading whale surfacing a few boat lengths behind us and the three then kept pace with us. We cheered again. When they next surfaced the leading whale was parallel and no more than a boat length away. The others were right behind him. The leader was perhaps 10 feet longer than PETRONELLA. The shoulders were massive. We were out here in the natural environment of this truly large creature. It could out-pace us, out-maneuver us and out-displace us. We watched in wonder as the huge creature porpoised lazily alongside us, slower and more elegant than any dolphin, rolling to watch us with its great eye, and then dived with barely a movement of its body or a ripple on the water. The others followed it down. Slowly it dawned on E and me that in ten minutes or so these whales would re-surface. Where would they be? A mile away? Right next to us? Or right under us? We were at their mercy.

The whales made three more nerve wracking dives before they slipped away to reappear half a mile away, back in the business of whatever they were doing before we had appeared like clumsy clowns to entertain them. They were massive but not aggressive. Seeing them so close, as a chance encounter during a voyage on my own boat has been one of the highlights of my sailing. The pleasure and wonder were all the sharper for the tinge of real fear at being so close to such huge wild creatures.

The Azores is a center for whale watching and we soon discovered the rules that professional boats follow. Never chase a whale. Never get too close. Stay behind them. Never frighten them by coming on them unawares. In a way we had followed these rules naturally. We were closer than a professional boat will go, but the whale made that decision, not us.

There are instances of yachts coming up on whales by surprise, often when they appear to have been sleeping, and in some cases of possibly running into the whale and seeing the reddish stain of blood on the surface after the whale has dived. I learned in the Azores that a frightened whale may defecate as it dives, leaving a reddish stain on the surface of the sea. Let us hope that this is the more common cause of the surface stain than the blood of a wound.

Watch out for the last leg

Beware the journey's end. Even sailors who routinely cross oceans can get demob happy as land looms up. There is almost an anti-climax about making landfall after days or weeks at sea that causes a laxness just when greatest care is needed. Eric Hiscock, doyen of British sailing authors, wrote that closing land after a long time at sea calls for the greatest diligence of the whole passage.

A buddy isn't crew

I can see the surface appeal of setting out on a testing venture like an ocean crossing with another boat nearby but I'm not sure if some of the expectations stack up with the practicalities. Buddy boating seems to run counter to the essentially solitary enterprise of ocean sailing. More importantly, the idea itself seems to run counter to the stern attitude of total self reliance that I think should sit over and above all else on a boat heading far offshore. When the geographical gap between boats widens as it must, the responsibility is all your own. Sailors should not see added security in the company of others. An unready boat gains no extra seaworthiness from knowing another yacht is just over the horizon.

> One singlehander told me that when he was half way between Bermuda and the Azores he realized the enormity of his solitude. It would be nice not to have a big storm or an illness or a broken arm but out here the ocean doesn't care or forgive. Self reliance is for real.

The VHF nets and the bar conversations of the Caribbean are full of chat about buddy boating, whether through the island chain or on excursions to Venezuela or as far as Panama. This makes a lot of sense. Journeys usually take only the daylight hours or if overnight, seldom more than one. They are punctuated by days or weeks at anchor exploring ashore when company or a boat guardian allows you to be more adventurous. I'm all too familiar with the frustration of anchoring in a new place and hardly setting foot ashore in case the weather changes or the anchor drags. Some of our most enjoyable sailing has been sailing with other boats between the islands of the Caribbean or the Azores.

For short-hop buddy boating the compatibility or similarity in boat performance or strength of crews is hardly important. A couple sailing an under-canvassed cruiser will arrive no more than a few hours later than a racing crew on a semi racer. No one need wait for or worry about the other. Conflicts in desired itineraries are easily managed if no one is too bothered whether they stay 3 days or a week or if they take a side trip and join the main plan later. Problems of broken gear and repairs, forcing timetables to be revised, are usually coped with sympathetically. Taking the view "There but for the grace of God go I" is easier when it doesn't actually stop anyone from doing what they want.

There are errors of judgment of course and mismatches but these are a step beyond what buddy boats should be asked to endure.

> The two boats set off from Trinidad to Grenada just before dusk. P and Q were steering by electronic autohelm so they "motorsailed" the whole way. Both P and Q thought they needed the motor element of that but in the lumpy seas off the tail of Grenada their primary fuel filter clogged and the engine shut off. Now that they had to sail the boat and handsteer they realized they couldn't manage this. They couldn't make the tacks along the south coast of Grenada so Q called the buddy boat, now already anchored, not for advice on how to change a filter but for a tow. The buddy boat slipped along the coast with the wind and current but then had to slog back into wind and current with the heavy boat in tow. The buddy boat arrangement didn't last much further.

Setting out for a two- to four-week ocean crossing is altogether different from the idea of buddy boating or a cruise in company. The scale of the ocean works against remedies for human mistakes. Boats, even of the same design, are badly matched for speed on long passages. When an ocean passage is measured in thousands of miles and VHF range is measured in tens of miles it is just a matter of time before yacht scale is swallowed by ocean scale.

In the flat seas and clear horizons of the Horse Latitudes we might see the sails of another yacht at about five miles and a supertanker at about 15 miles. The Horse Latitudes cover millions of square miles. No wonder we didn't see much of anything out there.

The range of SSB radio means you can trade total solitude for the company of one of the informal cruiser nets often set up in jumping off places like Bermuda to complement the weather nets. Boats can be in touch all the way across and then, since you may not have met many of these sailors before setting off, you get the pleasure of putting new faces to the familiar voices when you arrive.

The ultimate in buddy boating across an ocean is something like the ARC. With around 225 boats on the same route, VHF schedules and monitoring by satellites back at base, there is a great deal of comfort if things go wrong. The event has a number of rescues to its credit, even rescues of boats not on the ARC. But the 2002 ARC had the first man-over-board fatality. Other boats in the vicinity just couldn't get there in time to prevent the sad tragedy.

Beware: you might be buddy boating by accident. Yachts on the Trade Wind route leaving the Canaries in November might find themselves in a crowd of 226 as the ARC joins them. Try to arrange your departure date for a little later or head south and leave from Cape Verde or Senegal.

The Pony Express

Sailing is as unreliable a way of getting from one place to another as can be imagined. The problem is not so much making the journey safely but the when and where of your arrival. The fear that catastrophe at sea will prevent your safe arrival is, of course, what worries people ashore, but such final disasters are still relatively rare. Goodness me, if they weren't sailing would not be very popular. The problem for the sailor is that all predictions of where and when they will arrive are wrong from the moment the lines are cast off, and sometimes even before that. We live in a world of such wonderful shore based communications that it is hard to realize that once you are out of sight of land, as far as keeping in touch with others goes, you might as well still be in the era of the Pony Express or using carrier pigeons.

We are encouraged by coastguards and sail training manuals to post details of our next port so that the world knows we have arrived safely. Officials love this. They have made us live by their rules of simple order rather than by the more chaotic natural rules of nature and the sea. They have ruled that the non-event of a message not being received can trigger off something that in the past was dependent on a positive request for assistance or the actual observation that a boat was in danger.

More insidious than this is that we are deemed irresponsible if we don't nominate a person ashore to hold our passage plans, receive messages from us and trigger a search and rescue when we are overdue. Imagine what we are doing to such a person! They hold our lives in their hands and yet they know nothing of what is happening to us. It is not a responsibility I would like to have. I know how fickle winds and currents are, how often the satellite weather picture looks awful while the storm (if there is one) is somewhere else, how wrong an estimate of an ocean passage can be, and how events conspire to land us in a port other than the one we first thought of. And even knowing this, and knowing the problems G and I have had in far off places trying to find a phone that works or the small change in a foreign currency to make it work, I would be hard pressed to sleep at night if a friend was a few days late and I had been deputed to raise the alarm.

I am not of the school of thought that an offshore sailor in difficulties should have the courtesy to die quietly at sea like a gentleman. Personally, I make sure we have liferaft and grab bag and EPIRB and radio and flares as well as a cell phone and fully plan to use them when we are in trouble and when we need to ask for help. But I feel that these wonders of modern technology are there to give me a better chance of survival without taking away my responsibility for making that call myself, in full awareness of the conditions of the moment. People back home don't know that the weather is lighter than expected or that you spent two days at half speed without an effective headsail as you mended a huge split in the genoa. As a skipper in a gale I will have enough anxiety without worrying that mother back home might be making the wrong call and I need to do something to get us somewhere to tell her not to. As a skipper drifting in the calms of the Horse Latitudes I don't want to feel I must burn diesel every day, even when we have a gentle sailing breeze, so that I can make a phone call to say I am alright. As the repair man when the SSB isn't working, I would rather be reading a book on deck than fiddling with soldering irons and skinny multi-strand wires to send off the radio message on schedule. Concerns like that can take the fun out of life and only lead to the wrong priorities for the boat.

A skipper on passage from the Azores to Gibraltar found winds lighter than expected and their progress was mainly drifting. The estimated time for the 900-mile passage would be off by a few days, and their parents would worry once they went over the projected ETA. They were fine, of course, with food and water and fuel, able to stay at sea for six weeks at least, but they didn't want to motor through every calm and they didn't want to be too far off their ETA. The dilemma spoilt their enjoyment.

Of course you must let people know the when and where of your plans. It helps if you give them a list of alternatives and a journey time that ranges from your best estimate to three times this. Then it also helps if you leave this information with as many people as you know who have actual experience of your shocking failure to ever arrive on time.

Best of all, work to a different sort of calendar. Before the industrial age, time was marked by seasons. A lunar month was about as short a time period as you needed. Come the industrial age, we learned to live by the hour, so that we could start and end our shift. Now we all wear watches accurate to the second and some of us live by meetings that are timed to the minute. This precision of time keeping is appropriate to airline travel, not the ridiculously antiquated mode of sailing. Once you go to sea you go lunar again. Drop the "deadline mentality." It isn't safe. It isn't appropriate. The worst reason to rush a trip is to arrive when you said you would. The journey takes as long as it takes. The time to arrive is when it is prudent.

> The sailing couple on the heavy displacement 50-foot steel ketch MITHRIL have sailed the world, including the Roaring Forties and as far into the Antarctic as the little island of South Georgia, and come safely through weather the rest of us wouldn't care to think of. On their crossing from Venezuela to Britain they had family reasons to be in a hurry. When they were almost home, just 80 miles southwest of the Fastnet Rock off Ireland, they knew they were in for a vigorous depression but welcomed it, thinking it would speed them on their way. When the gale hit they were in the worst position to cope with it, 20 miles inside the continental shelf. A full gale, gusting to hurricane force, piled up ocean swells like waves on a surfing beach. Not high but curling and breaking like no others they had seen in the ocean. MITHRIL coped until The Wave. This wave was not much bigger than the others but the crest was curling round on itself. It threw the boat down on her side. It only took a moment for the boat to right but the contents of every locker had exploded. A saucepan lid dented the headlining inches away from the crew's head. Bottles left lethal shards of broken glass and their oily contents everywhere. The seas continued to bounce the boat around, even though they reduced sail to storm canvas. Clearing up was difficult. Hot food impossible for the next nine hours.

MITHRIL sailed into one of the deepest depressions recorded off Ireland. These experienced sailors knew they could have sat out the worst of the weather in deeper water. They learned several lessons: that glass and china on a boat are a liability;

that lockers and floorboards need stronger catches; that every storm must be prepared for as though it will be the most extreme. Lesson number one was that if you have a fixed timetable and an unchangeable destination, go by plane.

Are you ready?

The question of readiness is a sort of mega-question. It sits over the top of a thousand other questions which must each be answered in their turn. But of course, you can never answer so many questions, and what's worse, if you do check one off it will wriggle round and come back onto the list. Those questions never stay answered for long.

There is no way of knowing when you are ready. I've never yet cast off without a long list of jobs still to be done. Not all omissions are equally important.

> My old friend E was anxious to leave for the Azores but skipper D was prevaricating. The boat was never quite ready, even though not many others were left in the harbor by now and the sailing season was slipping away. "We haven't got a ship's bucket," D said. "Can't sail without a bucket. We'll have to wait till the shops open in the morning." E got in the dinghy and rowed round the harbor knocking on each boat. "Have you got a bucket you could sell us?" He came back and slapped the bucket down in front of D. They sailed at dawn, before the shops opened and D could add other "no-have" to the list.

By now you know the key parts of the equation that must be solved. Have you got the sailing skills and experience to take on the ocean? Do you have the right boat design to bring you through ocean weather? Is the boat seaworthy and the gear reliable? Have you got crew to see you through the hard bits as well as the fun bits? Have you thanked Aunty Wilma for the book on survival yet? These are not the full set of questions and yet even these questions (except the last) can be broken down into a hundred sub questions. I favor the Alexandrian approach to the Gordian Knot, as taught him by Aristotle. Cut the insoluble. Go when the season is right, the weather looks good and your stores are on board. Don't wait till your friends stop asking when are you going and start asking "if you are going."

9

New tricks and gadgets

Anchoring to stay put

Now that you are long-term sailors you will spend more time at anchor than you did back home. North America is so blessed with marinas that many sailors now don't even think twice about where they will be when they stop for the night. They sail from marina to marina. This is to miss the wonderful advantages of spending time at anchor. For one thing, you can go to much more remote places, or little fishing ports that have always lived with the sea but have not yet started to live with modern yachting. You have much less noise and shore dirt. You have privacy. And best of all, laying an anchor is much less trouble than bringing a boat alongside, setting fenders, running bow and stern and spring lines and then attending these lines for surge or tide.

You cannot enjoy being at anchor if you don't have the right ground tackle and anchor windlass. You will not sleep well and you will not be comfortable going ashore and leaving the boat unattended. In your new life as ocean cruisers your ground tackle is the most important equipment you carry. A good anchoring system is what stands between your home and that surf down to leeward, so make sure you have strong ground tackle even for every day anchorages but bear in mind that the time will come when you will also need to put out two or more anchors, whether to hold you to the swell, to cope with a night squall or because a big storm is on its way.

Don't feel that nature has picked you out as an example to others just because your anchor drags. We have dragged so many times that I regard dragging as the norm. If your boat isn't dragging then another one will be.

My thanks to Bill Clinton, the sailor's best friend. Since he turned off the selective availability system that deliberately introduced errors into civilian-channel GPS-systems it is possible to use the

236

anchor drag alarm on your GPS to see if you are on the move. Of course, given the other errors that GPS signals may suffer from, this is only a back-up to taking a look at your transits from time to time but it is a back-up that can come with a loud external alarm to raise you from the deep sleep of the unwary.

The solution to better anchoring is to carry the biggest bower anchor you can handle, choose your spot carefully, lay your anchor tenderly and put out plenty of scope. Look at your ground tackle with a critical eye. It is unlikely to be heavy enough. True, weight isn't everything. The surface area of the flukes is also vital to the grip the anchor can achieve. But heavier ground tackle is still your best insurance.

Different bottoms need different types of anchors, which is a good reason to carry more than one type of anchor. The other reason to carry several anchors is that you may lose one just when you need to anchor securely. Danforth-type anchors are good in sandy and muddy bottoms. So too are plough-type anchors, and these will penetrate weed better than a Danforth. The old fisherman-type anchor, useful for its ease of stowage, is a good anchor for rocky bottoms but needs to be very heavy to hold well in soft bottoms.

For a lot of cruisers the fisherman anchor is the pattern of last resort for when the big winds are forecast. This is because they can often carry a dismantled 100lb fisherman in the bilges. Such a heavy anchor should give you a lot of grip on the bottom but even an anchor that separates into its parts is useless if it is so big that you can't get it out of the bilge and ready on deck when the storm arrives. You might find a Danforth-type anchor can give much more holding power for much less weight, and still be disassembled to fit the bilges.

A coastal sailor may think two anchors is plenty. You need three or four now that you are an ocean sailor. We carry three substantial anchors and a lightweight kedge anchor which I haven't seen in years. I wouldn't feel complete if we only had two anchors. For main anchor we use one of our two 45lb CQRs and keep a 65lb fisherman anchor always ready to go from our second bow roller. I don't know how we would manage with only one bow roller.

A survey of long-term cruisers found the CQR to be the anchor of choice and that the preferred weight was always much heavier than recommended in the data sheets of almanacs or yachting magazines or those produced by yacht builders.

> The initials CQR are said to stand for SECURE. I have to hope that Professor Geoffrey Taylor, a nuclear physicist at the Los Alamos laboratory who invented the anchor for flying boats, was stating his intentions for the design rather than being ironic.

Our 45lb CQR is as heavy as most we see on 40 to 50 footers but really I think we need a 60lb CQR as our main anchor. The message is this: if you want to sleep easy, put down the heaviest anchor you can handle and don't bother with calculations of minimal acceptable weights. The second message is: don't bother with a main anchor for normal use and a heavier one for bad weather. Use the heaviest one you can handle as your main anchor. Bad weather always comes in the early hours of a dark and rainy night and this is not the time to be messing around laying second anchors.

> G and I carried out an objective and scientific test on the relative holding power of our 45lb CQR and our 65lb fisherman. We didn't intend to, but that is what it turned out to be when we set a river mooring using these two anchors. We put each anchor on opposite ends of a long length of heavy chain and connected PETRONELLA to a half inch chain riser in the center of this. After two months, ready to leave the river, we hauled up the mooring. It wasn't easy. The CQR was still nice and tidy on a length of chain. The fisherman had knitted itself into a great convulsion of metal. Unable to hold to the bottom it had been pulled towards the more secure CQR, twisting and knotting the chain as it went. It was the opposite of what we had expected.

The CQR, a sort of plough anchor, like all ploughs needs to wriggle and worm its way underground, mainly through the action of the sea and chain. The CQR likes to be on a long scope and I like to sleep easy thinking of the deep catenary doing much of the work and certainly not jerking me or Mr Secure upright in the gusts of the night, so we usually lie on a heavy chain scope closer to 5:1 than 3:1. Despite being generous with our weight and length of chain, and the holding power claimed for the CQR, the anchor has dragged so many times that we now lay it down like a rare piece of porcelain. We do not drop our anchor. That is too careless a description of what we do.

Ploughs need time to settle. Just about the worst thing you can do is drop the anchor and a bundle of chain then motor back to set it. You will achieve nothing more than a shallow furrow with your plough tastefully lying on top of it. When you have selected your anchoring spot, overshoot by a boat length. Let the boat drop back slowly as you lay the anchor on the bottom and feed out the chain or rode bit by bit until you have enough out for the depth of water. Then take five minutes or more to tidy up the deck, put on sail covers, debate the meaning of life and sit up on the bow admiring the scenery in general but some stable transit in particular. From time to time lay your bare hand on the anchor rode as it comes taut. You can almost always feel if the anchor is dragging and, if it is, re-anchor now rather than later. When you have waited twice as long as you first thought of, and your transits are steady, you may now use the engine to set the anchor. But come back easy. The point is not to see how many horse powers it takes to drag the thing back to the surface. Your anchor just needs a little encouragement from you to dig in deeper, and the rest is up to its designer.

We encourage our CQR to stay set by two little tricks:

- a snubber of nylon line to take up snatch. This needs to be 20 or 30 feet long to work in really snatchy conditions
- a weight on the anchor chain to increase the catenary effect. We don't bother with running an "angel" or "chum," as such weights are called. Much too troublesome to recover in the many crises my imagination conjures up. We just run a big loop of anchor chain behind the rope snubber. We wind this up on the windlass like any other anchor chain.

We like the CQR design for its holding power and versatility but not blindly. There are some days when we don't like it at all. Over the years in our search for a drag-proof anchor still light enough to handle we have taken great interest in the new designs. What has surprised us most is how many new designs there have been in the last 10 to 15 years, given how long mankind has been putting to sea in boats. Often they are developments of familiar designs such as spade and plough, Danforth type and fisherman, changing a key dimension or making use of new metals, such as the light weight but high tensile alloys of aluminum magnesium used in the Danforth-style Fortress. Others, like the Bügelanker from Germany and the strange looking Sarca from Australia, are more radical ideas. Some, unfortunately, are just cheaper copies of designs no longer covered by patent. The point is that each type of anchor has its strengths and weaknesses. Improving an anchor's ability to do what it does best doesn't mean you gain in the things it isn't designed to do. You still must choose an anchor for the particular conditions.

Such a widening range of yacht anchors demands better information for us users, but I find much published research confusing. Tests are often badly designed, so that, for example, the holding power of a ship-style anchor or a fisherman-type anchor on a sandy bottom is compared to a broad fluked yacht anchor. A ship-style anchor needs to be very heavy to work, which is why you never see them on a yacht. A fisherman anchor, even the improved Herreshoff version, needs very broad flukes to hold in sand or mud. That isn't where you would choose to use it. Such tests are inherently biased and may be providing misinformation. Look critically at the test data. Is like being compared with like? Was the test method rigorous and appropriate? Be cautious of any new and therefore relatively untried design which comes out well ahead in all tests in all conditions. Best of all, talk to other sailors.

> Tests by two major anchor manufacturers resonated with me. First, the test boats often failed to get the anchor to hold well enough to begin the test. And they were experts. Imagine how often we ordinary mortals are likely to fail? The man said: "You can never repeat the test or be sure what has happened. With anchoring you get good, bad and terrible days." Seabed videos of the way the anchor set showed that often the beast behaved in an unlikely or unpredicted manner. An anchor that seemed to have gripped would later drag, for no obvious reason. Some designs are very much better than others in certain types of seabed. But since it is not usually possible to see the exact nature of the seabed, most of us settle for the best on average. Make this your watch word: never assume it will hold, even if it has held all week in gales.

Straight line pull is only one test of an anchor but often it is the only test that you will read about. It is a test that a magazine or a manufacturer can do in an hour from a tug boat. A useful test is the anchor's willingness to reset after a change of current or tide but as the tests quoted above show this may not be such a quick and simple thing to observe. The best test of all is the test of time. This can measure such things as the anchor's resistance to impact shock loads and twist, things you may not immediately think of when you imagine your anchor down there on a dark and stormy night, but they are part of the stressful life an anchor must lead. I didn't really appreciate what such loadings could do until we watched a friend pulling up the remains of a Bahamian moor. He had been at anchor a long time in a place where wind and tide caused the boat to range around its anchors, especially when the rising tide and afternoon wind coincided. The downstream anchor had taken more of this ranging than the other one. Its shank had been bent by the chain wrapping around and jerking on it. An anchor shank is like a long lever arm. The longer the lever, the more chance of bending it. After that I found myself noticing many more broken anchors hidden away in boat yards. And they weren't all poorly made cheap copies of those old designs whose patents have expired.

> The much publicized dragging of the 246-foot MIRABELLA V in 2005, the world's largest sloop and biggest private sailing yacht, was in the usually tranquil Villefranche-sur-Mer, near Nice in the Mediterranean, when her "High Holding Power" design anchor apparently broke out. The forces imposed as she briefly ranged around in the suddenly strengthening and changing breeze before grounding on rocks were so great that the shank of her 1300lb anchor had been bent. It seems unlikely that the $130 million dollar MIRABELLA V would skimp on its anchors or chain. At the time of the grounding we were about to buy a cheap copy of the high-holding power Bruce-type anchor. Not now. We shall just increase our scope more often.

The moment will come when you will wonder about putting out a second anchor. My feeling is only to do this when you have to. A second anchor adds a dimension of complication that you may regret later. Apart from times of approaching storms I would only put out a second anchor in five very clear sets of circumstances:

- to hold the boat into a swell
- where a wind switch is expected
- where the current reverses and there is little swinging room
- where others are lying to two anchors
- when I need to make special arrangements to stay in a particular spot.

I would never lie to a bow and stern anchor if every one else near us is on one. With a stern anchor out I would always have ready a long line suitably buoyed for when I have to get out in a hurry leaving the stern anchor behind for collection later. The hardest thing is not the practical ways of temporarily jettisoning an anchor but the mental one of sailing off in the hope that the precious thing will still be there a day or two later when the conditions allow you to pick it up. I learned my techniques while in the Canaries, those sun-kissed Atlantic isles where the wind always seems to come onshore into your anchorage when you are least wanting it. Coming back for an anchor only seems hard to do when you have never left an anchor behind before. Believe me: when the time comes, do it.

When you need more holding power than your main anchor provides, think of putting anchors in tandem. Attach your next main anchor to 30 feet or so of chain and fasten this to your main anchor. Then lay them down in a line. This is much better than laying two anchors at 45 degrees to one another. With anchors in tandem, you have the combined weight and resistance of the pair. With anchors at 45 degrees, you have either one or the other taking the whole strain. You have two drawbacks to anchors in tandem:

- if you now start to drag, the conditions are likely to be so awful that you won't want to go near the foredeck to recover and reset the anchors. Cast them off on a buoyed line to return for them later, and be glad you still have another two in your locker
- recovering tandem anchors is never going to be easy. Main force will be needed to recover the second anchor once the windlass has pulled the first one over the bow roller. But think positively: at least you have all your strength after that good night's sleep.

You need stowage and a good roller for a stern anchor. This helps whenever you need to lay a second anchor to hold you to the swell or kedge off, but especially for cruising in the Mediterranean where it is common to moor bows on to a stern anchor.

You may have come across the Mediterranean method of mooring in Spain and Portugal before you arrive in the Mediterranean or in the Baltic when you anchor off little rocky islands. It works in areas with little rise of tide, so don't try it in southern Brittany. Local boats often moor stern to the quay but I prefer going in bows to the quay. It is more private but also protects your vulnerable rudder if a swell gets up. There is often very little water off the quays and the bottom can be hard rock. You will get the hang of the technique soon enough. Sometimes there is a stern buoy which you pick up as you drive in towards the dock. Cleat the line or use it as a brake as you come into the dock. In fishing harbors you may have to drop your own anchor instead. Drop it about three boat lengths out from the dock and make sure you have flaked out enough warp to reach the quay. Have boat hooks, lines and anchors ready, plenty of fenders out, and be prepared to ignore the instructions you are getting from ashore, even if they are in a language you understand. Tension up fore and aft so that your bow is clear of the dock. As you enter a little Mediterranean harbor you may think there isn't room for another boat. There usually is. Someone will start to make a space for you to squeeze into, and the six boats after you will somehow manage to squeeze in too.

Sailing textbooks advise you to run a trip line on the crown of your anchor if you suspect the bottom to be fouled and your anchor liable to snag down there. I have snagged anchors and I have used trip lines. My preference is to cope with a snagged anchor rather than the mess a trip line can get you in. A trip line round the propeller can be terminal in a crisis, which is what I consider the natural condition of much of my sailing. Think long and hard before you add this complication and source of danger to your anchor. It is nature's way to send currents and winds to turn the vessel round and round throughout the night, so that the safety trip line is now around the keel, rudder and propeller and has immobilized you.

The survey of cruisers also found that long distance sailors preferred all chain rode. It's the weight again, keeping the anchor in place, and the reassurance it brings. Also, I suspect, it is because self stowing chain gets rid of all that knitting on a wave-swept foredeck. If you want the stretch that a rope gives you in strong winds when the rode is taut buy a chain claw and put a line to your chain. We always put our chain on to a 30-foot rope bridle, because rope is quieter in the bow roller than chain. If we worried about the loss of catenary in strong winds we would just drop a big loop of chain behind the rope, as a weight.

Chain or rope? This is a question that divides two continents. You have probably used a mix of rope and chain for your anchor rode, carefully matching the relatively short length of chain to the depths you usually anchor in. Europeans and others usually use all chain. Now that you are likely to be doing more anchoring than ever before, I would recommend an all-chain rode. I like its self stowing character. I like the added weight it gives to the anchor when the breeze gets up. I like to think of how it won't be cut by coral or rock as it ranges around the seabed. I even like to think how it won't be cut by a passing fishing boat propeller in a tight little Mediterranean anchorage, but that is perhaps casting an aspersion too far. If you have a choice between two sizes, choose the bigger chain.

Make sure you have plenty of cable too. We have our main anchor on about 150 feet or 50m of chain extended by the same length of line spliced to the chain. We have yet to put out the line. In reserve we have two 300 feet lengths of line and 15 feet lengths of chain.

How much chain to carry? We wondered whether 150 feet would be enough when a bad storm came through. Our friend Ted gave me a useful tip. "We carried 300 feet of chain for years," he said, "and never put out more than half. When we came to look we found that the stuff that never left the anchor locker had turned into a heap of salty rust. We cut it off and bought 150 feet of new chain, which we carry separately so that it stays away from salt water."

The other aspect of frequent anchoring is recovering all that weight. Many blue-water crews rate the electric windlass as the single most desired or desirable piece of kit. I am no different, even though G and I vacillate over going electric. Reliable powered anchor windlasses for cruising yachts didn't really arrive until the late 1970s. PETRONELLA is of the age when manual windlasses were the norm. I am of the age when a bad back is the consequence. There have been more times when we have wished for the speed and convenience of an electric windlass than when we loudly bless the reliability and stubbornness of our manual windlass. Our manual windlass is powerful and we are practiced in letting the boat do most of the work in recovering the anchor, but sometimes we are short of sea room and blasted by squally showers and life could be more fun than cranking the windlass handle. We are a heavy forty footer. Weighing anchor with a manual windlass can be a bit of a battle even on a 35 footer if you're using it daily. How nice to just press a button.

If you don't already have a powered windlass then consider this. Now that you are a serious offshore sailor, choose a size larger than recommended for your boat. And when thinking over the pros and cons of older-style horizontal versus the neat and space saving vertical axis windlass, consider that the horizontal windlass is the more convenient when you set two anchors. And bear in mind that you may find yourself without the power to power the powered winch. Choose one that can be effectively cranked manually. Not all are equal in this respect.

Ship to shore—maneuvering with ropes

Sometimes the old ways are still the best ways, especially when every place you visit is new and strange rather than the familiar marina you have called home for the last decade. We often find ourselves using lines ashore to help us leave a berth when wind and current are against us. We may not be the best in the world at it, but at least we have this technique in our mental locker and we are no longer afraid to look silly playing with lines. It is better than losing control.

The old sailing ships and today's sailing schools probably know a thousand more maneuvers with shore lines than we do, but the two we know can be applied in a hundred variations just like you can get a long way knowing only two knots if the two you know are the bowline and a round turn and two half hitches. Taking a line from your stern to the shore will stop you as you reverse straight out of a marina berth and pull your bow round to face right down the exit lane. A line from bow to shore makes a wonderful pivot, so that when you motor forward onto it your little ship magically comes alongside the dock. Playing with lines helps you appreciate which way the stern will swing when you pull on the bow, and vice versa.

Ponta Delgada marina had boats rafted two deep along the main pontoon, but it was time for our friends to leave from their inside berth. The gusty wind blowing along the pontoon was helping to push boats off and our friends left simply in reverse. Their neighbors on a high-sided 50 footer were going to warp back in with us on the pontoon to help. They brought their stern line round the bow of our friends' boat and handed it to us to haul them back in. It went horribly wrong very quickly. The stern of the high sided yacht blew off at right angles to the dock. No matter where we stood the angle we pulled at dragged the boat forward onto the boats ahead of it. It was becoming slapstick. One of the helpers on the pontoon had heaved all the slack from the stern line when the panic stricken skipper tried to take out more. Two men pulling at opposite ends of the same line is not sustainable. Neither could cleat his end because the instant he stopped hauling the other would pull him into the water. G tried to organize the mate on the foredeck to shorten up on her line and persuade the skipper to motor ahead on it. Motor ahead!!! The boat was already going ahead every time anyone pulled on the stern line, and the only effect was to hit their neighbors. "The bow line will turn you and pull you back onto the dock," G said but they couldn't see it. It was too counter-intuitive. The skipper and mate were trapped in a routine of alternately hauling and slackening stern line and bow line, dragging the boat forward on the lines and then pushing it backwards with hands and feet as they fended off from their neighbors' windvane steering, radar mount and solar panels. After a while we left. We could do no more. Sailing half way across an ocean doesn't mean you have mastered the tricks of controlling your boat in harbor.

Thrust to the fore—fending off a bow thruster

What a thing of wonder is a bow thruster, an aid to maneuvering that can make us all better at parking. I have no objection to that. I have watched them help turn a clumsy boat on a dime when I would have been desperately trying to keep our bowsprit out of the cocktail party on the boat ahead. When G and I hear that unmistakable whine we always rush out to see some entertainingly closer-quarters maneuvering than we could manage.

But my respect for the bow thrusters is tempered. I have seen bow thrusters fail more often than main engines, and always at the worst possible moment. Of course they do. It's in their very nature. A bow thruster is intended to deliver turning force at no other time than the precise moment when you need it, when no other option exists because your reliance on a sideways push led you to commit yourself to that maneuver.

A bow thruster works in short periods of being on and then off. Stopping and starting any motor in mid-maneuver wears my nerves to shreds. In my sailing life, not every stop has been followed by the desired start.

On PETRONELLA the main engine is a plodder, running happily for hours or days. Yours probably is too, which means you should have a pretty good idea as you go hard astern whether the engine is about to die or not. The main engine will deliver most maneuvers if you plan them in advance. It won't allow you to push the boat sideways against the wind. But why are you trying to do that anyway? It won't make a long-keeled boat turn predictably in reverse. You can learn to live with such uncertainty and learn to maneuver with warps and advance warning to other yachts. And if you can't, the better solution is to sail a yacht with a fin keel.

We had more or less blown down into the tight little space the harbormaster had allotted us. A bit of engine ahead, a bit astern, a couple of roving fenders. We did it that way because we had no other choice. A few days later another yacht had to squeeze in near us. It came in rather fast by our standards and then we heard the whine of the bow thruster. Ah, that was the secret to their confidence. The bow pulled round, the stern swung, and the crew on the neighboring yacht yelled. Only the combined strength of their panic-powered limbs prevented the collision as the turning hull continued to drive forward. At the last moment in this maneuver the "skipper" had hit the bow-thruster controls instead of putting his main engine astern. It was a moment of mental aberration, like most operator errors.

Safety is not a harness and a through-bolted padeye

Who am I to take issue with the United States government? Try dinghying across a harbor like a millpond without a lumescent approved flotation device for every person and dog and officials will pounce and fine you for being anti-socially careless of human life. So why is it that in the real world of life far offshore all the sailors I know only put on a lifejacket when conditions get bad, and sometime only after conditions have started to improve?

I get a lot of misunderstanding about my views on safety harnesses and lifejackets, especially from my more nervous crews. I have been known to take my harness off and go forward to work on the mast in a gale of wind because the harness was getting in my way and making me unsafe. A harness? Making me unsafe? See what I mean about misunderstanding?

Safety at sea is in the head and in the instincts you develop. Harnesses and flotation devices don't stop accidents. They just change the outcome. They will save you only if used properly and adjusted to the conditions. When you are working on deck the tether should be long enough to let you do the job but short enough to make it impossible to go overboard. If you are working with too short a tether to reach everything, you will spend too long out of commission from the rest of the tasks that need doing, or end up taking risks undoing and re-doing the clip. If you go overboard on a long tether you are in danger of being towed under. No crew in the world is strong enough to haul you back on board at even three or four knots.

P was on his way back from the Azores. He and his skipper had been at sea for weeks now. Sailing was second nature. The wind had died to nothing, the sails flapped and fluffed and the sea was too inviting to resist. P tied a knot in a 150-foot long line and trailed it from the stern. Then he dived off the bow. When he came up the line was whipping past him and he only just managed to grab its end. He took a turn around his forearm because he knew immediately that he couldn't hold on for long. His skipper struggled to bring him back to the boat, hand over hand, hauling and cleating, hauling and cleating. It took more than an hour to get P back to the boat. Both he and the skipper were exhausted. There was no wind. The sea was flat calm. The boat was drifting at no more than one knot. P is a strong swimmer and a strong man. He was lucky.

I hold two views strongly about harnesses:

- they are your second line of defense, not your first. Get used to working on your deck. Work out the quickest routines for the hardest and least common tasks. Let the handholds become second nature to your hands. Make your feet learn where to put themselves. The more you work on deck, the easier it is to make decisions to go out and do things.
- the most important time to wear a harness is when you are in the cockpit and feeling safe. This might be in rough seas, when you could be caught by a ton of water unexpectedly riding over the bow and all the way back to the stern. Or on night watch in easy conditions, when you are relaxed and at peace and are caught unawares by a sudden lurch of the hull. The cockpit is less of a safe place than many realize. Most of us are pumped up to full alert by a gale but the worst seas and the most extreme movements of the boat often come when the strong winds die. Just when the danger seems over you are most at risk.

On PETRONELLA we run jacklines along our deck from bow to cockpit. We use webbing because I didn't like the idea of picking up a fast skid from accidentally standing on the rolly wire just as the boat lurches sideways at an unprecedented 10 knots. We made these jacklines ourselves and when I stitched the eyes at each end I had in mind how much force I might exert traveling six feet at full speed before the jackline stopped my progress. We lash the jacklines to strong deck points with many, many turns of strong light line. When we get to harbor we take the jackstays off. This is perhaps a short-coming of webbing over wire jackstays. You can leave wire on without too much fear of weakening it, but webbing can degrade in UV and we don't like to risk that.

Another thing about webbing is that it really is a "use once and discard" material. Makers of American and European safety gear have just added a load indicator to safety harness webbing. A thin tracer strand breaks if the harness is ever subject to shock loads in excess of 7,000 Newtons. I'm glad it's an automatic load indicator. I'm not sure how I would know if that sudden jerk across the deck was 6,999 Newtons or the terminal 7,001.

Think about how you use all your safety equipment. Never trust it implicitly. It wasn't so long ago that harness manufacturers changed their end clips from the one that opened accidentally when twisted at a particular angle in the padeye. Don't just assume that you are safe because you are using safety equipment. At sea a disaster can follow very quickly from any mistake. Your greatest danger in worsening weather is inactivity. Inactive sailors do not adjust themselves or the boat to the changing conditions.

When you make your rules for night and heavy weather sailing, as you surely must, make them simple. If that involves always wearing flotation vests and harnesses and whistles and strobe lights, so be it. It is your world and your rules out there so stick to them. Put on and practice moving around deck in your harnesses and tethers so that you get used to what you wear, so that you always feel comfortable in the stuff and you never have that nagging feeling of being unprotected when crawling along the high side in a rising sea.

Pumping policy

Emergencies sometimes follow from being caught in heavy weather. Bilge pumps are for emergencies. You need manual pumps as your main line of defense and electric as stand-by. Not the other way round. Carry spares for your pumps. The well worn handle of a bilge pump is less the mark of an offshore sailor than it used to be, now that the bilges of modern hulls need less routine pumping, but an ocean crossing and the prospect of bad offshore weather will give your pump some exercise.

Before you think that I have a Luddite attitude to boat electrics, let me assure you that we have an electric bilge pump with a float switch to run it automatically. Come the moment when we need extra hands to plug the hole and stem the incoming water, we will be grateful for the electric pump. But electric pumps never seem able to deliver the capacity stated on the box.

Manufacturers usually state pump capacity for zero head and open flow (i.e. no pipe connection and no water being lifted) and an input of 13.6 volts (i.e. the impractical theoretical maximum of a 12-volt battery).

Most yachts use a centrifugal bilge pump for the very good reasons that they can work when immersed, can self-prime, can tolerate running dry without burning out, and are less liable than other designs to get blocked by small pieces of solid matter. They are better for the job than the alternatives. Diaphragm pumps can be jammed open by debris. Flexible impeller pumps are power hungry and won't survive running dry.

The drawback to centrifugal pumps is that they suffer from "head pressure," the cumulative resistance of being connected to a discharge pipe and of having to lift water vertically up to the skin fitting. Just fitting them in a yacht's bilge and asking them to do their job drastically reduces the capacity stated on their box.

Locate your thru-hull skin fitting in the side of the boat to give your bilge water the shortest route over the side. Make sure this route has a steady, continuous rise. If your chosen route has low spots, water can fall back when the pump stops and be trapped. This trapped water can act as a blockage, air-locking the pump and stalling it.

Make sure that your carefully sited skin fitting is not below the waterline when you are heeled on a particular tack in case you get back-siphoning and flooding. You may want to fit a check valve in the pipe to reduce the chances of back-siphoning. Don't. Check valves give resistance equivalent to many feet of vertical lift, adding to head pressure. They may also trap water and become a blockage, stopping the pump from pumping. Finally, they sometimes jam open, resulting in the very back-siphoning you were trying to prevent. So leave the check valve out of the installation and add a few feet of pipe to raise the hose above heeling level and add an anti-siphon break.

When there is no more you can do to reduce the vertical lifting component, make sure that your pipework on the discharge side is smooth walled on the inside rather than corrugated. Corrugations, so useful in preventing the walls of the pipe from crushing under pressure, cause friction to the water flow and this means more head pressure.

Bilge pumps are vulnerable to voltage drop. Make sure your cables are sized to minimize voltage drop. The chances are that when you need your bilge pump for real you will have been running other electrical gear and now find the batteries are less than fully charged. You can't afford to add any further voltage drop to this. If your undersized wires reduce battery voltage at the pump by 10% and the batteries are already down to nearly 12 volts, the pump will be getting less than 11 volts. Factor in the other reductions from head pressure and you might be lucky to get 50% of the rated capacity of the pump.

Bilge pumps are awkward little suckers. They don't like low voltage but have a nasty habit which can reduce pristine batteries to being totally flat. Let's call it the "automatic float switch self cycling phenomena" for want of a more cumbersome expression. If your boat has small bilges, as boats with narrow bilges deep down in the keel often do, a small amount of water sloshing around down there may cause the water level to fluctuate and fool the float switch into turning on the pump. Water levels fluctuate in the bilge when a boat is hobby horsing into a head sea or rolling in following seas. The level can also fluctuate when a long discharge hose drops its water back into the bilge when the pump switches off. Imagine that. The float switch turns the pump on and the water rises up the hose but just before it gets pumped overboard the level in the bilge falls enough to turn the switch off. Down comes the water, on goes the switch. Up goes the water, off goes the switch. Down comes the water, on goes the switch. On and on and on until the battery gives up and dies.

So here is the answer. Two electric bilge pumps. Have a little pump without a float switch sited so that it can hoover up the last drops of water from your bilges. The trickle that drops out of the hose when this is switched off won't matter an iota. Install a larger pump, capable of coping with a serious inflow of sea water, with its automatic float higher up in the bilge, clear of dropped nuts and bolts and other detritus that can block the float switch.

And having done this, make sure your trusty old manual pump is in good working order. There is no guarantee that you will not suffer a hole in the hull but the nearest to getting such a guarantee that I know is to install numerous oversized pumps and make sure they are tested frequently and maintained scrupulously. Call it superstition if you must, but make sure you have a couple of buckets on lanyards too.

> We had frightened ourselves the night before by nearly running aground. Perhaps that's what made me look in the bilges the next morning before we started the engine to motor into our anchorage. "We're sinking!!" I tried not to scream out the news. I reckon our deep bilge can hold a hundred gallons before the water starts to slop over the bottom of the engine and the top of the battery box. It was slopping there now. A minute later we knew that the huge manual bilge pump was blocked even though its strum box was clear. E began to dismantle the pump. The rest of us hauled buckets. We never did find anything blocking the pump. The reason it failed was because we hadn't serviced it or even said Good Morning to it for the last two years. It was the buckets that saved us that day.

When the pumps and the buckets can't cope remember that your main engine is a pump too. Shut off the seacock and disconnect the water supply to the engine pump. Add some sort of strainer and put the hose end into the bilge water. Now start the engine. It is amazing how much water an engine pumps. It might just help delay the sinking.

The last pump

The US Harbor Pollution Act prohibits the discharge of sewage, refuse or oil in the navigable waters of the US and is strictly enforced by the US Coast Guard. International regulations prohibit the discharge of wastes within three miles of the coast of all countries and many countries now have national legislation to bring this into effect.

An increasing number of European countries require local vessels to have holding tanks. All the signs are that more will follow this lead and that more countries will demand the same of foreign vessels visiting their waters. Anchorages designated as "clean" will soon only be available to yachts with holding tanks. In the EU moves are underway to legislate not only for "black water" from toilets but "grey water" from washing up and "bilge water" i.e. contaminated with oil.

Popular, non-tidal areas like the Mediterranean take particular care over pollution. In the Baltic the Helcom agreement relating to non-disposal of sewage requires local vessels to have a holding tank capable of being pumped out at a shore station. Foreign flagged vessels don't need to meet this requirement but still must not pump sewage into the territorial waters.

The answer is that you should have a holding tank or a device that prevents you discharging any visible floating solids of sewage.

SECTION FOUR

Trials by Weather

10

Heavy weather sailing

Heavy weather is what I fear most. In reality I have met very little and you can probably avoid most of it by judicious choice of route and tactics in key places. But you still have to be fully prepared. Bad weather can always arrive unexpectedly. An Atlantic crossing at these latitudes always brings the chance of a gale or two. Dealing with the unexpected is what defines bluewater sailing.

> Heavy weather is when the weather is or will become sufficiently severe that the crew is obliged to change their cruise or passage plan solely for that reason. Preparing for bad weather holds a fascination for most sailors. You can make a really good start by reading the classic work on the subject, *Heavy Weather Sailing* by Adlard Coles, now revised and edited by Peter Bruce.

Talk to bluewater liveaboards and it is truly amazing how little heavy weather they encounter. This isn't because the bluewater life destroys memory cells or that such sailors are used to hardship. The real reason is that they take great care not to be in the wrong place at the wrong time. Round-the-buoys-racers who treat an ocean crossing as a delivery trip expect to swallow unheated dehydrated food and wear foulies as pajamas to make the wet spinnaker a more comfortable bed. They have a different mindset and a different idea of "fun."

Nor do bluewater sailors avoid bad weather by having the boat speed to outrun a low-pressure system. Fast yachts in good conditions might manage close to 200 miles a day but to outrun a large depression in the ocean you might need a boat that can sustain 200 to 300 miles a day. On a coastal hop of a day or two there is no excuse for running into a gale unless the forecaster got it really wrong. On such passages boat speed is often the key to staying in good weather. This just means sustained speeds of seven knots rather than five knots. It shouldn't require ten knots or more.

Most modern cruising boats, if sailed conservatively with a well-prepared crew, should be safe in a strong gale, even storm force winds. You were probably more at risk from bad weather when you were a coastal sailor. Then you lacked sea room to ride out a storm and probably didn't have the equipment either, or the inclination to use it. You probably relied on weather forecasts to keep out of serious trouble and often as not just accepted the information without wondering about the limitations on it. Now that you are bluewater sailing with all the equipment to ride out storms the onus of care has shifted to you. Now that you sail with climate rather than weather there probably isn't much more that a forecaster can do at present to better serve a bluewater sailor like you.

In heavy weather the discomfort and danger is in the waves rather than the wind. A Force 10 in protected waters might give some exhilarating sailing. A Force 8 gale in open ocean can bring impressively disturbed and breaking seas, and be profoundly worrying. It is the jet pressure of breaking waves that brings danger. It is surprising how small a breaking wave need be to threaten capsize. A breaking wave with a height one third of hull length will capsize many boats. A breaking wave two thirds of hull length will overwhelm almost all boats. So a 15-foot breaking wave can flatten a 45-foot yacht and a 30-foot breaking wave may capsize you. Some places in the ocean are worse than others for breaking waves. Avoid tide races and rips, ocean currents and massive changes in depth.

Even in such places and faced with breaking waves you can sail your boat to minimize their effect. Crests rarely break the whole length of a wave. Get out of the way of the bit that is. The greatest danger is when the wave begins to break. This is when it is most full of energy. Position your boat to delay the moment when the breaker strikes.

The sailors' ideal is to test the boat in bad weather in a place of their own choosing, before the final casting off. This isn't always possible. Some of the worst waves you are likely to experience will be when crossing the Gulf Stream right at the beginning of your journey. A storm that might not bother your boat in open ocean can cause problems here with the potential for the wind to blow against the current. When a two-knot Gulf Stream current opposes a near gale, every wave will be breaking. With luck you won't have a problem other than discomfort. But the potential for trouble is there.

Avoiding a bad Gulf Stream crossing shouldn't be beyond most cautious sailors. Even this huge ocean current is seldom more than 100 miles wide. In some parts, in some years it might only be 25 miles wide. With the weather stable and a good forecast you have a good idea of what will come over the next 24 hours. Even if a storm starts to form you should have a day at least of calm before the wind rises and seas kick up. Cross the Stream as fast as you can or use current charts to tell you where the edges are and get outside the Stream. Motor or motorsail to make better speed. A day under engine is worth more than two days trailing warps.

In this turbulent area a forecast of settled weather can still mean a gale. When the official forecast lets you down you must make your own assessment. For most small boat sailors the problem is not a lack of information. Internet, weatherfax and SSB routers pump out more than enough of that. Improve your weather knowledge to understand and use the information.

Coping with or missing a Gulf Stream storm can be vital to crew morale and keeping everyone interested in the rest of your Atlantic adventure. Fear and sea-sickness so early on can make some members of the crew want to finish the crossing right here and now, or Bermuda if the rescue helicopter is delayed.

On my first Atlantic crossing we set off for the infamous Bay of Biscay with a good five-day forecast but on day three the gales came, one after the other. A few years earlier, in the same boat, I had been in the busy approaches to the English Channel when a Force 8 gale came through which built to a Force 9, so I had previous experience to draw on. The Biscay gales didn't take me beyond my experience and my own definition of dangerous weather. We had the stormsails set and the reefs in and the social program organized before the deep secondary low arrived. The boat was happy to cope without us. True, we had split our genoa and heavy water was sluicing across the deck, but the main task for me that day was keeping crew morale up. We had sea room. Life would have been foul if we had been forced to thrash to windward. I was determined to enjoy the storm, and not transmit anxiety to the crew. They, not knowing any better, took their lead from me.

The second gale in Biscay was a more serious storm but shorter lived, as secondary fronts in these latitudes often are. The seas were around twenty feet, with breaking crests. The boat rode this endless line of crests and troughs predictably until some dreadful rogue suddenly stood up and hit us. When two big waves hit us in succession we first heeled the gunwales under and then were pushed bodily sideways. This was a novelty. From the cockpit we looked over a wall into a vertical drop beyond it. At night we hardly bothered with watches. There was little chance of seeing anything and nothing we could do if we did. The boat sailed on, more or less hove-to, tiller lashed, main reefed like a pocket handkerchief, tiny staysail steadying us. We ate and chatted down below and took turns to peer out at the seascape around us.

Waves in deep ocean are not the worst I have encountered. Once I had to ride out a three-day storm only one hundred miles offshore in the relatively shallow sea between England and Ireland. Unbelievably large square-shaped waves would erupt and stand like a five-story office block till they collapsed. There might be half a dozen in view at any one time. I had never seen waves like them and had no idea what created them. I wondered what would happen if one erupted under my little boat or decided to drop on my deck.

Similarly strange but bigger monsters were reported by a friend sailing from the Azores to the Mediterranean. Two days into a three-day storm he experienced waves far beyond those expected. The 20-foot waves rode up on the 30- to 40-foot waves to produce something nearly 60 feet high. He would have thought them freaks if they hadn't been everywhere around him. They rose where they chose. His task was to avoid them.

It is always worth sailing hard as bad weather approaches, to get as far from the storm center as possible. It is also vital to put sail back on as soon as you can. A storm will often leave you with light wind and disturbed wave patterns. The stabilizing influence of the strong wind is now lost and without sail to drive you the boat is at risk. Boats have been knocked down in this phase, when the crew thought they had come through safely. Sailors have been hurt or even washed overboard by the unexpectedly violent movement of the boat in these confused waves.

The approach of bad weather is the most vital time to take care of the crew. No crew is at its best when cold and wet, tired and hungry, unwilling to go below the heaving decks and afraid of the seas they see all around them. Warm, dry, secure accommodation will tempt the crew out of the cockpit and keep them rested for later.

The skipper has the main responsibility for crew morale and comfort although it helps if other crewmembers can do some of the practical jobs, from keeping up a supply of nourishing food to wringing out the soaked bedding.

> You still have to eat in bad weather. Make sandwiches in advance. Put hot drinks in a flask. Otherwise:
>
> - Have a bum-strap in the galley so that you don't need to use your hands to hang on
> - Cook in protective waterproof clothing
> - Put cups in the sink when you pour water into them, so that spilt water goes down the drain
> - Pass things into the cockpit rather than carry them up the steps.

Stay alert. Beware the lethargy of motion sickness and fatigue. Apathy is the single greatest enemy of crew morale. Make yourself get things ready in advance.

Take seasickness remedies early. Secure deck items. Dog down hatches, especially the anchor hatch if you have a deck locker. Remove canvas sprayhoods and cockpit dodgers before the sea does it for you. Block off the hawse hole. Restrain heavy items inside the boat.

Work through the sail combinations you will use as the wind and seas get worse. Have lines ready. When you put your deepest reef in the main, get the trysail on deck and lashed down. When the trysail goes up, get trailing warps or a drogue ready. When the trysail goes up, I hope this won't be the first time. Trysails are trickier than you think. They are unusual in the way they attach to the mast, tack down and are sheeted. They need their own leads. The time to work all this out is in a flat calm, possibly while at anchor, when you have time to play. Not in a howling wind when you can only just hear your crew ask where the sheet lead is.

Books will give you plenty of ideas for heavy weather sailing. Sailors will tell you how they survived particular storms. All of this is useful but the point is that there is no single way to cope with a storm. Be ready to try different methods if what worked last time isn't working so well now.

Your first line of defense when the boat is too uncomfortable to sail is to heave-to. Most boats can heave-to although heavy long keelers probably do this most comfortably. Comfort is what you are after just now. Rest and save energy for what might come later.

Heaving-to is a common practice for us and many other sailors, regardless of the weather. We do it to catch up on rest during the day or to stop the boat catching fishing pots over night. The Pardeys have written about heaving-to after a tense night sailing between islands in strong current or finding vital navigation lights were not on station.

> Slowing the boat's forward motion when heaving-to stalls the keel and makes it behave a bit like a parachute rather than the wing we usually think. Of course, a big parachute comes down slowly and a small one comes down fast. So it is with keels. Large keel area makes slow leeway while the small area of an efficient racing keel will slip sideways quickly. This can be of considerable interest if you have danger down to lee.

With luck heaving-to will be all you need to do as the weather worsens. The aim is to keep the bows at between 30° and 60° to the wind and make no headway. Practice this in strong winds before you have to do it for real. It isn't difficult to master but you will need to learn the particular way in which your own boat heaves-to, in terms of where the rudder is positioned, the amount of mainsail you keep up and whether you back the headsail or not. Some yachts, mainly smaller ones with narrow keels, may need to stream a sea anchor from the bow to keep the head up at the right angle to the wind. A sea anchor adds complexity at times of stress. It can put enormous strain on you and your boat's fittings. It reduces your flexibility to maneuver or to try alternatives when conditions change. And of course conditions will change, usually when the center of the low passes and you are in a different quadrant with the wind from a different direction. Even so, some skippers find their sea anchor so comfortable and effective that they do this almost as their first resort.

For us on PETRONELLA, lying a-hull is the step beyond heaving-to. This is when all sail is removed and lashed down. As with heaving-to, the boat requires no help and can get on with its job of looking after the crew.

If you find yourself caught in the troughs and beam on to the waves it is time to quit heaving-to or lying a-hull before you are broached. When, for whatever reason, you can't heave-to any longer but still have plenty of sea room, you must run off. I had to run off once under bare poles in a light and lively 24 footer when caught in a full gale. It wasn't exactly the Roaring Forties but I remembered the technique Bernard Moitessier borrowed from Vito Dumas when caught in a survival storm in his JOSHUA in the South Pacific, and in my little boat I did the same. I kept the sea slightly off the stern so that I didn't risk surfing or being pooped. As the breaking crest came through I slanted the boat to about 15 or 20 degrees, anticipated the pressure to turn up into wind, and kept the boat safe from broaching. I steered like that for half a night during the worst of the storm. That's the trouble with running off. You always end up hand steering for half the night or more.

When running before a gale don't let the boat outrun the seas. Running gives you two essential benefits which you must try to hang on to. First, boat speed reduces the speed and force of the wind. Second, you are not presenting your beam to the seas. But the trick to avoiding a broach or being pooped is to keep the boat under control. Light, quick hulls with plenty of topsides may need some help here. If you are going too fast under bare poles, stream warps or, better still, tow a drogue. This will help keep your stern to the seas and save you from broaching or, if in really massive seas, save you from pitchpoling. A drogue exerts less drag when the boat slows down, as it will in troughs, and so is less likely to kill your steering. Usually a tiny foresail, preferably on the inner stay, will help you run straight. A reefed main or trysail might be dangerous if it turns you into wind and leaves you beam on to the seas.

Drogues come in many forms. You can buy them from a catalog but they don't have to be any more hi-tech or expensive than your boat. The solo skipper of a plywood 28 footer from Florida designed a drogue to match his budget. He bought two five gallon buckets and attached line through holes drilled around their tops. His luxury was to drill four attachment holes instead of three. Four seemed more stable. Weight in the buckets kept them underwater as they dragged along behind. In theory, the drag would keep the sloop's buoyant stern to the waves and stop it surfing or broaching. He put theory into practice three days after leaving Bermuda when a Force 6 began to gust Force 8. He ran under double reefed main and jib until the wind freshened and the boat began to surf down the 20-foot waves. After going down one 25-foot wave at 10 knots he opted for prudence, triple reefed the main and launched his buckets. They worked. As the breaking wave started to push the transom the buckets snagged and pulled the stern into the middle of the white water. The little boat slid smoothly down the back of the wave. Later, in the Force 8 gusting Force 9 and breaking waves of 25 to 30 feet the boat still ran comfortably with its two buckets on the warps.

Of course, not all boats respond to two buckets or other forms of drogue and when towing warps the moment may come when the length of the warp is simply no longer appropriate to the wave length. The true bravery of Moitessier was not just to angle his stern to the seas, it was to cut his warps away despite the huge wind and sea. He had realized that the warps were killing maneuverability, slowing the boat's response to his steering and exposing him to being swamped. He gambled that extra boat speed would give him back steering without driving him too fast.

Modern hull design and materials enable some yachts to sail to windward in heavy weather. This survival technique was denied sailors even 20 or 30 years ago but is perhaps the safest direction to take a design that must present its ends to the seas, especially if it has danger down to lee. The boat will need strong well cut sails, first class performance, and a person at the helm.

Hull design is just part of the survival story. Some of our deck arrangements on PETRONELLA and most of our below-deck arrangements reflect years of sailing the Caribbean, when gales are unheard of outside the hurricane season and even in rough weather you are never more than a few uncomfortable hours from shelter. On PETRONELLA we probably gave more thought to securing things than actually doing it but by screwing floorboards down I at least kept the batteries, spare chain and anchors restrained. Our forecabin didn't look pretty and leg room in the heads and under the cabin table was not all it used to be, but we weren't carrying our dinghy or fenders or miles of warps on deck nor any fuel and water containers up there. I know it is often the mark of a long-distance cruiser to have water and fuel in containers lashed to planks along the side decks, but some of them have bicycles and prams on deck that were fine in harbor. At sea that stuff should be put away. The real shellbacks also carry a sharp knife and are ready to cut deck gear away in an emergency. If you really do have insufficient capacity for water and diesel, consider having extra tanks fitted.

A clear deck brings several advantages:

- less for you or your crew to trip over when you have to go forward
- less windage or heeling forces in strong winds and breaking seas
- less vital gear to be lost overboard and rip out guardrails when the bad weather comes.

I really hate watching our dinghy slip-sliding on deck as its lashing works loose in a storm at night knowing that I don't want to get up there and fix it and that with a little forethought and energy I could have stowed it below. The things to make secure are not just the heavy and dangerous but the delicate and vulnerable too.

On deck:

- Whatever can't be removed must be lashed to secure fixing points. If need be, install through-bolted folding deck eyes before you set off. Handrails are tempting but you will need them for yourself. Never tie gear so that your handrail ceases to be a grabrail. If you have a large cockpit reduce its capacity with sail bags.

Below decks:

- Restrain batteries, tool boxes, floorboards, ladders, chain, spare anchors, propane tanks, scuba tanks, water containers, stoves and cookers, heavy locker lids, glass items, books and computers. In short, anything that can take off to become a dangerous flying object.

Think of your crew too as loose, frail, vulnerable and potentially dangerous flying objects. With no delaying handhold you can work up a good speed across the saloon of a 40 footer as it broaches. It isn't just the damage that flying crew can do to fine furniture and irreplaceable glassware. You can smash skulls and a few ribs too.

Going for gale

I know I say only go to sea in a sturdy boat and be ready for anything but actually there is less and less reason not to know what the weather will do. G has made understanding weather one of her top priorities, perhaps because she feels I haven't.

> I asked a big ship's captain for a weather forecast. "We don't bother with them," he said. "When it is time for us to leave we go. Knowing the weather in advance would not help us." This, give or take a weatherfax or two, is roughly my own lax attitude but I don't have the tonnage to get me out of trouble.

I'm not proud to admit that I can't forecast weather but then nor can anyone else I've met. You can work with most of the weather you'll meet offshore. The rest you just have to live with. Any trip of five days or more takes you outside the forecast period and no broadcast forecast is so wonderfully accurate that it will be right for where you are at that precise minute. Keep well informed but don't blame a good forecast when you catch something you don't like.

> The Fastnet race disaster of August 1979, one of the worst disasters in the history of ocean racing, happened largely because of unforecast bad weather. When the skippers were preparing for the race they expected some strong winds, up to Force 7. They didn't realize that a small storm centered over Ohio was deepening at a catastrophic rate and would hit them the next morning with gales overnight developing into a full storm Force 10 and worse at the rock itself. As the storm developed and breaking waves the size of houses arrived, sailors with a huge amount of experience realized that this was something beyond anything they had met in the past. The report of the disaster by the Royal Ocean Racing Club, drawing on the eyewitness accounts of sailors, is one of the great contributions to coping with heavy weather. It wasn't just the storm that did the damage but where precisely boats were. Some boats were in seas that threatened their very survival. Others simply experienced a bad gale.

One sailor's definition of heavy weather compared to another's is usually a matter of experience and the chance to handle a boat in worsening conditions.

With luck, experience brings competence and so you win two long-term prizes for the price of a little fear and discomfort. The only way to get this is to go out there when the breeze is blowing hard and try all the tricks of reefing, raising storm canvas, heaving-to and running off. A passage in rough water need not be a long one to give you experience and the boat a test. Regard a spell of heavy weather as an essential part of your experience, an experience you will never get by sitting in harbor waiting for the forecaster to say you have a "weather window." You never want to knowingly set off into a gale but there is something very reassuring about coming through bad weather unscathed.

> I have learned two eternal truths from my offshore sailing. First, the sea can always blow up a storm when it wants to. Second, I might as well forget about meteorology and just keep practicing slab reefing.

The Horse Latitudes can lull you into a false sense of eternal Force 3s. You think you would like a bit more wind and say things like "Wouldn't a Force 5 be nice." Some crew might shout "Come blow strong winds and tempests all" and you get a vaguely fearful feeling in the pit of your stomach. The ancient gods of wind are not to be tempted or called, lest they come.

We had our Horse Latitudes "gale" when several hundred miles southwest of the Azores. It came with plenty of warning but after all our easy days in the Horse Latitudes none of this warning was credible. The barometer dropped from 1024 to 1016. As if that wasn't enough, the swell from the northeast came rolling in at 10 to 12 feet. Four-foot waves ran in confusion along the back of the swell. The sky clouded and squall lines ran across from the northwest. We had a Force 4 and expected it to increase to Force 5. E started his watch at dusk, kindly planning to do the whole night to let me catch up on sleep. It taught us the lesson that the sea can always teach a lesson to the unwary.

> **Lesson 1 at sea**
> Troubles happen when more than one thing isn't working. I wasn't working. Fortunately whatever had poisoned my system didn't get to E's until the next day, when I had recovered.

The strong wind came through in the dark, bringing heavy rain and such thick cloud that the big moon was put out.

Lesson 2 at sea
It is always a very dark night when the storm arrives, just when you want bright daylight.

The wind blew a steady Force 7 and at intervals rose to full gale 8. An unnoticed problem with the self steering forced E to spend nearly the whole of his watch at the wheel. With one reef in the main and full genoa the boat was not over-canvassed but she was badly balanced and hard to steer in the rising seas. Down below, I had no sense of a boat struggling with the seas and no sense that E was working too hard but at dawn when I came on deck we put in a second reef, rolled away half the genoa and hoisted the staysail. With better balance and a lower sail-plan we drove the boat harder, put one knot on our speed and made her steer straighter.

PETRONELLA's natural ability to sail herself on the wind had probably covered up Mr Aries' failure to work in the preceding days but she couldn't continue this trick without the right sail balance. Now she dashed along at six knots at 45 degrees to the wind and not a finger on the wheel even though waves hit her at all angles and water ran continually off the decks.

Lesson number 1 revisited
Reef down in daylight when both hands are on deck. We should have done this 12 hours earlier but were too complacent to suspect a gale and too badly organized when it came.

On this route from the Caribbean to the Azores you can't afford to waste a minute of a near gale. We had a 24-hour pussy cat compared to the harder winds further north where gales might blow for 48 or 72 hours and where gale can follow gale with ever increasing wave heights. In our 24-hour storm the seas didn't have time to become worrying never mind dangerous. Our little storm drove us straight and hard towards Horta but behind it came dying breezes as the pressure rose and then a flat calm for six hours. The new wind, when it came, was from the wrong direction and headed us too far north.

Lesson 3 at sea
Use the gale. We wasted precious wind by not reducing sail and pushing the boat faster.

Fearlessly forward

Bluewater sailors often debate the pros and cons of technological solutions to sailhandling compared to the older fashioned use of ropes and muscle. I have quit this debate when it comes to headsail roller reefing. I acknowledge that roller reefing can fail dangerously, and I admit that we get more snags with our reefing foresail than with any of our other sails, but I hope never to go back to the wet days of changing sails at the end of the bowsprit. Roller reefing does the vital job of keeping me and my crew off the foredeck in heavy weather.

But I will still enter the debate on in-mast and in-boom mainsail furling as against slab reefing. The keep-it-simple argument seems to appeal here to a lot of bluewater sailors. Slab reefing is simple. When it fails it is more likely to have failed safe than the other systems. With a couple of simple additions it can be made even simpler.

Lazy jacks are lines that run from the mast to the boom to catch the mainsail as it falls and prevent it from spilling all over the boom and deck. I first fitted them to my little estuary cruiser so I could drop the main without embarrassment when sailing onto my mooring. I have used them ever since. There is no reason not to fit lazy jacks to conventional mainsails. The design and fitting of the cheek blocks and lines is truly trivial.

I am also a convert to the boom gallows. This is a fine old-fashioned solution to safer reefing or just working on deck. A boom that swings even six inches when reefing or tidying away the dropped sail is potentially dangerous and prolongs the job. We drop the boom into the gallows as soon as we drop sail. And when the last reef goes into the mainsail, the one that you really are going to rely on in the filthy weather to come, I like to have the boom secure so my shaking fingers can knot the reefing line to perfection. But it wasn't just safety I had in mind when I fitted the gallows. Of all the annoying noises a boat makes when rolling in a windless swell—the click-clack of plates, the thump-thump of binoculars in their rack—none matches the smack-crash of the tightly sheeted boom slamming over the few inches that cannot be removed no matter how hard the sheet is cranked in.

Last of the simple essentials for slab reefing: the boom preventer. In strong winds on an ocean crossing you don't want an accidental gibe. You need a boom preventer that is always rigged or ready to be rigged, can be reset from the cockpit every time you tack or jibe, and is able to be let go in a breath. You can buy patent-protected ones off the shelf, or you can make your own. Ours is simple. Two lines go from near the outer end of the boom to the deck rail. One goes to port, one to starboard, each runs through a block with a becket. Each is led aft to where they can be cleated. We rarely need to use a winch on them. We also run preventers on our staysail and mizzen.

We love our self tacking staysail but we call the boom "Mr Whackit."
The generic term for booms is "widow makers." Delay your encounter
with this aspect of them.

Make sure your preventer blocks and fittings are strong. We carelessly blew out
two blocks during our Trade Wind crossing. We learned the tell-tale signs of a
half completed gibe. The blocks groan audibly, the line stretches thinner before
our very eyes.

Our old fashioned rig requires reefs to be taken in at the mast but we are used
to this and I never think it dangerous to go forward on deck. We have good
handholds as far as the main mast and then mast pulpits, which we call "granny
bars," to snuggle into. I'm not even sure I approve of having all lines led back into
the cockpit. It might make working the mainsail more convenient if you have a
powerful winch to overcome the friction of the many right angles in the leads but
I'm not sure it adds to the ultimate safety of the boat. It is Murphy's Law that
when some problem arises which requires you to go forward it will be in bad
weather. You will not be as used to being on deck in those conditions and you
may be too concerned with your personal safety to be safe.

When I go forward in bad weather I concentrate on the task at hand, not the
mind-numbing consequences of falling overboard. Getting the right frame of
mind seems to make the body more relaxed and each new move seems to be done
easily and smoothly. Get used to going forward on your own boat, letting your
hands find things to grab and your body used to the motion. On PETRONELLA we
often go out to the end of the bowsprit for communing with nature or to watch
the dolphins. Maybe it looks risky to some but familiarity with foredeck and
bowsprit pays off for us.

It was late, it was dark, we were 1,000 miles offshore and making six
knots into a sloppy sea when we reefed the jenny and pulled the reefing line through the stops. No reefing line; no chance of using the
jenny till we re-rove the line. We could leave it till daylight but by then
we might have a second problem and be in desperate need of that
jenny. I think one gear problem is manageable. When you have two
at the same time the ship is in danger. E had pulled the line out but
I know the boat better so I went forward. Grabrails take me as far as
the main mast. Rigging gives handholds to the inner forestay. And
then all it takes is a little canter to reach the pulpit. After that all I
had to do was straddle the bowsprit and wriggle forward a few feet till

I could comfortably reach the furling gear at the end of the bowsprit. I was there about an hour. When I was finished I realized E had been standing at the inner forestay, presumably to save me if a wave washed me off the bowsprit. I was appalled at his disregard for his safety. I didn't have time to tell him so before he cursed me for a fool at what I had done. But I had been in no danger once I had reached the bowsprit. All the danger lay in crossing the foredeck, which is what he had been planning to do. I would have sat on that bowsprit till dinner time tomorrow to finish the job rather than risk crossing the foredeck twice.

Try this

The storm trysail is a bit like the sextant. It is often regarded as the mark of the true bluewater sailor though few are likely to prefer it to the alternatives. If you ever need to use it, it is best if you have put in a lot of practice beforehand. It won't work if you haven't got all the rest of the kit that goes with it. And it's always under a pile of junk when the crisis comes and you need it.

On this Atlantic adventure it is probably only those sailing on the northern routes who will come across the storm conditions that require a trysail. But then the ocean is a funny old place and bad weather can catch out even us southern-route rabbits. I'm not superstitious, not in the least, but I have the idea in my head that the day we leave the trysail behind will be the one passage when we need to use it for real.

The cutter rigged Crealock 34 carried but never used a storm trysail and a storm jib. They never met more than a Force 8 gale on their route via the Azores and for this their working sails were enough. The third reef they had added to their main before leaving New England got plenty of use.

Like most sailors who follow the seasons I have never had to use our trysail in a life-threatening storm. But I did use it out in the deep ocean one day when I was desperate to stop the rhythmic rolling of the Trade Wind crossing and hoped that the trysail would give balance to the twin headsails. It didn't, but that is another story.

The purpose of a storm trysail in bad weather is to balance the storm jib and hold the head of the boat up to windward better than a deep reefed main. It is also built to survive the storm better than the deep reefed main, so that when the winds die down you will still have a mainsail and can get back to sailing. The trysail is also able to be sheeted without a boom, so it gives you an alternative when the boom is broken. Most coastal sailors will not carry a trysail. They will rely on the strength of modern sail cloth to bring them through most bad weather with just a third reef. But the offshore racing rules require yachts racing across oceans or in unprotected areas to carry a trysail, so there must be something in it.

The weather bomb that hit the Sydney-Hobart Race in 1998 proved to be a field test for the trysail and a major revision in thinking about its use. The first lesson was that too many boats were carrying trysails to preserve their expensive racing sails. When they sailed into truly extreme conditions their trysails were too large. The second lesson was that few boats had the ancillary gear to use their trysail in a survival storm.

The trysail needs to be small, probably less than the size of your third reefed main. It should be a heavier weight of cloth than the main, but softer so you can handle it. It needs strong track slides. All ours are aluminum though I've heard people argue that you can get away with plastic slides as long as you have aluminum slides at the top and the bottom. A sailor I met in Horta in the Azores wouldn't agree with that. He lost his mainsail in a gale when his plastic slides started to pop. He had replacements made in steel before he headed back to the ocean.

The preferred means of hoisting the trysail is on its own track, so that you don't have to reach above the stack of doused mainsail. We don't have a separate track but we can drop our main right out of its track. I have done that and can tell you that it is better than trying to feed a sail into track six feet above a heaving deck, but it still isn't really what you want to be doing in a storm. I have toyed with the idea of having a short, lower second track which links to the main track with a set of "points" like railways use. This used to be common in the days before I was born when sailors kept their trysail bagged and hanked-on whenever they went offshore. If I ever see a set of points that fit our track I will buy it. If you have in-mast or in-boom furling then you are at the mercy of whatever the designer deemed necessary. If I were you, I'd get the brochure out right now.

The Challenge Business runs round-the-world and ocean races that put its especially designed yachts through conditions that most cruisers would pay to avoid. They like trysails and have spent the last decade refining how to handle and use them. One major problem has been mast track. The mainsail track just couldn't cope, and the crews were unhappy trying to reach that high, so the first modification was a separate track for the trysail. Their second modification was to make the track stronger. A track designed to cope with 60-knot winds was getting bent and torn when waves slammed into the sail. Look at what you have on your mast and consider that in the conditions when you need a trysail it is hard to make any track strong enough.

The trysail should be sheeted direct to the stern quarter rather than to the boom, so that in severe weather the boom is not a danger to the crew or in danger of tripping and breaking on a wave. This means having blocks on the quarter and a means to restrain the boom when it isn't being used. We drop ours into a boom gallows. This is about as out of date on modern yachts as a set of mast track points but certainly beats trying to disconnect a boom vang or lash the boom to the deck. In less than severe weather you would probably be better off sheeting the trysail to the end of the boom, so long as the trysail can support the boom.

These practical matters are not trivial. Getting the details right makes for a quicker hoist, and that makes the crew and the boat safer at a time when safety really matters. You have a lot of details to get right, apart from those I have just mentioned. You need a rope tack pennant, because wire will cut your mainsail to ribbons. You need to bag the trysail so that the slides come out in the right order. You might want to mark the halyard so you know when you have the sail at the right height. You need to sort all this out in light weather while you and your credit card are still in reach of a chandler's. And even then you might decide to risk not bothering with a trysail. Why not, the debate seems fairly open to me. Modern sail cloth and construction methods make for immensely strong sails and a fourth reef seems an easier option than trying to hoist a completely new sail. If that leaves you open to blowing your main away, carry a spare main. Of course, a deep third reef or a fourth reef isn't kind to the rig. When the foot of the sail is so short, the loads on the leech are enormous.

The practicalities of setting a storm jib are more straightforward. I don't believe it is possible to hoist or set a foresail in a gale without a wire to give you luff tension. I have seen ways of hoisting a storm jib over a roller furled foresail, but I have never seen this done at sea. You should aim for a hank-on sail and a wire stay dedicated to it. Pulling a roller-reefed genoa out of its extrusion and slipping a new storm jib into its place is not something I would willingly consider during a storm. And then remember that your storm jib will need its separate sheets, ready fastened before hoisting to save you the entertainment of trying to reach the wildly flogging tack afterwards, and different sheet leads to your normal headsails.

Oddly, the trysail and storm jib may be even more important for the light weight, quick, racing-pedigree hulls than the heavy displacement boats that probably carry such sails as a matter of pride. The easily driven hull needs to slow down to be comfortable in really severe weather, or else it may broach or crash land and damage itself. Sailing slowly is a bit like heaving-to, but brings the light weight, short keel boat the added benefits of steerage. A design that heels easily is in danger of turning to windward, out of control and starting to broach. It might be saved from this by having enough maneuverability when sailing slowly for the helmsperson to be able to pick the best part of the wave crest to cross. Sailing slowly through a storm means having a trysail and storm sail small enough for the weather. Maybe you should kit yourself out with storm sails for a boat 10 feet smaller than yours.

There is a lot to be said for heaving-to or sailing through a storm rather than running with it. Chris, a twice around-the-world French singlehander, smiled when G asked him for his worst storm. It was when he was a novice, of course, just leaving northwest France to head south to the Mediterranean. He was caught by a storm from the north. He didn't feel comfortable heaving-to so he ran with it. The storm was moving at perhaps 15 knots. He was sailing at about six knots. Instead of having a gale for 24 hours he took a beating for four days. He was taking the gale with him. He figured his mistake out later and never repeated it. "If you're not going with it, you get through it quicker."

11

Light weather sailing

PETRONELLA was heavy before we loaded the tons of ocean crossing stores. Then her marks went underwater and stayed there. In crossing trim, any boat that once ghosted happily in Force 2 is wallowing in a Force 3. Working sails need reinforcements when the wind drops to a Force 3 or less. You'll be amazed how often that is. We were no sooner out of the Trades and into the Horse Latitudes than it dawned on me that we didn't have the right sails for this passage. Give plenty of thought to your light weather sails and with luck you will never need your storm sails.

Life ashore has taught me that when there are still a dozen solutions to a simple problem there isn't one that works. Light weather sails are a fine floating example of this.

Take the genoa. This is such an inadequate solution that most yacht designs come with genoas numbered from one to six or even more. The bigger the number, the firmer the grip the sailmaker has on your pocketbook. Even PETRONELLA has a sail plan showing four genoas. Where would I keep them? I can't hear myself saying to G, "Sorry, darling, you're off the crew list for this one. I need your berth for number three and four genoas. See you in a month or so." And as for the spinnaker, I regard this as so lethal for a weak crew at sea that I won't hear of having one on board. Unless, that is, it's of a rather wonderful design I'm still working on.

Why do we let sailmakers make us feel so inadequate? Decades ago I used to feel inadequate when I went into a hi-fi shop and was examined on woofers and tweeters and cross-over units. Now hi-fi has been replaced by computer and cell phone shops as the place where people of my generation go to feel inadequate. I don't understand why sailmakers feel the need to similarly test my ignorance. What's your J number? Do you want tri-radial or cross cut? They could be talking about marmalade for all I know.

Sailmakers expect us to add two spinnakers to the six genoas, at least one cruising chute and a multi-purpose genoa to cover the gap. They sneer at my cutter rig, beloved of generations of great ocean wanderers, with its tiny sail on its painted wooden boom, sweeping the foredeck like the Old Reaper's scythe.

Light as a breeze—set the spinnaker flying

Is the reason we don't have a spinnaker on PETRONELLA a principled stand that such sails have no place on a shorthanded bluewater cruiser or do I call it a principle because we don't have a spinnaker? Without a doubt a boat with a spinnaker, the gear and the crew would be flying it all the way through the Horse Latitudes. They would be getting two more knots in the Force 3 winds and enough steering speed in the Force 2. It would have saved us hours of rolling in calms when we were reluctant to motor and gallons of diesel when we pressed the starter button. A spinnaker could be worth 500 miles on this route, and that could be the difference between 20 days and 25 days at sea, between arriving with empty water tanks or coming in freshly showered, between finishing your last beer as you head for the Customs' dock or having finished it a week earlier.

On PETRONELLA we have no hands to spare when spinnaker poles and lines make for foredeck confusion and no spare crew to constantly trim the sheet. Also, we have seen the amusing disasters when the huge sail wraps around the stay or decides to give the foredeck crew a trapeze ride. Of course, we realized we had been over-cautious in the matter of spinnakers when we went sailing with Emm.

G and I watched in envy as Emm refused all offers of help in raising and dropping the big spinnaker, and did both without any drama. The secret is a symmetrical spinnaker that needs no pole and therefore does away with all the lines that poles need. His symmetrical spinnaker only needs sheets. It will happily sway 20 degrees either side of the bow and remain full of wind and pulling the boat. When it has to come down, it just needs a snuffer from the masthead to put the sail to sleep. Emm had designed the snuffer himself, after a lot of experimentation. It worked for him and he was modest enough to say it might not work for anyone else. Needless to say, we had a sketch of his ideas with us when we left his boat.

Our problem in the Horse Latitudes was that we needed a sail we didn't have. We needed a huge light cruising headsail that would catch and hold this weak following breeze. Our foresails were all too small and heavy, being designed for running down the boisterous Trades, and the nearer we came to a dead run the more they flapped uselessly, blanketed by the main and rolled by the swell. I craved a huge overlapping genoa of the lightest cloth for when we were close hauled or reaching and a huge light weight chute for when we were off the wind. On a truly dead run we dropped the genoa and hauled out the main and mizzen as far as the shrouds allowed. The preventers kept the booms out despite our gentle rolling, but nothing could keep the sails drawing well in such light airs. The slightest roll would spill the wind from the main, our best driving sail. With a consistent two knots more of wind we would have steadied the main and doubled our boat speed. Two knots is so little extra to ask but proved impossible to get.

In the flat seas of the Horse Latitudes we might have been able to sail goose-winged, but I have never found this comfortable out on the ocean when there is almost always a swell and watching others sail wing-on-wing usually adds a dash of comedy to any day.

> We came up on a Czech boat on our penultimate day before Horta. They were to the north and barely visible. To our surprise they had not sailed into our vision in order to sail out of it. We were closing on them. As daylight faded, even at a distance of two miles we could see the boat gyrating wildly for no reason we could fathom. When the wind fell to nothing they sailed on in this odd and uncomfortable manner while we hove-to to rest and set off again when the new breeze came four hours later. At dawn, with a good breeze at last, we came up fast on the Czech yacht. We could see why it was gyrating so horribly. They were goose-winging, their jib poled right out. The wind came first into the main, then into the jib, then they rolled their decks under with the swell. We roared by on a broad reach, PETRONELLA's sweet hull steady as a super-tanker. Perhaps being able to pole out a jib isn't always a good thing.

There is, my sailmaker friends tell me, a new generation of asymmetric reaching sails, some of which are small and cut flat for close winded work and some larger and fuller for off wind work. These are developments of the Flasher sail popular in Britain and the Multi Purpose Genoa which I remember fondly as a very useful addition to my previous boat.

Developments in materials and dousing methods have helped but the real breakthrough comes from the ability of sailmaking software to design the curves. One of these new general purpose light weather sails of 1.5 ounce nylon can cope with winds up to 15 knots and angles of 60 to 140 degrees. To be robust and forgiving enough for offshore work and able to be handled by a shorthanded crew, the sail will be about two thirds the size of a coastal reacher, but they will repay in diesel saved and extra miles covered in greater comfort.

SECTION FIVE

A taste of
ocean pleasures

12

Stable as the Horse Latitudes

Talking of Horses

I wrote to a Canadian friend who had for years been a boatyard neighbor of ours when we both laid up in Trinidad for the hurricane season. I feared he was spending more time with horses than with his boat.

> Dear John,
> Its time you saw more than the southern Caribbean. I have wonderful news for you. After you sail to the Virgins for a taste of Caribbean sailing without swell I want you to head north and east into the most fantastic calm emptiness of the ocean, and renew your reasons for sailing.

I shall never forget sailing in the Horse Latitudes. Reading the Pilot Charts hadn't prepared me for such docile solitude. As we left the domestic conviviality of the Virgins I waited for evil to strike. I counted the days, perplexed but anxious. Surely it would only be all the more terrible for being so long delayed? Gradually I realized that each morning here really is one of the most beautiful mornings imaginable. Such clear skies are impossible in the tropics and unimaginable among the Westerly lows. These clouds formed such pretty shapes to entertain us with art, not frighten us with raw power. And the sea ripples like a lake because there is no near-gale to turn ripples into waves.

It was hard to shake the feeling that the ocean was always going to do something unpleasant. After all, what's to stop it? It took time to learn I could rely on good weather. Every morning the shadows of blue and white and grey that defined the day were all at the horizon, five miles away. These gentle, almost transparent hazes overlaid the light blue of the sky. The beauty of the scene lay in its scale. The distance to the horizon was immense. Clouds rose in tiny patches and distinct shapes from horizon to zenith. You have to come here to realize what I mean.

Friends crossing in 2002 had been just as smitten. They didn't chase non-existent winds. They drifted, confident a breeze would return. "Didn't you think 28 days was a long time?" I asked. "It was the best month of my life," came the reply.

Slow as a mule

The miles we logged from noon-to-noon and the hours we motored tell a sad but powerful story. I found it odd that there was so much variation in daily distance, given so little change in conditions, until I realized that on our worst days the miles we covered were in zigzags looking for better wind.

I dislike motoring on ocean passages. I prefer the attitude that we can't motor across an ocean. Reaching for the starter button even once makes you more inclined to do it the second time. But we would have motored more if we had not been worried about running out of fuel before we reached the famous calms of the Azores High. We had a serious diesel bug and were not able to use fuel from all our tanks. Better to wait for wind in the Horse Latitudes where there is a chance of finding it, than in the Azores where you have no hope. In practice we found good wind close to the archipelago, as did other boats in different years. Perhaps the islands produce a local effect which allows a sailing breeze to live within the wide open isobars of the Azores High.

If you must motor through the Horse Latitudes then motor towards wind. One skipper north of us was receiving weather information and had a better idea than us of where to find wind. He would motor when becalmed, which for him was anything less than 3 knots. There was a price to pay. He did more sail changing, damaged more gear and did more hand steering. He beat us by four days. He worked a lot harder. I doubt he enjoyed the trip as much as I did.

A sad tale of the horse: in 28 days we logged 2,348 miles but on some days did as little as 40 miles. The 61 hours we motored probably accounted for 10% of the miles we traveled. We seldom motored for more than one or two hours a day.

Motoring slowly to Horta

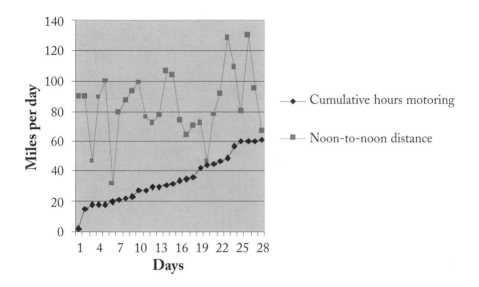

Horse Wisdom

We learned some important lessons sailing the Horse Latitudes.

You need patience. The winds will not rush you. You will be there a long time.

The wind was never where the Pilot Chart showed it should be. Perhaps the seasons were out of joint.

Days were similar but no two were the same in terms of wind strength and direction, cloud cover, cloud build up or sunsets. Wind tended to fade at sunset and die by midnight, to return around dawn. I wouldn't bet on the regularity of this.

Sunsets were wonderful although usually through a haze of red cloud. The drop in temperature after the Caribbean was noticeable, even with a south wind, yet the sun was always bright and hot.

No ships to see but in that stunning visibility no room for one to hide. At dusk, when clouds often filled in and obscured the sunset, there was still no question of reduced visibility. During the night this sunset cloud would often lift and stars would appear low down completely encircling us.

We saw birds and flying fish but not much of either. We were followed by three or four large dark gulls day after day. They would circle and flop down in the sea to watch us go by, then fly round again to flop ahead of us and watch us go by. I'm sure it was always the same few birds.

We discovered an odd life form—the Plasto-hog. It had a seemingly plastic upper body in the shape of a sail and could tack into the wind. It moved in the same shuffling way as a hedgehog. We captured one in the name of science, measured it, sketched it and put it back in the ocean and watched it hog off. Later we discovered it was a Portuguese Man o' War (Physalia physalis) and we were grateful not to have discovered its sting.

Physalia physalis is not a single creature. Underneath the blue or purple "sail" is a complex community working as a single entity. Some of these creatures have stinging tentacles up to 100 feet long. Don't touch them, even when they are washed up on the beach and apparently dead. One sailor between Bermuda and the Azores pulling in his heavy weather warps found they were covered in Portuguese Man o' War stingers. His hands were burning. He chewed some dried papaya to a pulp and covered the stings. The burning ceased and by morning there was no damage to his skin. I don't think we had dried papaya nor knew its medicinal value. Most meat tenderizer have dried green papaya in them, so they would do. And if you haven't got any use the ammonia in your own bladder.

We began to accept the absence of swell as normal. Swell, a wave produced by winds outside their present area, can penetrate up to 2,000 to 3,000 miles from the belt of Disturbed Westerlies and is a major irritant in most of the ocean. We expected to meet swell once we got north into the Westerlies and on the eastern side of the ocean. Delaying this pleasure made me all the happier with our Horse Latitudes slop.

On good sailing days we got up to five or six knots and would look forward to a 120 plus mile day, but no day had consistently good winds for us to manage this. The days grew more mixed the further we went, hence our better averages. With the extra wind came swell. This was nothing compared to the Caribbean but it could take the edge off boat speed and make nights uncomfortable.

The bow sends up white spray. Speed builds to six knots and then PETRONELLA loses her regular encounter with the waves. As she rises another wave slips under her so that she continues rising when she should be falling. The cushion of this extra wave can't be sustained. The falling bow hits the oncoming wave in a great explosion of spray. White water runs down the lee deck, the hull staggers, speed drops to four knots. We bear off, pick up speed and come back on course. Five knots build to six and then it happens again. It happens

> every two minutes, 30 times an hour, 360 times in the night. Every tenth one is a bigger rise, a harder hit. And each time PETRONELLA crashes off the wave I wince a little for her, tense my muscles and hope it was just water we hit.

If nature had planted islands in the Horse Latitudes they would be the world's favorite resort. Sailors tired of the unrelenting Trade Winds or the wild westerly depressions would drift here in flocks. We would be the lotus eaters—"Oh rest ye brother mariners we will not journey more." Our calluses would turn to silk-soft skin. Our moral fiber would decay. We would be fit for nothing but Force 3 breezes and millpond seas.

Out of the Horses

True to its nature, the Horse Latitudes seemed reluctant to let us pass. We saw signs of changeable weather and had periods of stronger wind which tempted us to believe that we were breaking free, but they passed and the familiar clear air, high pressure and soft breezes reasserted themselves.

> **PETRONELLA log, Day 18**
> Our good wind died at dawn and I came on deck to see as black a front as ever I have seen. Blackness stretched round the western and northern horizons and rain streamed down to the sea. We rolled in the swell waiting for the inevitable wind but all we got was rain. The only wind we got came behind the front. Our previous southwest wind was replaced by a northwesterly, which died after three hours. It was still the Horse Latitudes, but the sky was different. Cloud overhead was bigger and higher and more massed on the horizon. Atmospheric pressure was still 1024 mb but the sea had a livelier look that promised wind, we hoped.

In trying to explain why we failed to clear the Horse Latitudes I wondered whether a diurnal factor was at work as we went further north, so that we more clearly received cooler air from the high altitudes as it descended to sea level. Certainly we were getting cooler air. And I wondered what happened at night when the cold air from the troposphere met the warm surface of the sea, when there was no radiation heat from the hot sun to expand the air, absorb moisture and keep the air dry. Did this explain the build up of cloud in the late afternoon and the heavy, rain-bearing cloud we saw at dawn? At night, without a breath of wind, visibility at sea level seemed misty while still diamond bright in the high sky.

It was as though the falling cold air took heat and moisture and pushed it upwards in a sort of small area of low pressure which tantalized us until the morning sun burnt it off. Certainly, those clouds looked like convection clouds but by mid-morning there was nothing left in the sky but isolated puffs of candy floss.

My republic for a Horse

When we reached the Azores we asked other sailors for their reaction to the Horse Latitudes. Even I was surprised by the obvious enjoyment three Czechs on a 35 footer got from their 44-day passage. With the strict rationing that 44 days implied this had to be more uncomfortable than anything E and I had suffered.

> "Well," E said, "that tells us something about life in the new Czech Republic."

13

Life in the Azores

No time limit

The more G and I thought about it the more appealing a prolonged stop in the Azores became. We had just come back from a visit to the bottom of Faial's ancient caldeira and were having a drink in Peter's Bar, so no wonder we were wide open to this new idea. We realized that spending a year here was a once in a lifetime opportunity. Suddenly we were in no hurry to get to mainland Europe.

For us, as for the other boats crossing the ocean, the Azores began as just a convenient halfway stop. Like the others, we just intended to rest, restock and sail on. I don't know why we all want to keep going. Perhaps visiting yachts are put off by the changeable weather here, especially if the famous Azores High hasn't arrived. Also, most yachts simply don't have the time. Those heading for northern Europe still have a long way to go before the weather turns against them. Some of those heading for the Mediterranean are on a tight delivery for owners who like to winter in the Caribbean and take summer in the Mediterranean. Others have been away long enough already and need to get back to family and jobs. None of that applied to us. We needed a place to stay over the winter and till we got there the Azores weren't even on the long list. Also, we grew excited about exploring the nine islands of the 300-mile long archipelago. Most yachts just give themselves time to see Horta on Faial and take the ferry to Pico.

The British sailors we met in Horta were doing the Atlantic. The skipper had sailed his family across with the ARC, had done the Caribbean from St Lucia to Antigua, seen enough and was sailing home with a delivery crew of old friends. They had no deadlines but sailing was a driving sport for them and they saw no reason to stay in Horta longer than it took for the next weather window to open.

Our American neighbors on the marina wall had sightseen Faial in three days, assimilated the culture on their fourth and were off tomorrow to check out Terceira for half a day before mainland Portugal and the Mediterranean.

If we hadn't met J&L we might have changed our plan and gone with the herd. We had last seen them in Trinidad a year earlier. They were sailing from South Africa with no fixed destination but I had certainly not expected to moor opposite them in the Azores. They had spent a winter in Horta, seen most of the islands, and were planning to put down roots. After they had told me about their winter here I was hooked. This was the place.

The big question mark was whether the Azores was a safe place to spend the winter. The Azores are, after all, just little volcanic rocks in a huge ocean. When the ocean roars, the Azores just have to take it. The protecting band of high pressure slips south in the winter and although the islands are not in the worst bands of Atlantic weather they are open to big winter storms. We didn't want to discover that the harbor was dangerous in a huge winter storm and find ourselves forced to run for the mainland.

Faial, Azores. I was tempted to join the citizens of Horta on their regular New Year's Day swim, but I resisted. There are limits even to hedonism.

Year round wind and weather at the Azores

Month	Wind and weather	Likelihood of gales
May	From all quarters; mainly Force 5-6. Force 7 possible	No gales
June	Light, mainly W from S to NW. Rarely over Force 4	No gales
July	Calms and light winds. Mainly W from SW to N	No gales
August	From all quarters; mainly W from SW to NW. Force 6 max	No gales
September	Light winds from all quarters; mainly S	No gales
October	All quarters; mainly W from SW to North. Force 6 max	From W and NW
November	All quarters but mainly W	From NW east around to SE
December	From S to NW. Near gales from S	From NW
January	From S to SW	From S and SW
February	All quarters; mainly W from SE round to N	From S/SE and N/NW
March	Mainly S to NW	From NW
April	W from S to North, mainly NW to North. Possible Force 7 from NW	No gales

Source: Pilot Charts

We needn't have worried. The harbor at Horta has learned the lesson of break-waters. The little yacht marina shelters behind two of them and we tied ourselves to the inner wall on a dozen lines and big fenders. We burst a couple of fenders over the winter but replaced them with old car tires. So much more robust.

No two years the same

I was glad to have crossed in 2003, even though we had so little wind and others seemed to have so much. The year 2004 never seemed to settle into a comfortable pattern. It began badly for one 45-foot French yacht that had gone to the Caribbean in November 2003 and was in too much of a hurry to get home. She arrived in Horta with a delivery crew of three in January 2004. Ten days of her fifteen days from St Martin had been storms. The boat had destroyed its genoa, taken so much water below that all the electrics ceased to function, and never had windvane self steering. The three crew were also hammered. The skipper had been flung across the cockpit and broke two ribs. The other male member of the crew had dislocated his shoulder. The female crew was bruised from head to toe. G heard her in the showers singing, which we later realized was for the joy of being on land.

Even in the winter months new boats would arrive. A French Open 50 arrived for Christmas, just doing some sea trials ahead of a race later in the year. She was pretty enough to get the newspapers out taking photographs. A powerful steel boat came in as part of its circumnavigation of Africa. They had beat up from the Cape in foul headwinds and thought nothing of the storm they sailed through to finally reach Horta.

But the season of arrivals doesn't take off till May. Apart from the maverick singlehanders or skippers unable to read the weather charts, it is the big boats on delivery that arrive first in May and are the first to leave. They are on a schedule, making delivery trips from the Caribbean to the Mediterranean for the changing charter season or to be ready for their rich owners. These are huge and beautiful sailing ships in immaculate condition and with the latest high tech equipment. They have hydraulic rams and hot tubs where the rest of us have old fashioned turnbuckles and a bucket.

As the days pushed into May, the smaller boats arrived mainly from the Caribbean. Those coming from America were in the vanguard, and regretting being early. In 2004 they took a dusting from the Gulf Stream, which seemed to be wider than usual that year and throwing up bad cross seas. Casting off a week later would have made quite a difference to comfort. Even in late May the boats coming in from Florida were reporting bad weather.

Boats sailing to the Bermuda latitudes from the Caribbean in 2004 struggled against persistent, often strong northeasterlies. One boat spent a week sailing first north and then south, going nowhere with the wind but unable to motor into steep breaking seas. The rhumb route was a popular choice but one 46 footer spent a day running under storm sails in what I remember as the empty and calm Horse Latitudes.

> The longer the passage, the more chance of changes in the weather. A Czech boat, inappropriately named OK, pushed up Caribbean average passage times in 2003. They had what they called a "hurricane." Perhaps it was Ana. They had been on track for a slow 30 days but their "hurricane" blew them backwards for four days and then the skipper refused to motor in the week of windless calm and lumpy seas that followed. Their 43 days was a record breaker.

It seemed that 2004 was a hard year to forecast, but then I said the same about 2003. The reason for this gradually became clear. Forecasters reckoned that spring 2004 had been delayed by about three weeks. Boats leaving the Caribbean and America in early summer had set off too soon. The northern Caribbean was getting some unseasonably bad weather. Rains lasting more than a week in Haiti and the Dominican Republic in May had caused huge mudslides that killed over 80 people.

> Talking to new arrivals we could see that being a few days apart could mean very different times on the same route. The harbor data tells the same story. A group of boats would all arrive together from Bermuda in quick times of 11 to 12 days and then a week later another group would arrive with slow journeys of 17 to 18 days. A week later the better times come again. It isn't just the climate that determines conditions on these routes. It is clear that passages can be affected by weather changes week by week.

The synoptic charts for April and May showed slowly moving lows deepening as they dragged themselves eastwards from America. The Azores sat on the edge of a stationary high but the frontal lows brought the cloud down to head height. Yachts at sea in May complained that weather routing advice was running a day or two behind the actual conditions. Perhaps the routers were fooled by the slow speed of the lows. One boat traveling with three others from the northern Caribbean gave up on the routers advice and arrived three days before their more compliant buddies. They had gone north of the prescribed route and found fine sailing conditions while their buddies wallowed in uncomfortable seas and light winds.

We didn't use the services of a weather router. To get the best out of such a service you need a fast and powerful boat able to take position on either side of the depressions coming through. If you don't have such a boat you have two choices: take what comes or take a conservative route and keep clear of the most frequent gale tracks.

> The little steel sloop BRILLIG had mixed winds on its crossing from Florida to the Azores. They went up to 34°N looking for wind but didn't catch much for 10 days, by which time they were just north of Bermuda. After that they had mainly fair winds and a single brief gale. A yacht 100 miles north of them caught much more of the gale than they did and had to heave-to for two days. One hundred miles makes a lot of difference, as their weather router pointedly told them over the SSB.

We listened with delight to the stories of calamity and comedy in Peter's Bar, the meeting place *par excellence* in this ocean crossroads. Of course, not all accounts might be wholly accurate. Some, no doubt, were fuelled by relief and alcohol. These are, after all, tales told by sailors. One boat reporting monster seas and 70-knot winds might have been exaggerating. One can only hope so. But they did have the scars of tattered sails and the little sail repair shop was busy since May began. Huge sails are heaved across decks and fill up the back of his van. The engineering shop on the dockside was also busy. Taken together their work load tells the story of a hard start to the season. Chain plates renewed. Steel sail slides replacing plastic. Roller furling gear stripped down and repaired.

> The aero rig had taken a beating at sea and the owner gave it another when it arrived in Horta. Part of the hi-tech extrusion had jammed. The owner wanted to remove the broken length so he took his hammer to it. When this failed, he went to buy a bigger hammer. When this failed he went to John to borrow a sledgehammer. John is a sailor who decided to stop in Horta and open a little engineering workshop. He says he isn't an engineer but he's the closest we have so sooner or later we all end up at John's shop. John declined to lend his big hammer and instead took a look at the extrusion. It was, he said, a miracle of fine engineering, with clever hidden collets and other devices to hold the tubes inside one another. John looked and thought and then he made a tool that reached inside the extrusion

and unlocked the broken piece. Then all he had to do was repair the damage that nature and owner had done together.

One yacht leaves with three reefing points added to their in-mast furling mainsail and a new arrangement to raise and lower the sail the old fashioned way. They were halfway from Bermuda in a lumpy sea with howling winds and the sail wouldn't go in or out, up or down. They weren't going to be caught like that again. I thought it a shame since I was on the verge of overcoming my long-term antipathy to in-mast furling. G and I have spent many a happy hour noticing how many bluewater yachts now have in-mast furling and convincing ourselves to give it a try on our next boat. All that convenience. Such effortless reefing and un-reefing. Always having the right amount of sail. What a joy. What a dream.

Several boats make fiberglass repairs. The hull of a 30-foot French design was badly rung by the twisting motion during some of the rougher weather and took water through their anchor well. Others are fixing things at the tops of their masts. A charter yacht moving to its Mediterranean summer pastures needs new masthead fittings sent from the States. At least one other boat is checking its electrical wires. It was lucky not to have a serious fire in mid-ocean when some insulation abraded and caused a short. They could smell burning. When they located the damage the wires were no longer glowing but the timber and the fiberglass were deeply charred and blackened. Their mahogany paneling is less attractive since they levered it off with a wrecking bar but at least they don't have the mess that comes when a fire extinguisher is used.

G and I have our own jobs to attend to, but they are nothing more than routine maintenance. Our singlehanding Swedish neighbor on his old fashioned and simple 30-foot fiberglass double-ended sloop finished his maintenance the day after his arrival and has been playing his guitar and socializing and sightseeing. He came from New York and didn't have any weather to complain about. Next to him the 32-foot thirty-year-old timber yacht heading home to Poland to finish its second circumnavigation had a hard beat up from South Africa but the skipper has nothing much to do except dry the bedding and on his first evening in harbor went with us to a concert. It reminds me of the mantra of Lin and Larry Pardey, who claimed to have suffered no gear breakages on their tough little SERAFFYN on their journey from San Diego to Europe via the Chesapeake. The smaller and simpler your boat, the more time you have to sail and socialize. I know that to some the attitude and standards of the Pardeys are as out of date as flat earth theories, but their ideas speak strongly to me. And not just to me. There is a whole gaggle of us here in Horta, mainly on traditionally rugged 30 to 40 footers built of steel or concrete or those early fiberglass hulls built two inches thick. We point to sleek and beautiful 50 footers with every labor saving device on deck and below decks and inconceivably fast average cruising speeds of eight to ten knots and say reassuring things to one another such as "I wouldn't put to sea in that!" as our over-active imaginations conjure visions of containers floating awash halfway between here and Lisbon. And we are right, though we still do our washing by hand, and we know what people mean when they call their savings "freedom chips."

Winter into summer in Horta

Horta in season is the fourth busiest yacht harbor in the world. By the time we left at the end of May, party time was back in full swing and Horta had turned itself into the best, biggest and most varied boat show in the world. Forget Annapolis. Forget London. This is the place to see the finest, newest, oldest, most *avant garde*, most traditional, most elegant, must idiosyncratic boats. You want to know how to combine simple slab reefing with finger tip hydraulic control? Ask the 60-foot aluminum yacht designed by Chuck Payne. Does junk rig work on a trawler hull? There's one out of Fort Lauderdale you could ask. Does aero rig work? Ask that British 65 footer. Are the oldest boats the prettiest? Check that steel 65 footer built in Belgium in 1942. She is beautiful.

> We were checking out a Russian oligarch's 200 footer. A friend had been fixing her outdoor sauna. Her blocks and turnbuckles cost more than PETRONELLA. Each, that is. We walked back and forward on the quayside trying to decide what had gone wrong with the design. Too much height? Too much beam? Too much money? As we stepped back for a better view we bumped into the unmistakable spoon bow of a J class. We had the answer. VELSHEDA! We forgot the Russian boat. We had a J class to look at, the most beautiful yacht I've ever seen.

A boat show always has something of the circus about it. People who arrived in Horta three days ago shake their heads in disbelief as a new arrival sneaks up the narrowing fairway to find a place to tie up. But three days ago we were saying that of their boat. The harbor fills and empties, the speed depending on the weather forecast. There is always room for another, even if the marina staff must juggle with the nearly infinite combinations of length, beam, depth, displacement, length of stay and fragility of topsides. Not to mention maneuverability. Two boats combined to help each other moor. One had an engine that worked.

The other only had a bowthruster. They came up the narrow fairway and slid sideways into a tight space with boats rafted four deep ahead and astern of them.

Last to leave

At the end of May the queue to leave gets longer, delayed by a few days of wet and miserable weather as a depression to the north disturbs the prevailing high. Boats are in a hurry now that they took longer than expected to get here and their intended three day stopover has stretched to a week.

We are delayed only because we are off to the neighboring island of São Jorge and the south wind will be pushing an uncomfortable swell into the harbors. This south wind would be good for Europe, getting us clear of the islands, but it isn't obvious what will follow. Our Israeli-American neighbor headed for the Mediterranean wonders if he will be closing the busy Straits of Gibraltar with half a gale from the west. He doesn't want that.

Then suddenly the weather system moves and the boats start leaving. We didn't get the forecast right and neither did many of the others we met up with later.

> M&R left the Azores expecting fair winds for southern Portugal but four days of easterlies had them on course for Britain. Then the wind went through south to southwest, northwest to north and put them back on track for Cape St Vincent and the Algarve coast.

Leaving the Azores was as hard as leaving Horta. We called in at Terceira for a day and stayed a week to enjoy the company of other sailors, the island scenery and the beautiful city of Angra. It was fiesta time and we watched the bulls running through the narrow back streets a ten minute walk from the harbor. In the end we dragged ourselves away to São Miguel to moor up for two weeks but we stayed longer to explore this large and beautiful island. The capital, Ponta Delgada, lacks the charm of Terceira's Angra. It is bigger, and the fine Azorean-style buildings that might have covered the waterfront have been now been replaced by slab style hotels and offices and shops. Also, Ponta Delgada is a true city, large enough to have poverty and slums. In the other islands this poverty must exist but it always seems manageable when in rural areas rather than the brutal city. The gap between affluent visitors and city workers or local and foreign yacht owners and the local poor is always a jolt. The Azores may be part of Europe but they are on the margins and part of one of Western Europe's poorer countries.

There was no imperative for us to leave and the weather was no impetus. Up to the north the great depressions ran across the ocean to bring unseasonably foul winds and rain to northwest Europe, Ireland and Britain. Under the well established benign Azores High we had clear skies, hot sun and not a worthwhile sailing breeze. We told ourselves that the strong local breezes around the island would persist out at sea but we were only kidding ourselves. We had seen the weather charts. No wind could be hiding in those well spread isobars. We had heard from sailors who had already left. No wind for two hundred miles. When we left it was like going back into the Horse Latitudes, but this time with full tanks of clean diesel. Huge empty blue skies. An ocean of ripples, not waves. A T-shirt to keep off the burning rays, rather than for warmth. These were, indeed, the best of times.

From the Azores to Spain

The weather on this last leg was typical high pressure. Sparkling visibility during the day even if the night skies were often cloudy and obscured. Very little rain but fierce lightning storms to the north and west. Day temperatures between 80°F and 85°F dropping to around 68°F at night. The sea state was flat to very flat and often flatter than that. There was rarely much swell.

Once clear of the Azores most shipping was hull down on the horizon and best visible at night. We saw an abundance of flotsam. Plastic bottles and bags that seemed to follow tide lines of their own. Fortunately nothing large or life-threatening. We were curious about the floats and buoys that we passed. Some were clearly drifting. Others seemed tethered to the seabed. But this was a thousand miles offshore in depths of two to three miles. Surely no one wants a seabed marker so deep and so far away.

A good place to arrive

The Rias are a wonderful cruising ground and a good place to arrive for those like us who have been a long time out of busy yachting centers.

Bayona was a more developed town than when I was last here. G would have none of my grumbling. I was forced to see Bayona through her eyes. We were, it turned out, in a pleasant little resort town full of Spanish holiday makers enjoying themselves. Nice beaches, lots of restaurants and street cafes. At a jazz concert in the town square on our first night we re-discovered how nice it is to listen to world class jazz trios from midnight to 2 a.m. instead of standing watch at sea.

Epilogue

So what comes now? You made it. You sailed to Europe and then crossed back west to the Caribbean and now you are parked up somewhere in the Grenadines or the Virgins, nearly back home, back where you started this journey. What is different from when you started is you. Crossing the ocean in a small boat is a life-defining event. On this dark tropical evening you are wondering if you will still see the stars so clearly or the flittering fireflies or hear the parrots returning to their roost in a month's time when you are cleating your lines to your old marina berth.

Maybe you knew when you set off that this is not a journey that ends. Maybe you know it now. This book was not intended to persuade you to sell up and go sailing. It was only intended to help you make an ocean crossing. But an ocean crossing is a good test of whether you want to return to your old life ashore or try your hand at small boat cruising. When I made my first Atlantic crossing the crossing was all I had in mind. By the time I made my second crossing I had turned into a liveaboard, cut a lot of my ties with the land, and felt I was living a very privileged existence.

This book contains a lot of what I have learned from living the sailing life, and it's there to help you if you chose to do the same. If you think the life might suit you, then give it a try and do it now. It is never too soon to start. People dreaming of the cruising life always have a hundred and more good reasons to delay taking it up, but none of those reasons are good enough and none stack up when they actually do it.

Liveaboard cruising is not quite like a one-off trip around the Atlantic. It needs a simpler approach, a greater freedom from getting and spending, a boat and lifestyle pared down to the minimum. Most cruisers are on the edge of financial catastrophe most of the time. It isn't a problem, just something you learn to live with. It helps if your boat is small enough and simple enough to make shopping trips really short. In the last decade the list of "must-have" items specified by sailing journals and even by government agencies has expanded exponentially and the cost of the items gone up just as fast. If you want to get a good idea of what every one "must have" but which you might have to spend another decade working to afford, turn back to Sea time and shore time in Chapter 7. If you take this route in fitting out your sailing boat you may find a private income

Gloria isn't very big, but she looks like a giant next to the 14-foot Swedish yawl ARRANDIR in Horta on the return leg of its Atlantic circuit.

would be a great thing. But don't be put off if you don't have one. We don't and neither do 99.9% of the cruisers we meet. The Hiscocks didn't sail with this much-touted gear because most of it didn't exist in their era. The Pardeys didn't sail with it either. They didn't have the boat to carry it, the bank balance to buy it or the mind-set to want it.

You can save money by not investing in a lot of gear. That way you also save money in not having to repair it when it fails and you save time which would be better spent sailing or reading a good book in a pleasant anchorage. We continue to upgrade our boat gear in the hope of upgrading the quality of our life, but not everything adds to this end. Some new gear still lies in the box it came in, hardly used or the victim of a "better" plan. This is a disappointment to me, of course, but it shouldn't come as a surprise. It is a failure of choice common to sailors, as you can see by the range of unused/still-in-a-box offerings at any boat jumble.

Don't get suckered in to thinking that sailing is for when you retire and have a pension. Bring on the pension, by all means, but to wait till pension age is to put the best cruising years of your life on hold. Youth's a thing that's not for keeping.

If you have finished (or even only half finished) your Atlantic adventure and feel ready to take to the cruising life, don't feel that you have to continue with it if you find the sea too hostile, the life too insecure or the family too far away. Not everyone can cope with the huge insecurity of what is seen by many onshore as just a carefree hedonistic life. Don't feel you have to stay with it if you aren't having fun. Cruising can be as painful for some as it is pleasurable for others, and you didn't make this major life change to suffer boredom or discomfort.

G and I take frequent breaks from sailing, not all of which involve leaving the boat, and if we didn't I fear we might have seriously mistreated our brains or even left them somewhere and forgotten where. Sailing needs to be mixed with other challenges, especially intellectual challenges. The more remote the places you sail to or the more that you come to live wholly within the sailing community, the more you will need to mix in other lifestyles. So far, every break we take just makes us feel even more grateful and privileged to be cruising. It's a charmed life we live.

Appendix One

PETRONELLA, the boat

PETRONELLA is one of the JOSHUA class made famous by Bernard Moitessier, drawn by Jean Knocker and built by META in France. Moitessier became the doyen of single-handed sailors for his circumnavigation in his JOSHUA but he made international fame for his manner of leaving the Golden Globe race of 1968. The entrants in this first ever singlehanded non-stop round the world race were an unusually eccentric group even by the standards of the English, Irish, Border Scots and French who made up most of the fleet. Boats could start at any time between June and October. A trophy went to the first person home, and £5,000 to the fastest finisher. Englishman Robin Knox-Johnston, the winner and only finisher, in a punishing time of 313 days, left five weeks before Moitessier but Moitessier's JOSHUA was the faster boat and as he turned Cape Horn into the Atlantic Moitessier knew he would take the prize. Then, with a Gallic shrug, Moitessier wondered why he should bother. He had no wish for a silver cup or English pounds. He had no mantelpiece to put the cup on and no wish for one in his life. He had discovered himself on the voyage and he was not a match racer. He sailed on Tahiti, to become a legend in his own lifetime. His books are true treasures in the sailing archive.

> "I do not know how to explain to them my need to be at peace, to continue to the Pacific."

Moitessier's JOSHUA in the sailing museum in La Rochelle, France continues to attract idiosyncratic French sailors. When Bernard Peignon hadn't got his own boat ready for a singlehanded Atlantic race he asked to borrow JOSHUA. Of course, the museum replied, but only for the 500-mile qualifier. On no account must you sail her in the race. Of course, Peignon's boat was not ready when start day came so he raced in JOSHUA On arrival in the US he was arrested, deported

Petronella layout and rigging drawings

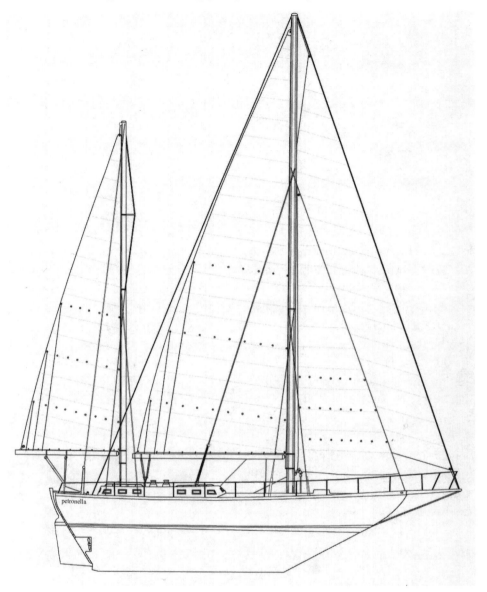

to France and given a nominal sentence of one day in prison. Another French sailing hero in the making.

Our JOSHUA is a double ended, ketch rigged, centre cockpit, heavy displacement 40 footer. She is made of rolled steel plate, has a long keel, a transom hung rudder and a short bowsprit. She is unmistakable. Afloat or on the hard she attracts the attention of all French sailors who are passing and some other nationalities too.

She is not fast by modern standards nor close winded but she can make quick passages. Her seaworthiness inspires enormous confidence. She can sail herself on the wind for days at a time, even without the rudder lashed. She has a few more luxuries than my previous boat but at heart she is a simple boat with simple systems and we remind ourselves of the advantages of this when we sometimes crave an extra luxury.

Appendix Two

Measures of wind strengths

Admiral Beaufort developed his scale of wind categories to indicate appropriate sail setting in Britain's sailing warships. It remains a useful mind-set for modern sailors even if today's instruments read out exact wind speeds and encourage us to work in knots. Usually I care less about exact wind speed and more about its likely average range. I know that a Force Five might rise to or gust up to a Force Six, and I know that I am comfortable with that. A Force Six, in my experience, can rise to or gust up to Force Seven, and I'd like advance warning of that. The sea state and the set of my sails will relate to the average wind speed rather than the top or bottom of the day's range. Also, European forecasts give wind speed in the Beaufort scale.

The Beaufort scale

Force	Wind speed in knots	Name of wind force
0	<1	Calm
1	1-3	Light air
2	4-6	Light breeze
3	7-10	Gentle breeze
4	11-16	Moderate breeze
5	17-21	Fresh breeze
6	22-27	Strong breeze
7	28-33	Near gale
8	34-40	Gale
9	41-47	Strong gale
10	48-55	Storm
11	56-63	Violent storm
12	>64	Hurricane

Wind speed is less relevant than the wind pressure it produces. The Beaufort scale deals with steps in pressure changes still significant to a yacht. It also describes sea state, and this is often much more relevant than wind speed.

Beaufort was a practical man. He took his scale up to hurricane Force 12 and left it there. Why categorize winds "which no canvas could withstand." Saffir and Simpson (respectively an engineer and the then director of the National Hurricane Center) developed their scale in the 1970s to indicate the potential damage of a hurricane ashore rather than danger to small yachts at sea. Their scale relates wind speed, barometric pressure and storm surges.

Saffir-Simpson Scale

Name of Feature	Wind Strength in Knots	Central barometric pressure	Tidal Surge Height
Tropical Depression	25 – 33		
Tropical Storms	34 – 63		
Category 1 Hurricane -minimal	64 – 82	Above 980 mb	5 feet
Category 2 Hurricane - moderate	82 – 95	965 to 979 mb	8 feet
Category 3 Hurricane - extensive	96 – 112	945 to 964 mb	12 feet
Category 4 Hurricane - extreme	113 – 134	920 to 944 mb	18 feet
Category 5 Hurricane - catastrophic	>134	Below 920 mb	Over 18 feet

The Saffir-Simpson Scale rates storms by maximum sustained wind. Gusts can bring much higher winds. Very few hurricanes reach the full ferocity of a catastrophic category five but winds may gust at 50% more than the maximum for their category. Recently a new class of hurricane has been informally added. Category five hurricanes blowing at over 155mph are called super-hurricanes.

Appendix Three

Liferafts and grab bags

G has made a study of survival at sea in which I hope we never have to be examined. But thanks to her I bring you this snippet of information to add to the whole books and magazine articles you might read on the subject.

Liferaft

My personal preference is for a liferaft that can be sailed, so that we can harness our own efforts to survival rather than wait passively to be blown to salvation. They exist. They can be your dinghy and your liferaft, all in one. But they all suffer drawbacks, mainly the impossible strength needed to hoist them over the side. So we have a conventional canister type raft stowed on deck. We seldom sail far offshore with more than three people on board, but we bought a six-person raft. Obviously. Because even G is too long to lie down flat in a four-person raft and if you want to be comfortable for endless days and nights you need to lie down. The one problem with a bigger liferaft is that they rely on more bodies to keep them ballasted. Without this they may flip in big seas. Ballast the raft with whatever comes to hand.

Of course you will never come to use your liferaft because they are tokens to ward off giant waves and rogue cargo vessels but just in case read the manufacturer's instructions so you know how to use the model you've got. The only advice to add to this is: only abandon ship when you can step up into your liferaft. Sinking yachts often never sink. They have been known to make their way ashore like homing pigeons. They are your mother ship. A liferaft, however, is an unknown quantity. It is your absolute last resort.

The remarkable Frenchman Dr Alain Bombard died in 2005 aged 80. He was convinced that more sailors torpedoed during the war could have survived in liferafts if given simple training and equipment such as fish squeezers, plankton nets and better fishing gear. In 1952, to prove that it was possible to live off the sea, he put his life on the line. He left the Canaries in an inflatable boat and 62 days later drifted ashore in Barbados, 55lbs lighter and no longer wearing toenails. The boat was barely suitable for the task, but the man was. His journey became the basis for his long running contributions to survival at sea. He obtained fresh water from juice squeezed from fish and got vital extra protein from plankton. Some findings still run contrary to conventional wisdom. In particular, most official advice is not to drink seawater under any circumstances. How many officials have been out there testing their advice? Bombard claims to have drunk more than a pint a day, diluting the salinity with fish juice. His life and work make fascinating reading. His little inflatable was called L'HERETIQUE. *Naturellement.*

Don't leave your dinghy behind if you can take it with you. Maralyn and Maurice Bailey, who suffered 117 days in their raft, said that having their dinghy and its pump was the difference between surviving and not.

Grab bag

I know very little about grab bags. I'm not even proud of what little I know. On my first Atlantic crossing I bought all sorts of harnesses and survival suits and wrote an impressive list of safety gear for the "grab bag" and called myself prepared. We went through two Biscay gales without me feeling well enough to search out the harnesses. The survival suits would not have helped either, being stuffed at the back of a clothes' locker. The grab bag never even came to mind during those gales. Even the liferaft was buried under two sails and some very wet and smelly oilskins. We had the gear. Getting it had been vital to my preparation. Having it useable was not.

I have adjusted to the ocean now, and if I hadn't G would still have a grab bag filled and handy. Along with the items above suggested by Alain Bombard we have these things packed into our waterproof containers. This is not an exhaustive list but it reflects our priorities and may make you think of something not included in the books and magazine articles on the subject:

- GPS, hand bearing compass, chart and pilot book, survival book, notebook and pencil, spectacles
- flares, EPIRB, VHF, binoculars, signaling mirror, flash light, watch, cell phone, spare batteries

- bailer, raft mending materials including sealant, clamps, sewing kit, duct tape, assorted line
- water in containers, solar still, food, can opener, knives, spoons, plates and mugs
- fishing tackle, spear, fish processing equipment: scissors, pliers or vice grip, hammer to stun fish, chopping board, pegs and line for drying fish, plastic bags
- wet weather gear, life jackets, space blanket, sleeping bag, bucket or two, bowl with lid
- first aid kit with routine medication, seasickness remedies and vitamins, sunscreen and hats, sponges and clothes, towels, toothbrush, etc.

Official advice is to take ship's papers, passports and money. Of course you should but remember that when you take to the liferaft your priority is survival. Take what counts.

Some items are so vital they need expanding a little.

Flares

Most of us carry plenty of out of date flares because we don't know what else to do with them. This is not good enough. Make sure you have some that are in date too. When you need to send off a flare it helps to have done it before, when your nerves were less in a jangle. I never realized how much of a bang they make till I tried one out. That bang, to the wrong person, could be a cue for a heart-attack. Also, I don't find the instructions very clear and on a dark night without my reading glasses would be quite nervous about whether I was gripping the holding end or the business end. So there is another reason for finding an opportunity to let some flares off for educational purposes.

You need a mix of flares. There are official guidelines and regulations on this. If you are over 45 feet overall and British registered you are subject to the Merchant Shipping Class Regulations. Their requirement isn't a bad one. I wish flares stayed in date a bit longer so that I wouldn't feel so mean about investing in such an overdraft of flares. This list is a minimum. Take more if you can.

Type of flare	Merchant Shipping requirement	Sensible offshore minimum
Handheld red flares	6	4
Handheld white flares	4	4
Buoyant orange smoke signals	2	2
Red parachute flares	12	6

A waterproof portable VHF

A VHF Mayday call is a more effective call for help than a flare. Your low aerial height when using a handheld VHF limits the transmission distance to about three miles. To send your signal even this distance you must make sure that the electrical wave part of the radio wave is in line with the receiving aerial. Fixed aerials are always vertical, so your handheld VHF's aerial must be vertical too. Holding the radio like a cell phone degrades the signal.

Make sure you know how the handheld's battery performs when the set is switched off. Some sets are discharged by their soft keys. The battery can go flat in three or four weeks even when switched off. If you disconnect the batteries they can hold their charge for about four months. When you put your spare VHF in the grab bag, put in some spare batteries too.

A cellular phone

I certainly hope to have the phone with us when we jump. It isn't just because in our daily life we have come to rely on the phone as a clock, a calendar and an alarm clock but because I hope to emulate those Cornish fishermen who set fire to their fishing boat and were able to put in a call to the Coast Guard. Cell phones are seldom watertight. Put it in a waterproof bag.

Appendix Four

Garbage disposal

I like to think that the big ships have given up throwing all their garbage into the sea and that most yachts are more ecologically aware than ever before but we saw a lot of floating and half floating trash in the wide empty spaces of the ocean.

The ideal (and only fully legal) policy is to carry all your waste with you and dispose of it ashore but over 15 to 30 days offshore the ideal can become a stinking mess of black garbage bags leaking or splitting on the aft deck and possibly dropping the wrong stuff overboard when you are not looking. We have a policy of limited waste disposal when offshore. No plastic of any sort is ever thrown over. Plasticized paper counts as plastic. I'm sure some plastic exists which degrades and rots in sun and salt water but it also floats, takes a long time to disappear and does a fish or marine mammal no good at all to eat. All vegetable matter and waste food is thrown over. This gets rid of the worst smelling rot and feeds the fishes. All glass and cans are thrown over but in a manner to ensure they sink. Never ever with a top still on!! Cans are ripped or punctured. Bottles and jars filled with seawater to sink them. Once on the sea bed these materials will rot or grind away. That is recycling of a sort.

Paper is a grey area. Some gets thrown, some doesn't. I'm not happy about throwing any of it overboard although I have little doubt that most of it will soon degrade. The thing is, the hand is quicker than the conscience and sometimes the paper is flying off to leeward before I know it.

I suspect the worst paper to throw over is toilet and kitchen tissue. Thor Hyerdahl reported decades ago how this turned into an almost undegradable cellulose drifting across oceans at the speed of his balsa wood raft, though less inclined to sink.

As a result of our eco-trash policy we can arrive with a manageable quantity of garbage to be disposed of ashore and still take the moral high ground when we see plastic containers and the like floating by.

Appendix Five

Web sites for sailors

Information - charts	British Admiralty Hydrographic Office	http://www.ukho.gov.uk
Information - charts	UK and Europe charts	http://www.tideplotter.co.uk
Information - almanac	Reeds OKI Almanac	http://www.reedsalmanac.co.uk
Information - tides and navigation	European and World charts	http://www.marinecomputing.com
Information - health	US Center for Disease Control	http://www.cdc.gov
Information - radio amateur weather net	Maritime Mobile service network	http://www.mmsn.org
Organizations	British Cruising Association	http://www.cruising.org.uk
Organizations	Royal Cruising Club	http://www.rcc.org.uk
Software - tides and navigation	UK and European tidal and navigation software	http://www.neptune-navigation.com
Weather	NOAA Marine Advisory	www.noaa.org
Weather	Ocean Prediction Center	http://www.opc.ncep.noaa.gov
Weather	Caribbean Weather	http://www.caribwx.com
Weather	US Coastguard Gulf Stream information	www.nws.noaa.gov or www.opc.ncep.noaa.gov
Weather	Excellent information on tropical storms	www.wunderground.com/tropical
Weather	Good general weather information	http://www.weatheronline.co.uk/sail.htm

Weather	British Marine Weather Services	www.marinecall.co.uk
Weather	Meteorological Office - UK. Shipping forecast	http://www.metoffice.co.uk
Weather	Meteorological Office - French	http://www.meteo.fr
Weather	Meteorological Office - Portuguese	http://www.meteo.pt
Weather	Atlantic coast and Mediterranean	http://www.metmarine.com
Weather	Inshore wind forecasts worldwide	http://www.windguru.com
Weather	Sources of radio weather stations in the Mediterranean	http://www.franksingleton.clara.net
Weather	Commercial site for mediterranean weather	http://www.mediterraneanweather.com forecasts.htm

Index